Hacked, Attacked & Abused

Digital crime exposed

Peter Lilley

KOGAN
PAGE

First rule of computer security: don't buy a computer. Second rule: if you buy one, don't turn it on.

Dark Avenger

For my parents, Reg and Nell Lilley

Also by Peter Lilley
Dirty Dealing

First published in 2002

Apart from any fair dealing for the purposes of research or private study, or criticism or review, as permitted under the Copyright, Designs and Patents Act 1988, this publication may only be reproduced, stored or transmitted, in any form or by any means, with the prior permission in writing of the publishers, or in the case of reprographic reproduction in accordance with the terms and licences issued by the CLA. Enquiries concerning reproduction outside these terms should be sent to the publishers at the undermentioned address:

Kogan Page Limited
120 Pentonville Road
London N1 9JN
UK

© Peter Lilley, 2002

The right of Peter Lilley to be identified as the author of this work has been asserted by him in accordance with the Copyright, Designs and Patents Act 1988.

British Library Cataloguing in Publication Data

A CIP record for this book is available from the British Library.

ISBN 0 7494 3874 6

Typeset by JS Typesetting Ltd, Wellingborough, Northants
Printed and bound in Great Britain by Biddles Ltd, Guildford and King's Lynn
www.biddles.co.uk

CONTENTS

PREFACE: WIRED FOR CRIME

I never think of the future. It comes soon enough.

Albert Einstein

I'm sorry Dave, I can't let you do that.

HAL, the seemingly all-knowing computer of 2001:
A Space Odyssey

You can phone virtually any country from a mobile phone as small as a packet of cigarettes. That mobile phone can receive and send endless text messages to another phone, or a computer. If you use text messaging regularly you will probably communicate in a shorthand language that is (thankfully) indecipherable by others. You can receive news, stock prices or sports scores on the same phone as well as convert one currency to another or carry out any other mathematical calculation.

Access your computer, log onto the Internet and the whole world is yours. You can bank online – you can even open your account online. That account no longer has to be in your native country, let alone the bank in your home town. You can choose and order your groceries online. You can trade stocks. You can book flights, hotels, taxis and anything else you need for your travel plans. You can search for old friends, or advertise for new friends. You can access and download newspapers, books, film scripts, research papers and millions of other documents. You can consult telephone directories, company filings, university student registers and an almost unimaginable number of other public (and some not so public) records. You can – even after the Napster controversy – download your favourite musical track. And you can get a palmtop computer, like I have, that measures 18 centimetres by 10 centimetres with a long battery life, which can do all of these things from anywhere on the planet.

You can work from home and communicate with anyone, anywhere by e-mail with a click of a mouse. You can give a telephone number in Switzerland but when it is dialled the caller is seamlessly transferred to a telephone thousands of miles away. You can even have a phone number in virtually any country of the world which when answered records a message and sends it as a file to be accessed by e-mail. When you pay for goods you are now probably more likely to do it with a piece of plastic that is validated and processed electronically – standing, for example, in Singapore but taking money electronically from your account in Spain. And if you should need cash, you can get it 24/7 from an electronic machine in a wall, anywhere in the world.

We now live, work and play in a Digital Age. In computer terms, digital refers to any system that is based on discontinuous data or events. Computers, for example, are digital because they can only distinguish between on and off, positive or non-positive or one and zero. All digital data must be encoded as a series of ones and zeroes. Each of these state digits is referred to as a bit; and when strung together in a format that a computer can address individually as a group as a byte. Digital has entered our vocabulary with a vengeance in the 21st century: every form of media has been digitally remixed or remastered; we have digital cameras, digital photographs, digital libraries, personal digital assistants, digital television, digital images, digital scanners; Web sites abound with 'digital' as a prefix or suffix – digitalwomen, digitalmedia, digitalproducer, digitaljournalist, digital-audio and somewhat obviously, digitalsex. Ironically much of the Digital Age relies on conversion from analogue to digital and vice versa: modems convert digital information to analogue signals for phone line transmission (and the other way around for incoming data); compact discs store analogue forms (music) in a digital form, but when they are played the CD player reconverts the digital information back into analogue form so that we can listen to it.

We live in world that has changed beyond recognition in the last 10 years: it is now almost possible to live your entire life online or through technology. Increasingly we have been sold this vision: not only as individuals, but in the business world too. Manufacturing companies suddenly turned themselves into cutting edge high-tech concerns; analysts and financial institutions put complete faith in technology investments; small companies were told that unless they had an Internet and e-commerce plan they were doomed. Dot coms were the future – and everything else was junked, until of course the dot coms themselves became junk.

But just like real life, the high-tech existence came with risks, and a dark shadowy side. Not that it was envisaged in the early days of this brave new world or appreciated that such a dark side would exist, but exist it does. The Internet simultaneously liberates and imprisons – pornography, paedophilia, hate sites, grudge sites, terrorist information – you can find it all, in glorious detail on the Internet. Want to rob a bank? Want to learn how to build a bomb? Want to rubbish a company or person? Want to stalk? You can do all of these things online. What has become obvious is that the tremendous advances and opportunities that technology has delivered have simultaneously opened up a 'Pandora's box' of possibilities for darker, sometimes evil, deeds. Terrorists, organized criminals, fraudsters, money launderers have all grasped the advantages offered by the Internet and other related technologies. Hackers, crackers, virus creators have all tried – and succeeded – in subverting the online environment. We have been sold the lie that technology provides us a safe, sterile, forward-looking environment: whereas the simple truth is that all of the risks and dangers inherent in normal life are magnified online and in high technology. Magnified, but to a large extent, ignored. It appears increasingly that we are unaware of the dangerous roads we are travelling along.

Cyberspace is not a real place (or is it?). Some of us probably think of cyberspace as the images that appear on screen when we participate in a Playstation game, when we drive an imaginary (but strangely realistic) rally car, or kill an opponent in a war game, or score a goal in soccer. Cyberspace may not be real, but it is not false either: very real events happen in cyberspace. Many of our personal details are there or can be accessed through there; many of our conversations (whether they be via phone, mobile phone, e-mail or fax) pass through there; the actions we take in cyberspace (what Web sites we access; what calls we make; what programmes we watch) can be recorded and monitored.

This book does not seek to present an alarmist vision of the Digital Age. But neither does it attempt to airbrush out the grave risks and dangers that are ever present in this brave new environment. This is not a technical book, in that it does not reproduce lines of software code that will magically solve all of your digital security problems. What this book does attempt to do is describe and analyse the risks inherent in the sustained and continuous reliance on technology. Primarily this is viewed from a business focus, but as ultimately we are all customers, the perspective cannot be a narrow one.

It continually strikes me that we do not realize the fault lines that we tread on each day when entrusting our communications, personal details, confidential material or whatever else to technology. In early 2001 the FBI warned that a successful hacker attack against the United States' banking and financial system could cripple the country within three days. Alan B Carroll, who supervises the analysis and warning component at the FBI's National Infrastructure Protection Center, observed that 'We cannot afford to let our dependence on automation become our Achilles heel. Our challenge is to button up the holes in our critical infrastructure, and believe me, there are holes'. The FBI has identified eight critical infrastructures that are heavily dependent on technology, and thus prime targets for attack. These are:

- utilities;
- oil and gas;
- telecommunications;
- transportation;
- banking and finance;
- water;
- emergency services;
- government operations.

At the opposite end of the panic spectrum are the merchants of doom who continually and repeatedly bang the drum warning of an electronic Pearl Harbor. These observers warn that because 21st century technology offers an infinite number of points of attack, the possibilities for future wars or individual battles lie in the digital domain. They write (endlessly) about attacks on mobile phone networks, cash dispenser systems and similar global structures. I used to have some sympathy with their views, but after the horrendous events of 11 September 2001 I have severe and abiding doubts about these predictions of so-called doom. In the end, who cares if the world's ATM networks crash? Is it the apocalypse if your mobile phone fails to function? Certainly interference or sabotage of such safety critical networks such as air traffic control would lead to dire consequences. Yet the indescribably tragic events of 11 September 2001 do not suggest to me that the digital world is the new global battleground: rather that our reliance on technology actually dulled our responses and left us open to attack. The suicide pilots basically stole four planes and then (in three cases) converted them into highly efficient flying bombs, ramming them into key physical structures populated by thousands of innocent people. The hijackers (in the actual outrage) made little use of technology *per se*, but, even more alarmingly, all of the technological systems that were supposed to warn against such attacks failed completely. Moreover the background support of intelligence collection by electronic methods was also shown to be utterly inefficient. None of this is to underestimate the technology that was almost certainly used to achieve effective, coded communication between the terrorists – or the computer wizardry employed in the subsequent military attacks by the United States or its allies.

Perhaps the safety controls that were in place did not react, or swing into action quickly enough, because there was no prior knowledge or expectation of what occurred. Blame the hardware and software systems that were supposed to protect us, then. Well, no. . . all technology ultimately is human created, programmed and maintained. In the marvellous, ground breaking film *2001: A Space Odyssey* Stanley Kubrick brought to life, so to speak, HAL. This 'Heuristically programmed ALgoritmic computer' was supposed to be as near to an artificially created intelligent machine as possible, so much so that HAL ultimately thought that it (or should that be he?) knew better than the human occupants of the space ship and promptly cut off their life support systems. However clever and independent of humans HAL thought it was, ultimately a human could terminate HAL's existence by cutting off its critical functions. Similarly, all technology that we use today, however advanced, is human dependent. We cannot blame 'the technology' – we created that technology. In business the convoluted (but no doubt necessary) procedure to design and install a new system begins with the user specifying its needs and requirements, and should end with an ongoing review of whether those needs have been met by what has been delivered. Trap doors exist in systems because the designers and/or programmers left them there; computers may 'be hacked' but the hacking is done by (probably) a male Caucasian aged under 20. This morning I phoned up my bank to make a very general query about my account, only to be informed (on three different occasions) that the system was down – which is a description not a reason. For the bank's system to be down, somewhere back along the line was a human error(s).

More prosaically, and closer to home, one e-mail that I recently received from an e-mail service that (fortunately) I use infrequently stated:

> *Dear Client*
> *We are currently performing unscheduled maintenance to your e-mail server due to unforeseen circumstances and the service is temporarily unavailable. E-mail residing on the e-mail server has been lost and will be unrecoverable.*
> *Your e-mail service will resume again shortly. Please try accessing again later. We apologize for the inconvenience caused.*

In other words, if you held all of your present and past correspondence in e-mail form on this server, you had just lost all of it forever. But most e-mail users rely heavily on this communication channel, until they receive a message like the one above.

This same provider warned customers a few months earlier that their Web hosting system was struggling to operate because of sustained denial of service attacks which were crippling the entire setup, making it impossible for Web sites to be accessed.

Even more surreal was the unsolicited e-mail that I recently received from a pornography Web site. Never mind that my e-mail address had obviously been obtained from my Web site via a 'sniffer' program. What amazed me was not the financial offer made to me, but the problems that had been previously experienced:

> *Site XXX raises the bar again and increases payouts.*
> *Site XXX reduced payouts in response to Webmaster fraud a few months ago. Now with vastly improved fraud detection technology, Site XXX is pleased to announce that payouts have once again been raised above all other programs available to adult Webmasters.*

Pornography and gambling have increasingly become the two business areas that are perceived as being able to generate profits via the Internet. While many observers would argue that these two sectors are prime representations of the dark side of technology, or the effects of it, both pornography peddlers and online gambling sites are vulnerable and frequent targets of criminal attacks.

Online gambling is surely one of the most interesting business sectors of the Internet: a sector that is solely based on money and could already be worth US $2 billion. The Internet is populated by thousands, if not millions, of online gambling sites, many ostensibly operating from obscure offshore locations. On reflection, such sites are an obvious target for fraudsters and hackers. It is now becoming evident that hackers are regularly obtaining large sums from these sites. In August 2001, a Canadian company that handles online casino games confirmed that a hacker had corrupted one of its games so that players could not lose: so for a few hours gamblers on the site obviously thought that they had accessed their idea of heaven. In that short time period 140 gamblers won a total of US $1.9 million. Then to compound the situation, in some instances, the intruders blackmailed the online operators, demanding large sums from them to 'guarantee' that further such attacks would not recur. While never confirmed in the public domain by relevant operators, it is widely suspected that some attacks and subsequent extortion requests originate from Eastern European organized crime groups. Like much hacker activity, attacks on gambling sites take a variety of forms: there have been various denial of service outrages which disable the relevant site. Such denial of service attacks, if timed to coincide with major sporting events, can very effectively deprive the operators of massive sums of bets. These incidents happened at real sites; there have also been various fraudulent gambling Web sites created. Such sites give the appearance of being a legitimate betting forum but in fact are nothing more than a scam. Keen punters fill in their credit card details so that they can place bets. These customers will never see any winnings but will, when they receive their credit card bills, realize that the criminals behind the site have used the credit cards as much as possible.

Even more frighteningly, the forward march of new technology is already impacting on our personal lives in sinister and previously unimagined ways. As an example, it is now very easy to buy software that records all activity on a computer. Such software can be used, for instance, by employers to monitor their workers' Internet and computer activity. It could also be used by a company to spy on a competitor or rival. These software programs can also be used in the domestic environment: the advertising material actively promotes such usage to monitor the computer activity of partners and children while you are absent. There have already been examples (and court cases) where an estranged partner has hacked into the computer of the other partner and installed software which then e-mails him or her (without the user's knowledge) details of all key strokes, Web surfing and Internet communication. You don't have to be paranoid about all this, but it certainly helps.

And strange, unpredictable events occur in the Digital Age: one survey in the United States conducted by Cyberatlas in early 2001 showed that 8 per cent of US adults and 12 per cent of US teens use the Internet for religious or spiritual experiences. In Brisbane, Australia, in October 2001 a man was jailed for the seemingly obscure crime of hacking into council computers that control sewage. He succeeded in, among other things, getting a sewage pumping station to overflow thousands of litres of 'material' together with pumping raw sewage into public waterways. In all he was found guilty of 30 charges including computer hacking, theft and environmental vandalism. His motive was pre-revenge against his former employer (the installer of the sewage system) and the council which had turned down his job application. An even darker side of Web activity are the claims (which have surfaced in relation to a number of separate events) that the Internet has been used to facilitate murder. Ofir Rachum was a 16-year-old Israeli boy who apparently established an online relationship with an older female US tourist who was staying in Jerusalem. The relationship moved from chat rooms to e-mail to telephone conversations. After meeting his online friend once in Jerusalem Rachum met her again in January 2001. Whatever the girl's original intentions, it appears that she was persuaded by the Palestinian Tanzim group (armed militia) to lead Rachum to them. He was shot 15 times. His body was found in the boot of a car on the outskirts of the Palestinian town of Ramallah.

This book seeks to provide an overview and evaluation of crime, fraud and risk in the Digital Age by exploring how we got where we are now, where we are going and what risks we face on this journey. To chart this journey we begin by reminiscing about the good old days, when computers were mainframes and mobile phones were the province of science fiction. From there we travel to the Digital Age of the 21st century, looking at key milestones en route: such as the fact that in 1995 each American used an annual average of 731 pounds of paper, more than double the amount used in the 1980s – so much, then, for the paperless society that technology was going to deliver. After considering just how far and fast technology has developed and impacted on our personal and business lives, we then turn to evaluate just how and why our considerations of computer and electronic crime have always been underestimated and subject to fatal ignorance. This ignorance has been transmitted into the legal and investigative process, where even now the concept of a global technology driven economy, with all the risks inherent in that is not sufficiently (if at all) embedded in the legal system.

Chapter 2 concentrates on the various forms of attack that occur on technological systems and programs together with the use of technology to facilitate criminal activities such as money laundering. And what a mixed bunch of attacks and attackers we face in the Digital Age: from hackers, self-inflicted errors, money launderers and virus writers to name but four.

The Internet itself forms the basis of Chapter 3. In 1993 Bruce Sterling saw the Internet as 'a true, modern, functioning anarchy' – a borderless community with very few, if any, rules and regulations. So the scam Web site that an investor has just lost money to may quote an address in New York, but in fact the crooks behind it are in Russia using a first stage bank account in the Caribbean. Multi jurisdictional crime such as this is difficult to prevent, investigate and prosecute; if only because of the immense problems encountered where different country laws, official bodies and – it must be said – turf guardianship abound. The Internet is truly global, but there exists no international body to police, regulate and control it.

While I am sceptical of the claims of an impending electronic Pearl Harbor, in Chapter 4 consideration is given to the claims made that some countries are already using technology extensively to 'attack' other nations. Moreover, and just as critical an issue, if countries are doing it, why can't businesses use identical techniques to grab competitive advantage from their rivals?

One of the key issues raised by the Digital Age is the loss of privacy that is implicit in many of the transactions conducted on the Internet, records held on computer or conversations conducted across the ether. Chapter 5 tries to quantify what information about us (as users, customers, subjects) is collected and stored. How is this information then used – and at what stage may that usage become unethical?

If by that stage of this book you have not become too distressed or despondent, go on to Chapter 6 which describes what practical steps technology users can take to manage and minimize the risks presented by electronic/digital crime and fraud.

Whether the Digital Age ultimately warrants such gloom is open to question, but I would not necessarily place any great reliance on a 'security' product available in the United States. This is a gargoyle which is placed next to your computer and wards off modern day evils such as viruses, hackers and system errors. Just one version of such a security device has sold over 100,000 units – which either means that this number of people have computers wide open to attack, or the rest of us need a gargoyle immediately to protect us as these 100,000 wise users have already protected themselves.

TERMINAL VELOCITY

In physics, terminal velocity is where the driving forces are cancelled out by the resistive forces. Once an object has reached terminal velocity, the object is not accelerating, therefore it is not speeding up or slowing down. It is in constant velocity unless either the driving forces or the resistive forces change.

In aviation, terminal velocity is the maximum speed that a particular aircraft or other body can achieve under given conditions.

> *There is more to life than increasing its speed.*
>
> Mahatma Gandhi

> *E-mail – when it absolutely positively has to get lost at the speed of light.*
>
> Unknown

> *TRS-80 Model II is a second generation computer unit intended for small businesses. It includes CRT display with 8-inch floppy disk drive built into the same housing. The keyboard pad has lower-case as well as upper-case letters; the display is 24 lines and 80 characters per line. The lowest price unit comes with 32k of RAM. Another 32K, additional disk drives, and a printer can be added. Price of the 26–4001 with 32k is US $3,450; of the 26–4002 with 64k, US $3,899.*
>
> *High-tech equipment, 1980s style from the 1980s* Whole Home Electronics Catalog

TIMELINES OF TECHNOLOGY

Evolve or perish.

Epigram on the Hacked Net Web site

This is a story of speed: the speed of change, the velocity of thought and above all how everything that has gone before suddenly seems meaningless when compared with the cataclysmic changes of the last few decades of the 20th century. This is also a story of the effects of speed in another way. How, in the imaginary car chase through cyberspace, the bad guys almost always have the faster vehicles than those on the side of law and order. On the odd occasion that they're not faster, the bad guys are always more nimble and cunning than the chasers. This is a narrative of how it took from 1642 (when Pascal invented a primitive calculator) to 1980 to invent even the most rudimentary small computer. But forget that 338-year period of development, because what is important is that which has happened since 1980. Today, less than 25 years later, I can communicate with people in any country, access information in any language in real time (and then get it translated into any other language on the Internet), transfer money online from my bank account, operate my own 'secret' bank account online, check what flights I've been on recently, book new flights, order books, do my shopping. . . all on my PC, or laptop (or increasingly palmtop or mobile phone).

The NATO Parliamentary Assembly report on Information Warfare and International Security crystallized the speed of change when it commented that:

> *The pace of technological change and our increasing reliance on technology are even more impressive. Five years ago, a computer chip could carry the equivalent of 1.1 million transistors. Now the number has increased to 120 million and engineers believe they can reach 400 million and even 1 billion. Capable of 256 billion multiplications per second, the latest desktop computers have acquired the speed of yesterday's supercomputers. This has accelerated the dispersion and use of the Internet. To achieve mass-user status, it took radio 35 years, television 13 years and the Internet only 4 years. Microsoft experts assert that Internet traffic doubles every 100 days and, according to other estimates, one billion people (one-sixth of humanity) will be online by 2005.*

This is both staggering and terrifying. Ultimately the developments in technology we are going to chronicle and examine present not doubts but only possibilities to the agile criminal mind. The criminal can envisage new and lucrative opportunities in the rapidly shrinking global marketplace. This marketplace is interconnected with technology the likes of which never existed before. Law enforcement bodies are quite probably unaware of these technologies and the opportunities they offer for criminal activity. The real levelling factor (and catalyst) in all of this is that the equipment required to commit electronic crime and fraud successfully is no longer expensive, and the entry price is dropping all the time. Moreover, what can be done easily in this new Digital Age is increasing at an exponential rate. Want to get into the bootleg music CD market? Download the entire album off the Internet and then buy a CD duplication system and copy unattended up to 150 CDs at a time. The current cost of the equipment? £800.

But, as all good stories always start, once upon a time – when the Tower of Babylon was being built the abacus was invented in Babylonia, in around 3000 BC. At least that is what we suspect. What we know is this primitive calculation method involved drawing marks in the sand; this process was then superceded by trays and eventually grooved trays with balls. There is some dispute as to which country and ancient civilization invented the more sophisticated rod and bead abacus: some commentators claim that the Egyptians were at the cutting edge of this new technology way back in 500 BC; others think it was far later, in China during the Ming Dynasty (1368–1636). The rod and bead abacus is still in use today, and was certainly a key instrument in business and trading until paper and pencils took hold in the Western world. After the abacus nothing much happened (relatively speaking) until John Napier, a Scottish mathematician, developed logarithms in the late 16th century. This enabled William Oughtred to invent the slide rule, which in one of its early incarnations was circular. Under normal circumstances I would present a lengthy discourse on the workings and merits of the slide rule, but as I have never understood how this instrument works (and more importantly why we need it) I will pass quickly on. In 1623–24 William Schikard designed and built the first four function mechanical calculating clock at the University of Heidelberg. Yet from the first abacus in around 3000 BC it took until the 1960s for handheld battery powered calculators to appear on the scene (with their appearance causing relief to students everywhere).

Unfortunately Blaise Pascal had no calculators in 1642, and thus had to invent his own adding machine – the Pascaline. This machine could add and subtract with eight movable dials, but was too expensive to be practical. In Hannover 30 years later Gottfried Leibniz built a mechanical calculating machine that adds, subtracts, divides and multiplies (Leibniz also invented differential and integral calculus – so if you are looking for someone to blame for these subjects, it's him).

In 1752 Benjamin Franklin proved that lightning and the spark from amber were one and the same thing. It was not until 1832 that Michael Faraday discovered that electricity could be produced through magnetism by motion. He discovered that when a magnet was moved inside a coil of copper wire, a tiny electric current flows through the wire. But even then it took another 40 years for a practical Direct Current Generator to be built by Thomas Edison in the United States. Yet already we are examining inventions that were made only 200 years ago: we have briefly dismissed everything that went before. From here on in, progress begins to come thick and fast, with the acceleration of the progress becoming frightening by the end of the 20th century.

In the early 19th century various general adding/computing machines were invented, such as the Arithometer. This was invented by a Frenchman, Charles Xavier Thomas de Colmar, and could perform all of the four basic mathematical functions. This machine remained in use until the first decades of the 20th century. Simultaneously those in the Luddite movement began destroying machines, believing that such inventions (presumably of the devil) threatened civilization as they knew it. By 1829 the first mechanical writing machine, the typewriter, was patented by William Austin Burt. It was slow and clumsy, but it stands as the first machine of its type. Within a decade the telegraph was invented and in 1844 Samuel Morse sent the first telegraph between Washington and Baltimore with the message 'What hath God wrought?'. Between 1822 and his death in 1871 Charles Babbage, in England, created (at least on paper) the Analytical Machine that followed instructions from punched cards. Well, it would have followed these instructions if it had worked. The Analytical Machine was intended to be powered by steam, and would be an automatic calculator together with having such features as branching, looping and sequential control. Babbage had the ideas, the design and the vision but sadly not the technology to build what would have been the world's first computer. But just in case you think that this machine would have looked like a modern day computer, prepare for a disappointment. The Analytical Machine would have been the size of a steam engine comprising thousands if not millions of minute clock-work parts. If one of those small components had failed, heaven only knows what would have happened to the monster itself (thus ironically it had something in common with a modern computer!). However, in 1991 a group of British scientists did what Babbage was never able to do a century earlier: build this monster of a machine that calculated precise figures up to 31 digits long. Working with Babbage was Augusta Ada Lovelace, Lord Byron's daughter. She is now thought of as the first computer programmer as she wrote programs in binary for the Analytical Machine.

In 1855, based on Babbage's work, George Scheutz built the first practical mechanical computer. In the same decade George Boole, an Irishman, published 'The Mathematical Analysis of Logic' that described a binary system, which ultimately became Boolean logic, and thus the basis for all computer logic. Before the end of the 19th century Alexander Graham Bell was to invent the telephone (in 1876) and William S Burroughs produced the first adding machine with a printer. In 1857 Elisha Graves Otis put total faith in his safety braking system by cutting the elevator's cables as it ascended a 300-foot tower.

By this time in the wider world, Sigmund Freud had been born, potato chips had been invented, the American Civil War had begun (and ended), Coca-Cola had appeared and various icons of the 20th century were just around the corner: the hamburger, the hot dog and the paperclip. Fraud, on the other hand, did not suddenly materialize: primarily because scams have been with us since the beginning of time. The oft quoted 'original' financial fraud – the South Sea Bubble – is not the start point of this genre, merely a larger version of previous events. That being said, the story of the South Sea Bubble does bear to be remembered, if only to stand as a reminder that nothing which happens in the dot com era is in the least part new or unique. In 1841 Charles MacKay wrote *Memoirs of Extraordinary Popular Delusions and the Madness of Crowds*; somewhat fittingly this book is now available in its entirety online. MacKay was a Scottish poet, journalist and editor who was best known in his life for his verse, some of which was set to music. This book was first published in 1841 and then updated in a two volume second edition in 1852. In the introduction to the book MacKay writes:

> *In reading the history of nations, we find that, like individuals, they have their whims and their peculiarities; their seasons of excitement and recklessness, when they care not what they do. We*

find that whole communities suddenly fix their minds upon one object and go mad in its pursuit; that millions of people become simultaneously impressed with one delusion, and run after it.

Mackay then singles out the Mississippi Scheme in France, the South Sea Bubble and Tulipomania in the Netherlands. Tulipomania occurred when the tulip bulb was introduced in the late-16th or early-17th century and the citizens of the Netherlands went to extreme extents (such as selling their houses and possessions) to own one. Because the bulb was perceived as being so valuable, it was of course inappropriate to plant it! Just imagine what global demand could be manufactured for such a valuable commodity now, by marketing it via the Internet. . .

In 1880 the American Census had taken 7 years to be manually counted, analysed and tabulated. There were great fears expressed that the results of the next census (in 1890) would take over 10 years to compile, which was somewhat problematic as the next but one census would have already begun by then. As a direct result of this quandary a US inventor, Dr. Herman Hollerith, invented the first electromechanical punched card data processing machine, not exactly a catchy title, but this machine's contribution to the speed of technology is clear. Instead of the predicted 10 years, census workers completed the compilation of results in 6 weeks. Babbage had worked on the theory of using cards to give his machine instructions; Hollerith used cards to store data, which were then 'read' by his machine to compile relevant results. Each of the cards stored up to 80 variables: each punch represented one number, and a combination of two punches representing a letter. Such technology was then brought into the business world – which continued to use it up to the 1960s. In the 20 years prior to 1890 working inventions had been coming quick and fast: the Electric Dental Drill (1875), the Phonograph (1877), the incandescent light bulb (1879), the hearing aid (1880), the electric fan (1882), the first skyscraper – 10 storeys high, in Chicago – (1885), the Kodak Camera (1888) and the Dishwasher (1889).

Hollerith created a company, the Tabulating Machine Company, which launched his data processing machines onto the business market in 1901. Ten years later this company merges with the Computing Scale Company and the International Time Recording Company to become the catchily titled Computer-Tabulating and Recording Company. Thomas J Watson, who became President of the company in 1914, obviously had similar reservations about the marketability of such a company name, because in 1924 he changed it to International Business Machines. Two years later the first public demonstration of television was given (in black and white) – but it would take until 1940 for the first colour television broadcast and then virtually the rest of the century for the multi channel digital television world we now know to emerge.

In 1935 IBM introduced the electric typewriter. A year later an Englishman, Alan Turing, published 'On Computable Numbers' which adapts the notion of algorith to the computation of functions. This lead to the first Collossus computer being built in 1941 and Mark II being built in 1944. The machine played a crucial part in the war against Germany by decoding secret messages transmitted by the Germans on their Enigma code machines.

In 1946, two engineers at the University of Pennsylvania, J Presper Eckert, Jr and John William Mauchly, built the first general purpose electronic digital computer. They called it ENIAC (electronic numerical integrator and computer). ENIAC contained about 18,000 vacuum tubes, which replaced the relays that had controlled the operation of Mark 1. The machine weighed more than 30 tons (27 metric tons), occupied more than 1,500 square feet (140 square metres) of floor space, and consumed 150 kilowatts of electricity during operation.

The invention of the transistor in 1947 led to the production of faster and more reliable electronic computers. Transistors control the flow of electric current in electronic equipment. They soon replaced the bulkier, less reliable vacuum tubes. In 1958, Control Data Corporation introduced the first fully transistorized computer, designed by American engineer Seymour Cray. IBM introduced its first transistorized computers in 1959.

Miniaturization (relatively speaking at that time) continued with the development of the integrated circuit in the early 1960s. An integrated circuit contains thousands of transistors and other tiny parts on a small chip. This device enabled engineers to design both mini-computers and high speed mainframes with tremendous memory capacities. Despite the shrinking size of their components, most computers remained relatively large and expensive. But dependence on computers increased dramatically. In 1965 Digital Equipment Corporation launched the PDP–8, the first successful commercial minicomputer.

By the late 1960s, many large businesses relied on computers. Many companies linked their computers together into networks, making it possible for different offices to share information. However, computers at this stage meant mainframes. These needed air-conditioned warehouses to house them and they did less than a high speed desktop PC does now – and did it slower.

The first personal computer, the Altair 8800, was introduced in 1975. While this machine was billed as 'the world's first microcomputer' only electronics hobbyists bought one. In 1977, two American students, Steven P Jobs and Stephen G Wozniak, founded the Apple Computer Company and introduced the Apple II personal computer. The Apple II was much less expensive than mainframes and had a printed circuit motherboard, switching power supply, keyboard, case assembly, manual, game paddles and obviously the most important thing – a game on cassette tape called 'Breakout'. As a result, computers became available to people other than computer specialists and technicians. In 1978 the 5.25 inch floppy (which it almost literally was) disk became the standard medium for software.

In 1981, IBM entered the personal computer market with its PC, which was based on the Intel 8088 chip. The machine was even more successful than the Apple II. Just to prove how successful it was, IBM clones began hitting the marketplace. It was also in 1981 that Microsoft created MS DOS which quickly became the operating system common to most PCs – although I remember only 10 years ago when you had to boot up a machine using MS DOS on a floppy. The speed of change was now accelerating rapidly: 2 million PCs were in use globally in 1981, a year later the figure was 5.5 million. Although no one really knows what the figure is today, estimates put it around 500 million. Unbelievably Windows only really came on the scene in 1990 – and then things really did speed up, both metaphorically and literally.

In 1987 IBM launched its PS/2 Machines, which made the 3.5 inch disk drive standard. The 3.5 inch disk drive had been introduced around 1984 – which begs the question in today's terms as to why it took three years for it to be widely accepted – and remember those wonderful machines that had both 5.25 inch and 3.5 inch disk drives which users at the time though were the height of progress! In 1993 Intel launched the Pentium processor, following it with the Pentium pro in 1995.

There are some observations to make here. It took 101 years to move from a static telephone to a mobile phone and then less than a further 20 to move to the point where I could stand at Singapore airport, having flown half way across the world, and use my GSM mobile to telephone another mobile in Finland (or Russia, Spain, Italy, Belgium, etc etc) and have crystal clear reception – so good that the person I was speaking to couldn't believe I was in Singapore. It took from 1642 to 1980 to invent even the most primitive small computer – that's 238 years! The desktop terminal in its most primitive form only really landed in the early 1980s.

The Internet, in an obscure way, has a direct link to Sputnik, the first artificial earth satellite launched by the USSR in 1957. As a response to that and the feeling that the United States was already falling behind the USSR in the space race, the Advanced Research Projects Agency (ARPA) was formed within the US Department of Defense to lead the way in military orientated science and technology. But even though the 1960s may have swung – the decade achieved it without the Internet – in the background the ARPA project had spawned ARPANET, a small network that was aimed at sharing supercomputers among researchers in the United States. By the early 1970s the ARPANET had grown to 23 hosts networking government research centres and universities around the United States. But something unexpected had occurred: the main purposes of the network were to facilitate the sharing of data and accessing remote computers. But the most popular feature, by far, was e-mail as users communicated with each other as never before. By 1973 the ability to e-mail colleagues went international as ARPANET established connections to the Royal Radar Establishment in Norway. By 1981 ARPANET had 213 hosts with a new one being added every 20 days. Already the first USENET newsgroups had been established, and on 1 January 1983 the host protocol of ARPANET was changed from the initial Host-to-Host Protocol (NCP) to TCP/IP. The following year saw the introduction of the Domain Name System (DNS) as the host database had become so big that it was not possible to store the list of hosts on one computer, thus DNS was created to allow the database to be distributed across numerous individual servers.

On 15 March 1985 the first registered domain was assigned to Symbolics.com, a company that was the premier producer of special-purpose computer systems for running and developing state-of-the-art object oriented programs in Lisp. The first.edu domains appeared in April 1985, the first .gov in July and the first .org.uk names in July. By 1987 the number of Internet hosts exceeded 10,000 and an e-mail link had been established between Germany and China. The inexorable speed of change had now taken ahold, but simultaneously flaws were beginning to appear: on 1 November 1988 a malicious program called the 'Internet Worm' appeared and succeeded in disabling approximately 6,000 of the total Internet hosts. Other new words and concepts were seeping into the language: in 1984 William Gibson created the term 'cyberspace'; people were speaking about hackers, crackers, phreakers and electronic break-ins. In August 1989 after the successful introduction of TCP/IP, ARPANET was turned off for good, and the faster NSFNET took over. Although the Internet has existed since 1973, and was turned over to the private sector in 1984, the World Wide Web was only developed in 1989–90 by Timothy Berners-Lee to enable information to be shared among internationally dispersed teams of researchers at the European Organization for Nuclear Research (CERN) facility near Geneva. This began with a hypertext project which had the intention of making it easier for users to search and retrieve information.

From that point to now, the velocity of development and growth became unstoppable (even taking into account the much hyped millennium bug, which although invited to New Year's Eve parties in 1999, mysteriously didn't quite make it):

- In 1989 America Online came into being as Quantum Computer Services chose this name for its online service.
- In 1992 CERN confirmed that it would not charge fees for Web use.
- In June 1992 an article entitled 'Surfing the Internet: an introduction' by New York Librarian and Internet pioneer Jean Armour Polly was held to be the first *documented* use of this term. To this day Jean is known as the Net-Mom and is now a successful author.
- In 1993 InterNIC was founded to provide directory and registry facilities. In the same year the World Wide Web grew by 341,000 per cent in a year.
- Somewhere around 1994 or 1995 the first Internet banking services began, although there is some doubt as to which bank was actually the first to offer online transactions, as opposed to just using the Web to have an online brochure.
- In 1994 Netscape was founded, based on a free Web browser that one of its co-founders had helped to write. It was purchased by America Online in 1995.
- Various Web sites that are now taken for granted were launched in this period: Yahoo (1994); *The New York Times* (1994 in a test form and in a full format in 1996); in 1995 *The Wall Street Journal*, Amazon, Alta Vista.
- At the height of dot com fever the domain name of Business.com was sold for US $7.5 million; DotTV, inc paid US $50 million to the island of Tuvalu for the rights to their .tv top level domain space.

- In May 1999 Shawn Fanning, a freshman at Northeastern University, founded the Napster online music service which was known as peer-to-peer file sharing. It allowed users to easily trade music encoded in the MP3 format (which had been introduced in 1992), which compresses recordings into small and portable files without sacrificing quality. It didn't take long (just until the end of the year) for multiple record companies to file a massive lawsuit against Napster accusing it of encouraging the illegal copying and distribution of copyrighted material.
- By 2000 the Millennium Bug had gone and not come – the predicted apocalypse had not quite materialized. Neither, in many cases, had the phenomenal profits predicted by thousands of dot com companies. The Love Bug and Melissa viruses did materialize though. The Iridium satellite system, which promised to revolutionize global communications dramatically fell to earth, with the great fear that its satellites might do the same.

Virtually (no pun intended) every piece of hardware that we now come to rely on to conduct business and pleasure has been invented since 1960. In 1964 the first electronic switching system was placed into service, a year later the first communication satellite came online. By 1968 cable television systems had been developed: but it took another four years for the first cellular phones to be demonstrated. Until 1980 all our music was predominantly played off vinyl – the CD has only been around since then; the CD-ROM appeared in 1984. Fax machines (which have now been somewhat superseded by e-mail) only became popular in the mid 1980s. In fact basic e-mail programs had already been invented and used in the early 1970s. The mobile phone was not widely introduced until 1989, at which time the Internet had 100,000 hosts.

A WINDOW ON OPERATING SYSTEMS

Many years ago (before 1985 actually) there was no Windows, and we all had to type text commands into the massive machine with the black and white (or was it green and white?) monitor that sat on our desks. In simple terms an operating system (OS) is the program which, after being initially loaded onto a computer, manages all the other programs on that computer. Increasingly, and almost exclusively, computers are now bought from your friendly local computer super-store with an OS and relevant 'essential' software preloaded, Yet, one day not so far back, you booted up your PC every day by inserting a 5.25 inch floppy disc. This is the short history of how we got from there to today in less than 30 years.

1973: CP/M was invented by Gary Kildall and is an operating system for 8-bit computers. Strangely this program still has its fans today – even though they are all still working on the most recent version, which emerged in 1982. CP/M stands for Control Program/Microcomputers. The great breakthrough of this program was that it loaded from a floppy disk.

1981: IBM launched its first personal computer and chose to use MS-DOS (Microsoft Disk Operating System) instead of CP/M. CP/M fans claim that MS-DOS is nothing more than a copy of their preferred OS.

1985: Windows 1.0 manufactured by Microsoft was launched in November and promised an easy to use graphical interface. To impress those of us around at the time the Windows 1.0 package included a calendar, cardfile, notepad, clock, control panel and many more amazing facilities.

1987: Windows 2.0 and Windows 286 and 386 were released. Unfortunately many computers around at the time struggled with being able to run the software properly.

1988: OS/2, a 16-bit operating system that had originally been developed jointly by IBM and Microsoft kind of came and went, but as with other redundant operating systems, still has fans today.

1990: Windows 3.0 was launched in May, at about the same time as Intel's 386 processor. Microsoft now had the most successful operating system ever, selling more than 10 million copies.

1992: Windows 3.1 was released in April and sold over 3 million copies (including upgrades) in its first two months. IBM continued on their own road with a second version of OS/2.

1993: Windows NT was launched, targeted at network servers, workstations and software development machines. In November 1993 Benny S Lee of Everex Systems Inc achieves the distinction of being the first person to achieve a prison sentence for software counterfeiting in the United States. The sentence was for a year, and the counterfeit software he manufactured and sold was MS-DOS.

1994: Version 1 of the Linux Kernel was released. Linux is an operating system with a source code freely available to everyone. Created by Linus Torvals in Finland, this OS has been developed as a collaborative effort across the Internet, involving over a hundred developers.

1995: Windows 95 was launched in August – a 32-bit system which ran independently of MS-DOS (a first for Windows).

1996: Windows CE 1.0 appeared in November. It replicated the look and feel of Windows for handheld and palmtop computers.

1998: Windows 98 was released in June. A browser-like interface was introduced and the OS now focused on the Internet. By now a new version of Windows is a major world media event.

1999: Around this time I visited a makeshift street stall next to Red Square, Moscow (which is probably still going to this day). There I was presented with a choice of about a hundred different software and OS packages – all counterfeit and all available for the rouble equivalent of US $15. In 1999 it was estimated that the computer software industry is losing up to US $20 billion per year because of piracy and counterfeiting. Organized crime groups undertook a substantial volume of this illicit activity. In some countries up to 90 per cent of software (including operating systems) are illegitimate copies.

2000: Windows 2000 and Windows ME were launched; however both appeared to be facelifts (to varying degrees) of previous versions of Windows.

2001: Windows XP was launched on 25 October. It promised a faster OS enabling users to do more with their computer and the Internet. Some users still swore by CP/M or OS/2, and thus remained distinctly underwhelmed by Microsoft's new product. Linux is now one of the fastest growing operating systems in the world with millions of users, and increasingly becoming more mainstream as opposed to a novelty. And of course those rather useful Apple Macs have none of this Windows paraphernalia, but run very well on their own MAC O/S.

The dazzling array of viruses, computer attacks and related events are far too numerous and extensive to hope to catalogue. However, here's a chronological selection of the most notable:

A SHORT TIMELINE OF VIRUSES

1983: Fred Cohen formally defined a virus as 'a computer program that can affect other computer programs by modifying them in such a way as to include a (possibly evolved) copy of itself.'

1986: The first PC virus was created in Pakistan. It was named the Brain virus – although somewhat comically it is misspelt as 'Brian' in some commentaries. This was a boot sector virus and thus only infected the boot records of floppy disks, but not hard drives. It spread by users trading disks (those were the days!). It would occupy space on the disk so that it could not be used. One novelty with the virus was that it contained the name, address and phone numbers of its creators. While it is not entirely clear why this was, one story is that the creators (two brothers running a computer store in Lahore) wrote the virus so that it would infect any computers running a bootleg copy of a software program that they had written.

1987: The Christmas Tree Exec worm (actually a Trojan horse) spread on IBM PCs, forcing many systems to shut down, including the worldwide IBM network. A user would receive an e-mail Christmas card that included executable code. If executed the program claimed to draw a Christmas tree on the user's screen. It did actually do this: but it also sent itself to everyone on the user's address lists.

1988: The first anti-virus program was compiled in Indonesia; two years later Norton AntiVirus was launched by Symantec.

1988: Robert Morris (a graduate student at Cornell University) launched an Internet worm program. It replicated itself over 6,000 hosts with the inevitable result of bringing almost all of the network to a stop. He was arrested, fined US $10,000, sentenced to three years' probation and ordered to do 400 hours' community service.

1988: Jerusalem (aka Friday the 13th) appeared. It was activated every Friday the 13th affecting various files and deleting programs that ran on that day. It also executed a software loop that would slow down computers. It was widely imitated.

1991: The first widespread polymorphic virus was found. Polymorphic viruses change their appearance at each new infection.

1992: Remember the Michangelo virus? Discovered in 1991, this virus would erase IBM hard disks on March 6, the birthday of Michelangelo. Hyped by media reporting (and misreporting) a solemn and serious estimate was given that 5 million computers would crash. No one knows how many did – but the highest estimate is 10,000 worldwide (the lowest estimate being zero!). Apocalypse avoided then, but awareness of the problem raised substantially.

1994: Post ironic or just plain stupid? One of the first e-mail hoaxes, Good Times, told you by e-mail that a malicious virus would erase your entire hard drive. All you had to do was open an e-mail titled 'Good Times' – which presumably you had just done, to read the warning. The hoax kept coming around every 6–12 months.

1995: Word Concept – an interesting development because it showed that Microsoft Word could be used as a platform for viruses. When opened it executed a series of macros that made changes to documents on templates. It spread as users swapped Word files.

1995: On November 15 Christopher Pile (alias 'The Black Baron') appeared for sentencing for 11 offences under the Sections 2 and 3 of the Computer Misuse Act at Exeter Crown Court, England. Pile had already pleaded guilty to all charges and was sentenced to 18 months in prison. The viruses were inspired by the British comedy/science fiction series *Red Dwarf*.

1998: The first of many Trojan viruses to steal information from AOL users was launched.

1999: The Melissa virus, which infects Word documents and then very kindly e-mails itself to 50 people in your address book, spread like wildfire. The virus also infects Word documents and e-mails them as attachments (there goes confidentiality then). It spread faster than any other virus.

1999: Disguised as a Y2K fix, Babylonia appeared. It is a virus capable of downloading and updating itself from the Internet.

1999: The Love Bug/ILOVEYOU Virus hit Outlook, like Melissa. The virus came as a VBS attachment and proceeded to delete files (MP3, MP2 and JPG to name but a selection). The Virus also sends usernames and passwords to the author of the virus. It was one of the first viruses that used Visual Basic scripts to execute commands on a computer.

2000: VBS.NewLove.A virus appeared – it overwrites every file on the user's system not currently in use.

2000: The Anna Kournikova virus (aka VBS/SST) appeared – offering a picture of the tennis star. It operated in the same way as Melissa and The Love Bug.

2001: The Code Red I and II attacked computer networks. It is a worm, as opposed to a virus, and took advantage of a vulnerability in Windows 2000 and NT server software. Microsoft itself admits that it was affected.

The terminal velocity of viruses:

- In 1986 there was one virus.
- In 1990 estimates of the number of viruses ranged from 200 to 500.
- One year later the highest estimate hit 1,000.
- By 1992 estimates ranged from 1,000 to 2,300.
- In 1996 the highest estimate went over 10,000.
- In 1998 the top limit went over 20,000.
- In 2000 the maximum number of viruses exceeded 50,000.
- In May 2002 Sophos Anti-Virus detected 73,553 viruses while Symantec listed 61,086.

A HISTORY OF HACKS

1960s: The first hackers appeared at MIT (Massachusetts Institute of Technology). The name they adopted was one that the model train group at the school used to describe what they did to electric trains, tracks and switches to make them run faster. 'Hacks' were essentially programming shortcuts to make things run quicker or better.

1970s: As crazy as it sounds, the phenomena of phone phreaking (hacking into national or international phone networks to make free calls) started from a breakfast cereal box. John Draper found that a toy whistle given away free in Cap'n Crunch cereal produced a 2,600-hertz signal. This was exactly the same tone that was used to access AT&T's long distance telephone switching system. Draper – who forever more will be known as Cap'n Crunch – constructed a blue box that when used with the free whistle allowed free calls. *Esquire* magazine subsequently published instructions as to how to make your very own blue box, and a whole new crime was born. With another one of those ironies ever present in this story, John Draper is now developing intrusion detection software, details of which and his life story can be found on www.webcruchers.com/crunch/.

1978: Randy Seuss and Ward Christiansen from Chicago created the first bulletin board system where hackers exchanged information, tips, stolen passwords and stolen credit card details. There are now over 40,000 bulletin boards worldwide.

1980: Hacking groups began to form, the primary ones being the Legion of Doom in the United States and the Chaos Club in Germany.

1983: The film *War Games* starring Matthew Broderick was released and proved to be highly influential. In it a teenage hacker accidentally broke into the military's nuclear combat simulator computer. When the film was released the Cold War was still in full swing, and the events showed the United States and the USSR coming closer to war.

1984: The hacker magazine *2600* was launched. It provides tips to would-be hackers and comments on the key issues of the day. The magazine is now sold in the United States at major book shops and operates a Web site (www.2600.com). A year later the online 'zine Phrack began.

1986: The United States Congress passed the Computer Fraud and Abuse Act which established two key felony offences: one established to address the unauthorized access of a federal interest computer with the intention to commit fraudulent theft, the other to address 'malicious damage,' which involves altering information in, or preventing the use of, a federal interest computer. A malicious damage violation would have to result in a loss to the victim of US $1,000 or more, except in cases involving the alteration of medical records. The law did not cover juveniles and it presupposed that individual states would enact similar legislation.

1989: As Clifford Stoll, a systems administrator at the University of California, Berkeley, was later to describe in 'The Cuckoo's Egg', five West German hackers were arrested on espionage charges. The hackers had perpetrated systematic intrusions into US university and government systems and then sold the information to the KGB. Three hackers were convicted, but because the stolen information was not classified, they never spent any time in prison.

1989: Enter Kevin Mitnick, who was convicted of stealing software from DEC and long distance access codes from the US telephone company MCI. He served a year in prison and on his release was ordered, as part of his probation, not to use computers or associate with any other hackers.

1990: Why do we continually debate whether it is possible to hack into critical infrastructures when the first jail sentences were handed out for such offences in 1990? Four members of the Legion of Doom (a southern US hacking group) were arrested for stealing the technical specifications of the 911 emergency telephone network of BellSouth. The company spent US $3 million on improved security as it was found that the hackers had also stolen passwords, logins and connection addresses. Three of the hackers are found guilty.

1990s: A Texas professor received (somewhat out of the blue) death threats as a result of a hacker who had broken into his e-mail and sent 20,000 racist messages out from it.

1991: During the Gulf War, the US General Accounting Office later revealed, Dutch teenage hackers changed or copied unclassified (but still sensitive) information from the Defense Department systems. They then tried to sell the data to the Iraqis, who thought that they were the subject of a hoax.

1993: Kevin Poulson was already a wanted man for breaking into phone company systems. But instead of lying low, he hacked the phone systems of three Los Angeles radio stations, so that he and two of his friends would effectively be the only callers in phone-in contests. The prizes they won included two Porsches, US $20,000 and various holidays.

1994: 'Data Stream' hacked into numerous systems including NASA computers, the Korean Atomic Research Institute and the Griffith US

Air Force Base. Master Criminal? Ace foreign spy? No – a 16-year-old British boy.

1995: 'Come in Mr Mitnick!' In February of 1995 Kevin Mitnick was captured in Raleigh, NC, by federal agents and charged with stealing 20,000 credit card numbers. Mitnick was imprisoned without trial until March 1999, when he pleaded guilty to seven felonies. He then served a further 10 months in prison, finally being released in January 2000 on parole. Vast over-reaction surely? After five years of this Mitnick was put on parole and is not allowed to use computer equipment until 2003 without permission from his probation officer.

1994: The stuff of Hollywood films seeped into reality: in July 1994 customers complained of US $400,000 mysteriously 'disappearing' from two Citibank accounts. The saga ended with Russian hacker, Vladimir Levin, being tried in New York and pleading guilty to stealing US $3.7 million from Citibank – with the original charge specifying an amount of over US $10 million. Levin was a graduate of the St Petersburg Tekhnologichesky University who had accessed the Citibank system, broken user identification codes and customers' passwords. The stolen funds were transferred to accounts in Finland, the United States, Germany and the Netherlands. Levin used a laptop to achieve this, and finally ended up with a three year jail sentence and an order to pay back US $240,015 to Citibank. This sentence was, strangely, less than the one served by Kevin Mitnick. . .

1997: AOHell was unleashed, which enabled almost a whole generation of teenage would-be hackers to terrify America Online: for days on end genuine AOL users logged on to find their mail boxes flooded with mail bombs and chat rooms decimated with Spam messages.

1997: An Israeli youth nicknamed 'The Analyser' was arrested for, in the words of the Deputy Defence Secretary 'the most organized and systematic attack on the Pentagon'. Two teenagers from California were also arrested. The Israeli youth, Ehud Tenebaum, is today reported as being the chief technology officer of a computer consulting firm.

1997: A Croatian youth successfully intruded on computers at a US Air Force base in Guam.

1998 and 1999: Rumours abounded that hackers had stolen classified software that enabled them to control a military satellite. This was reported as being either a British or US satellite.

1998: In testimony before US Congress the L0pht hacker group claimed that it would take less than 30 minutes to shut down nationwide access to the Internet. L0pht urged far more robust security measures.

1999: Numerous Web sites were attacked and defaced in May and June. Victim sites included the US Senate, US Army and White House.

1999: In December the DVD industry sued 72 hackers and associates for posting information and links to software that unlocked the system that was supposed to prevent illegal copying of DVDs. The system was supposed to be 'Hacker proof', but a Norwegian group called the Masters of Reverse Engineering obviously hadn't read that part of the press release.

2000: In February Denial of Service attacks abounded with eBay, Yahoo, Amazon, CNN and various others being flooded with massive volumes of data requests.

2000: In October Microsoft admitted that hackers had accessed its corporate network, and at the very least source code for future products had been examined. One US report describes this event as 'a possible national security risk'.

Just quite where this terminal velocity has taken us is open to question:

- According to *PC World* magazine in September 2001 the world-wide shipments of PCs would total 129.6 million in that year, down from 131.7 million units in 2000.
- The worldwide Internet population nearing the end of 2001 was, it is estimated, between 250 and 500 million users. According to Nielsen//NetRatings in July 2001 this includes the following home Internet access: 165.2 million users in the United States, 27.9 million in Germany, 23.9 million in the UK, 18.7 million in Italy, 11.6 million in Taiwan and 9.7 million in Australia.
- In November 2001, according to Netnames, there were 36,149,297 Internet domains registered on a global basis and 22,373,097 registered dot coms.
- The oft quoted but true (as far as anyone can tell) fact is that the most popular search term on the Internet is 'sex', with 'pornography/porno' not far behind – in something like fourth place of terms searched.
- The *Chicago Tribune* reported that secret monitoring by the US Treasury Department of Internet usage by IRS employees discovered that 51 per cent of their time online was spent on such activities as personal e-mail, online chats, shopping and checking personal finances. Such high usage of workplace facilities for personal reasons is borne out by numerous other surveys.

- Somewhat frighteningly, according to emarketer.com, 32.6 per cent of workers have no specific objective when they surf the Internet.
- New York research company Messaging Online estimated that at the end of 1999 there were 569 million e-mail accounts. E-mail, in many surveys and polls, is the most frequently used application by over 90 per cent of Internet users. According to e-marketeer.com, the average number of e-mails received each day in the United States is 13.8 (although other surveys have put the figure much higher for e-mails received by workers).
- By May 2001 in excess of half a billion GSM phones were in use on a global basis; 10 million of these are in the United States (where the system has only recently taken off) while in China there are 82.4 million GSM customers. The reasons given by the GSM Association for the exponential growth rate of the system are that these phones work seamlessly in any city or country and one telephone number can be used on virtually a worldwide basis.

If you really want to know about technology though, ask the people who have never known anything different – teenagers. They are the obvious reference point for all of your technology queries, from how to set the video to how to download and play back MP3 files taking in, along the way, instant messaging and programming your top of the range mobile phone. Thus it is never any surprise that all statistics (such as they are) confirm that it is precisely this group who are at the cutting edge of technical ability (and legality) when it comes to all flavours of digital crime.

DOUBTFUL DEFINITIONS – FROM COMPUTER CRIME TO THE DIGITAL AGE

Computer crime in one form or another could well be part of virtually every investigation in the coming years.

Donald K Stern, US Department of Justice attorney

According to Interpol the chances that a US adult will have the skills required to commit some form of e-crime is 1 in 11. Thus 9 per cent of technology users have the know-how to become digital criminals.

However, as recently as the 1990s our perceptions of what was then termed 'computer crime' were radically different from such perceptions now. In 1990 the UK Audit Commission published a 'Survey of Computer Fraud and Abuse', which at the time was viewed as an excellent summary of the risks posed by current day technology. The 33 page report was accompanied by a supplement of almost 100 pages that listed 180 cases of computer fraud. Looking at the report now, it seems as much a historical document as the Magna Carta or American Declaration of Independence. A glance at the typologies used to define and record computer fraud and abuse will show just how far we have moved on. The headings used were:

- Unauthorized alteration of input (36 cases).
- Destruction, Suppression, Misappropriation of Output (23 cases).
- Alteration of Computerized Data (17 cases).
- Alteration/Misuse of Programs (24 cases).
- Theft of Data and Software (11 cases).
- Use of Illicit Software (24 cases).
- Hacking (17 cases).
- Sabotage (7 cases).
- Viruses (53 cases).

The section on viruses was new and, judging by the number of examples quoted, was a harbinger of things to come. In total the 180 cases examined generated a financial loss of £1,140,142, giving an average hit of just over £6,000 per case. Apart from hacking, sabotage and viruses, which were all new or newish events, the threats relating to technology were firmly centred in an internal environment. That said, the report made clear that even in this now quaint but controllable atmosphere it was becoming difficult to manage and avoid risk. None of these comments should be viewed as being disparaging – merely that the terminal velocity of change has rendered such studies irrelevant. The authors of the report implicitly acknowledged this, with their opening lines which as much as anything written at the time, were deeply prophetic:

> *The benefits of information technology are well documented; in the next decade there will be changes which will make today's advances seem quite unremarkable. But as with all benefits there is a cost and part of the cost of the advantages which technology brings is the need to protect the investment.*

This 1990 report offers two further insights as to where we were then – and how far we have got from there. Firstly there is no mention of the Internet, simply because what we now take for granted did not exist in any form that would be recognizable today to the mainstream user. Secondly – and crucially – the definition used for computer fraud was deliberately wide, stated as 'any fraudulent behavior connected with computerization by which someone intends to gain dishonest advantage'.

By the mid 1990s reports and surveys on computer fraud and related issues were coming thick and fast – although in retrospect one does wonder about the usefulness of some of them. The 1994 'IT Security Breaches Survey Summary', part authored by the UK Department of Trade and Industry, concluded that the average cost of a security breach exceeded US $9,000. This document then showed a graphic reason of why digital crime would be (and still is) such a problem by concluding that 'Fire is the most feared security threat but computer equipment failure is the most common breach'. At around the same time the Audit Commission returned to the fray with 'Opportunity Makes a Thief: An analysis of computer abuse', a well informed and thought provoking document which in many instances still remains unanswered today. The subtext of the entire report can be summarized by the phrase 'Management often fails to understand the risks which computer abuse presents'; this is then broadened out into three key areas of risk:

- disregard for basic control procedures;
- ineffective monitoring procedures;
- ineffective internal audit.

Crucially, in a move away from much that had gone before, this report realizes the significance of attacks from outside, rather than focusing on crime perpetrated by insiders. This is made abundantly clear by comments such as 'Computer abuse is often carried out at a distance so that detection of the perpetrator is difficult'. However, the definition of computer abuse remained deliberately wide, referring to it as an umbrella term embracing various types of deliberate criminal acts each of which calls for different skills and techniques in detection.

In the area of computer crime there are more problems with definitions than any other comparable topic. This is because there are so many incidents which are conveniently (or rather inconveniently) bundled together under a catch-all heading. This semantic issue is further complicated by the origins of 'computer crime'. As can be seen in the late 1980s and early 1990s many learned reports were issued on the subject – but they appeared to confuse what exactly they were examining. The cases they quoted were essentially frauds which, in their perpetration, involved the use of a computer. For example, where accounting records had been fraudulently misused and this data had previously been held manually but was now held on a PC, this qualified as computer fraud. Using this logic in the 21st century would mean that virtually every financial crime committed is a computer crime – as somewhere during its execution a piece of IT hardware or software will be involved. Even the collective term to cover such acts has never been agreed upon, so come on down any of the following (or variants thereof): computer crime, computer related crime, computer assisted crime, computer abuse, computer fraud, electronic crime or fraud, digital crime, e-crime, cyber crime. Even more perplexing and confusing in equal parts is what any or each of these terms comprises. The UK Audit Commission had included the following types of problems in their studies:

- fraud;
- misuse of personal data;
- illicit software (which in turn includes counterfeit software and genuine software used without the requisite licence);
- private work;
- viruses;
- sabotage;
- hacking.

Then there are 'attacks' made on computer systems for a variety of reasons and motives – many of which do not necessarily involve theft/fraud:

- Military and intelligence attacks made by espionage agents or military personnel.
- Business attacks made by competitors or their agents.
- Financial attacks made on banks and businesses by criminals.
- Terrorist attacks made on computers in governments and other related institutions.
- Grudge attacks made on companies by disgruntled customers, employees or ex-employees.
- Fun attacks made on all types of organizations by crackers.

In the early 1990s the 'United Nations Manual on the prevention and control of computer related crime' commented that:

> *There has been a great deal of debate among experts on just what constitutes a computer crime or computer related crime. Even after several years, there is no internationally recognized definition of those terms. . . There is no doubt among the authors and experts who have attempted to arrive at definitions of computer crime that the phenomenon exists. However, the definitions that have been produced tend to relate to the study for which they were written. . . A global definition of computer crime has not been achieved; rather, functional definitions have been the norm.*

Little has changed since then, except that numerous 'definitions' of this critical phenomenon have come in faster than your PC boots up!

One interpretation defines computer crime as any criminal act which involves one or more computers either as the object of the crime or as an accessory or facilitator in its commission. This broad definition is then subdivided into two categories – computer related crime (CRC) and computer assisted crime (CAC). CRC is where the computer or its contents are the subject of a criminal attack, often quoted examples of this are hacking and denial of service attacks (we will leave aside for the moment the vexed question of whether hacking in its truest sense is a criminal act). CAC is where the computer is merely a tool to enable a crime to be committed, which would have been committed by other means if the computer was not there. In this category the most obvious example is financial fraud, which predated computers by a few thousand years.

But this is merely one interpretation: another one has it that there are three key types of computer crime: unauthorized use of a computer, releasing a malicious computer program, and harassment and stalking in cyberspace. These three types are typified by the following forms:

- ■ Unauthorized use
  - – accessing and reading confidential information
  - – changing and/or deleting data
  - – denial of service attacks
  - – altering Web sites.
- ■ Malicious computer programs
  - – viruses
  - – computer worms

- Trojan horses
- logic bombs.

■ Harassment and stalking. This final category shifts us into something else entirely; but however distressing the experience of cyber harassment is for the victim, are not these events merely computer related crimes in that stalking has been transposed into a new medium and delivery mechanism?

Confused already by the choice of definitions available? An anonymous paper on the Internet returns us to another broad definition, 'Computer Crime is generally defined as any crime accomplished through specialist knowledge of computer technology'. The types of crime that are then listed include white collar crime, physical attacks on computers, computer viruses, embezzlement, viruses, burglary, sabotage, espionage, murder, forgery, hacking, trespassing, copyright infringement, piracy and vandalism. So there we have it: computers are responsible for almost every crime that is perpetrated. Don't such definitions of computer crime miss the point? The fundamental point, working on the KISS principle, is that computers don't commit crime, people do. Just as computer crime against large organizations has, in the past, been viewed as a 'victimless' act (which of course it isn't), various definitions of computer crime seem to suggest (or at the very least imply) that somehow the computers themselves commit crimes without any human intervention. So when the Canadian Criminal Intelligence Service comments that 'Increasing use is being made of the Internet as a means of facilitating criminal activity, including prostitution, drug trafficking, the distribution of child pornography and fraud', the critical word is not 'Internet' but 'facilitating'. The Internet, for example, doesn't lure young girls into prostitution, people do. The Internet simply provides a new delivery mechanism for customers to get details of, or to contact, prostitutes.

Peter Grabosky defines various varieties of crimes that 'involve information systems as instruments and/or targets or crime' in his 2000 paper 'Computer Crime: A criminological overview'. These are:

■ theft of telecommunications services;
■ communication in furtherance of criminal conspiracies, such as drug trafficking, gambling, money laundering, illegal weapons sales and child pornography;
■ information piracy, forgery and counterfeiting;
■ dissemination of offensive materials;

- electronic money laundering and tax evasion;
- sales and investment fraud;
- illegal interception of telecommunications;
- electronic funds transfer fraud.

Such attempts to determine typologies are obviously helpful, but in many ways they muddy already clouded waters. Of the eight types listed above, I would argue that only two are true 'computer crime' – theft of telecommunications services and illegal interception of telecommunications. Whereas the other types – although important – are merely new variants on old themes that the brave new world of technology has made more prevalent by providing a new omnipresent and omnipotent delivery channel. We constantly appear to find it difficult to judge whether when, for example, a computer is stolen, is it a computer crime or just a simple theft? The answer, of course, is ambiguous: not only does it depend on the jurisdiction the theft occurred in, but it is also impacted by the motives behind the theft. Was the computer stolen because of its value as a piece of hardware? Or was the real motive to obtain the contents of the hard drive, in which case the computer itself was merely incidental.

As we have seen the types of crime that can come under the umbrella of 'computer crime' or the many other terms used to describe this phenomena are many and numerous. Thus it is important to devise or select a working definition that both encompasses all of these topics and simultaneously distinguishes between them. In essence the most workable definition has three categories:

- The computer as a target. This would include hacking, viruses, theft of telecommunications services.
- The computer as a tool of the crime – where technology has replaced other methods such as fraud, money laundering, counterfeiting using new technology, and cyber stalking.
- The computer as an incidental accessory of the crime. Examples would be a criminal's accounting records held on a computer (as opposed to an old fashioned sales ledger), an anonymous letter that was composed on a computer rather than being handwritten.

This, admittedly, is a very basic attempt to categorize a complex problem. Additionally it must be accepted that each category is not necessarily mutually exclusive. All of this being said, the advantage of seeing electronic crime in such a way is that the 'umbrella' concept is still retained, but an attempt is made to determine what importance the computer (or piece of technology) played in the execution of the crime.

This is a book about crime, fraud and risk in the Digital Age. Why the Digital Age? Because although we as humans experience life analogically, the world we inhabit is increasingly a digital one with computers and related technology at its centre. Computers effectively control transport networks (air, train, buses), hospitals, global weather services, national security, governments, military organizations, banks. There remain very few business that could operate without information technology – hence the attraction for criminals: computers now contain most of both the money and information they want. In the wired age, where connectivity is all, no one is safe from attack. More than ever before the World Wide Web transcends the traditional restrictions of location and security. Geographic location becomes increasingly unimportant (it doesn't matter where you are or where your bank is). The flip side of this coin is that criminals can attack from anywhere across the globe and disappear just as easily. If it hasn't already done so, the Internet will transform the way we:

- communicate;
- obtain information;
- use financial services;
- conduct business;
- govern countries, states and individuals.

Thus the Internet and the Digital Age will change the nature and operation of crime and risk beyond recognition, if for no other reason than that's where the money is going to be. Technology is an ideal forum for crime because:

- Digital crime can be anonymous.
- Crime can be transacted at a great distance without any need to meet or confront your victim. The criminal no longer has to be anywhere near the traditional scene of the crime – a financial fraud can be orchestrated from just around the block or from St Petersburg – the list of possible locations is actually infinite.
- Digital crime is viewed as a 'victimless' act – which it isn't of course.
- Crimes can be carried out quickly and almost invisibly without leaving traces.

- The increasing level of global interconnectivity makes crimes easy to commit: no physical borders to cross, no customs controls, no security checks. Moreover, whereas physical break-ins require a certain level of stamina, if not brute force, only to discover that the confidential documents you seek are in fact in another storage facility entirely, in the digital world you just click your mouse to access another file or server.
- In the digital world, all that is being transferred is bits of information. In 1997 Daniel Geer, a security expert, commented to a US Government Subcommittee that 'If I want to steal money, a computer is much better than a handgun. It would take a long time to steal US $10 million with a handgun'. But it's even more than that – in a normal suitcase you can fit (I am told, but have no personal experience of this) US $5 million. Thus to steal US $10 million one ends up with two heavy suitcases. Steal US $10 million by digital means and you move the figure one and seven zeros from somewhere in cyberspace to a new home that you control. In a more fundamental way, any financial amount you steal in the digital environment is a series of ones and zeros. Whatever the sum, the money has no mass – thus it is as easy to steal S 10 million (or US $100 million, or more) as it to steal US $1.
- Vast amounts of technical knowledge are not necessarily required. All hardware and software providers see the creation and development of a user friendly environment as their prime aim – drag and drop, point and click, plug and play. Need a virus creator? Download it from the Internet. Need to know how to hack? Read detailed instructions on the Internet.

The analogue or atom based culture has seen that much of what defined it can now be stored digitally: access the complete texts of Shakespeare's plays online; store your innermost spoken thoughts digitally on a handheld dictation machine; take photographs of your friends and loved ones without a film, download them onto a computer and then upload to share them on the Internet; rip your favorite CDs and vinyl records onto your hard drive and then convert them to digital MP3 files. The facilitators of the Digital Age have increasingly become the speed at which technology moves forward – particularly in terms of processor speed and storage capacity, combined with continually decreasing prices. Looking across my desk now I probably have as much power and capacity there as was to be found in massive air-conditioned silent computer suites 10 years ago. The laptop I am writing this on has a 550mhz chip, a 6Gb hard drive – and even better than that, plays music CDs! My mobile phone, which is not much larger than a cigarette packet, has so many features that I've given up understanding it. My main phone is a digital hands free one with an inbuilt digital answering service that records pin sharp messages without a tape. Additionally it too has so many features that I'm afraid to press any of the non-numeric keys. My main computer is wired to the world through an ISDN line, and connected to everything else through an Ethernet network, or USB connection to my palmtop. The oft quoted laws applying to this constant change – those of Gordon Moore and Robert Metcalfe – seem to be still holding true: Moore's law stating that every 18 months processing power doubles while cost holds constant; Metcalfe's law stating that the usefulness, or utility of a network equals the square of the number of users.

Networktivity – a wired world – is the third part of the equation with increased power and decreased price that has reshaped our world. We now exist in a connected digital world upon which we heavily depend. However, for every high speed computer that is purchased and wired into the Internet, to enable homework to be done, online chatting to take place, or even books about the subject to be written on it, there is the possibility that a criminal (or criminally inclined individual) can be appreciating the possibilities and opportunities of the Digital Age.

SCALES AND JUSTICE

According to my calculations, the problem doesn't exist.

US car bumper sticker

If you have come here for a definitive and objective evaluation of the scale of digital crime, then I'm going to have to disappoint you – sorry. To attempt such an evaluation can at best be described as a challenge while the opposite end of the spectrum renders it an impossibility. Whatever you might read, hear or see no one has the faintest idea of how much such crime there is, or has been – or for that matter will be. The subject of the level of such crime is a breeding ground for vested interests: hackers exaggerate; victim organizations deny the problem; journalists see it as good copy; security consultancies use 'definitive reports' to sell their services; law enforcement agencies have other priorities. While researching this book I came across a news clipping that I had kept from 1994 headed 'Computer fraud rises sharply'. It came as very little surprise that subsequent research from then to now essentially produced numerous repetitions of this view. In an attempt to avoid clichés, I will endeavour to discuss this subject without using the following words, terms or phrases:

- 'Tip of the fraud iceberg' as in stated figures (of any amount), which are a vast understatement of the problem.
- 'It's going to get a lot worse before it gets better', which presupposes that we have some idea of what the state of play is now so that we can measure when it gets worse (before it subsequently gets better).
- 'Fivefold rise in computer crime' or '10,000 per cent increase anticipated in crime losses' or in fact any percentage increase. All that we may know now is the reported level of digital crime (and it is impossible to gauge even this on a global basis) so talk of increases are meaningless.
- 'Digital crime set to soar' or claims of 'an exploding crime problem' – particularly suspect when quoted by a company trying to sell you an anti-virus, firewall or other security program.
- 'Just how serious is online/digital/Internet/computer fraud?' Numerous articles have run with this title, with diametrically opposing answers – it is more serious than you dare to imagine, or the media have hyped this problem out of all proportion (presumably through articles of the first type).
- 'Is there a security problem in computing/the Internet/the wired world?' Why bother writing (or reading) an article with a title such as this, when the answer is unequivocally 'Yes'?

Just because there is no accurate or reliable way of measuring national never mind global figures for digital crime hasn't prevented a wide range of individuals, companies and regulatory bodies attempting to do exactly this. That is not to say (necessarily) that any such reports or evaluations are incorrect or ill conceived, rather they are based on limited data which at times is questionable in its accuracy. More crucially, with such restricted information it is probably unwise (if not downright foolish) to attempt any meaningful conclusions or predictions. But these caveats haven't stopped a multitude of efforts, some of which are detailed in the following points (presented in chronological order). The figures quoted should not be taken as facts.

▪ In 1987 an American Bar association survey confirmed that 72 out of 300 corporations and government agencies polled had been the victim of a computer related crime in the preceding 12 months. Losses ranged from US $145 million to US $730 million.

▪ As far back as 1993 four out of every five computer crimes investigated by the FBI involved unauthorized access to computers using the Internet.

▪ The British National Computer Centre 1994 study into IT Security Breaches and failures reported a highest single loss uncovered in their survey as £1.2 million.

▪ The American Bar Association reported again in 1996 when a survey of 1,000 companies showed that just under half of them (48 per cent) had experienced computer fraud in the previous five years.

▪ In the same year the UK Association of British Insurers gave an estimate that the cost of computer crime was £250 million – but this was only 20 per cent of the actual loss.

▪ In February 1998 police statistics confirmed that computer crime was costing South Africa more money than armed robberies and cash in transit heists (which are the more publicized events). Losses were estimated at R 326 million. Computer crime is perpetrated by organized crime syndicates, disgruntled employees, embezzlers and hackers. South Africa's computer criminals have an added advantage – there are no laws to prosecute them with that cover computer crime.

▪ In March 1998 the San Francisco based Computer Security Institute published its 'Computer Crime and Security Survey' which is authored with the participation of the FBI. The data is taken from 520 respondents and contained the following frightening conclusions:
  – 64 per cent of respondents reported security breaches in the previous 12 months.
  – 72 per cent acknowledged suffering financial loss from such breaches – but only 46 per cent were able to quantify such losses.
  – The most serious losses were due to unauthorized access by insiders (18 respondents reported total losses of US $50,565,000 – which means an average loss of US $2,809,166); telecommunications fraud (32 respondents with a total loss of US $17,256,000: average loss US $539,250); and financial fraud (29 respondents with a total loss of US $11,239,000: average loss of US $387,552).

- The number of organizations reporting that their Internet connection as a frequent point of attack rose from 47 per cent in 1997 to 54 per cent in 1998.
- 63 per cent of respondents had no policy for preserving evidence for civil or criminal proceedings after a successful intrusion (a further 15 per cent didn't know whether they had one!).
- Only 17 per cent of intrusions were reported to Law Enforcement agencies.
- 74 per cent of unauthorized usage came from outside the organization but 70 per cent originated inside the organization.
- In the two year period 1997–98 there were 55 incidents of financial fraud which generated losses of over US $35 million.

■ In March 1998 the Jeddah Chapter of the Institute of Chartered Accountants of India cautioned banks about the growing number of frauds involving computers, which are estimated to cost the Saudi Banking sector £5 per employee per day.

■ In March 1998 the FBI told a hearing of Senators that it had recorded a significant increase in its pending cases of computer intrusions in 1998 from 206 to 480 – an increase of 133 per cent and up 250 per cent on two years previously.

■ US telephone companies lose more than US $1 billion to hackers annually (generally, the average age of hackers is 13–14).

■ It has been estimated that computer crime in the US exceeds US $8 billion each year: fraud exceeds US $555 million. Banks are the biggest victims with losses to fraud estimated at US $1 billion. (These figures are continually updated. A 1997 report for the Democratic members of the House Banking Committee puts the loss figure for thefts from US financial institutions by computer attacks at US $2.4 billion).

■ The US National Computer Crimes Squad estimates that between 85–97 per cent of computer crimes are not even detected. Glennok Wahlert, Manger Corporate Planning of the Australian Federal Police commented in 1998 that 80 per cent of companies who had suffered security breaches were not aware that a breach had happened.

■ Fewer than 10 per cent of all computer crimes are reported (even this figure may be too high – the true figure of reported computer crime could be less than 5 per cent of the total).

■ A 2001 report from the Computer Emergency Response Team at Carnegie Mellon University concluded that attacks on Web sites increased from 2,000 in 1997 to 21,000 in 2000.

- The Cybersource Fraud 2000 survey stated that the average percentage of revenue lost to online fraud was around 4 per cent.
- The Internet Fraud Complaint Center (IFCC) reported that cyber-crime incidents in 2000 were over 21,000 as opposed to the 1999 total of 10,000.
- Reported losses due to computer crime in Hong Kong for the first six months of 2001 totalled US $9.4 million against US $1.9 million in the second half of 2000. The total was made up of: US $5.6 million worth of criminal damage to computer systems; US $2.9 million from Internet shopping fraud; and US $546,000 from e-banking.
- The 2001 Information Week/PriceWaterhouseCoopers global security study estimated the annual global cybercrime bill at US $1.5 trillion (which only includes large business and not small/medium sized businesses, individual consumers or governments).
- February 2000: detected fraud in UK local government (but not necessarily all online related) exceeded £100 million.
- On March 15 2001 *The Daily Telegraph* reported that organized crime gangs are believed to be making around US $55 billion per annum from telecoms fraud.
- By 2001 the Computer Crime and Security survey reported that of the 538 respondents to the survey, 186 quantified their financial losses, which totalled US $377,828,700. The average losses over the three years prior to 2000 was US $120,240,180.
- In 2001 the Confederation of British Industry reported that two thirds of UK businesses have experienced a serious online incident such as hacking, virus attacks or credit card fraud.
- Current estimates put global credit card fraud at US $400 million per annum, damage from hacking at US $12 billion and software piracy in the United States at over US $1 billion per year.

Are you suffering from information overload yet? The dominant under-current of these various (and varying estimates) is that digital crime is a severe problem that is almost certainly under reported. Beyond that we may be venturing into the realms of producing large numbers for effect. Logically though, one way of if not estimating, then at least attempting to appreciate the possible level of digital crime, abuse and risk, is to examine the environment in which it thrives. More figures, I'm afraid:

- In rough terms, more than a billion PCs have been sold world-wide.

- The current total number of global Internet users with access in 2001 is between 500 and 600 million, with a projected total of around 750 million for 2002. The current total is predominantly in three geographical regions: the United States and Canada with around 180 million users; Europe with about 155 million users; and Asia/Pacific totalling around 145 million users.
- Online sales in the United States alone are predicted to reach US $65 billion in 2001.
- 12 billion text messages are sent to PCs, mobiles and personal digital assistants each month – and this is predicted to keep growing at an annual rate of 50 per cent.
- In 2000 the UK Link network of ATM cash machines which comprises 33,179 machines dished out a total of £32,495,613,939. On May 25 2001 the most transactions ever processed in a day (at the time of writing) was reached – a total of 5,955,863 which in hard cash terms was £237,490,577. Normally about 20 per cent of the week's withdrawals are made on a Friday.
- If you live in South Korea you will, based on 2000 estimates, use your credit card for 36 per cent of your total purchases, while in Sweden credit card expenditure is only about 1 per cent of the total. After South Korea, Canada comes a distant second with 24 per cent, Australia 21 per cent and the United States and UK with 18 per cent.

Yet however advanced we may claim to be, the undeniable truth is that all we can do is estimate such figures – there are no certainties, merely approximations. If we consider the digital world to be any piece of non-analogue hardware that is networked in some way, then it is impossible to calculate or calibrate the extent of this new environment; we simply do not know the numbers of:

- Mobile phones and national networks that they can access (and the routes taken when a phone from one network is used on, or calls another network such as when used out of the phone's home country).
- The total number of PC owners and users, and what online access they have. What we do know suggests a massive ongoing take up rate of PCs and Internet access. For example 93 per cent of PC owning households in the United States had Internet access, according to a survey undertaken by the Yankee group in 2001.

- The total of global Internet users, and the routes taken to access the Internet and individual Web sites.
- The total number of all Web sites.
- The extent and scale of corporate intranets (or networks), their global spread and connectivity and their interfaces with other non-public and public networks.
- The number of the world's cash dispenser machines and the telecommunications networks used by them which in turn all interconnect with the records of individual financial institutions.
- The number of credit and debit cards in circulation on a world-wide basis and the technical infrastructures used to process payments and debits.

The US Department of Defense (just on its own) runs more than 2 million computers, 100,000 local-area networks and 100 long distance networks. In 2000 the Department's unclassified networks were successfully attacked 215 times: but the total number of incidents was 23,662. The vast majority of these incidents involved the use of encoded hacker tools widely available on the Internet. The Department itself admit that it has no accurate way of knowing whether these attempted intrusions are by children, terrorists or hostile governments. Many of them appear to be 'routine' probes or scans sent by automatic hacking tools randomly probing for network vulnerabilities that could be used for future electronic break-ins.

Another simple example to illustrate these concerns, and simultaneously demonstrate the possibilities for crime, is an online transaction using a credit card. This is not, by the way, a technical explanation. I am certain that with the aid of numerous technical terms, world maps and diagrams I could offer (if I understood it) a convincing explanation of what occurs: however, such a reasoning may miss the point. Every day millions of Internet users purchase goods and services over the Internet. Again, the exact level and extent of such online activity is difficult to gauge, but some estimates have put online activity at traditional businesses (particularly in the United States) at up to a quarter of their business turnover. On most days, as an example, my firm accesses company records online using Web sites in the UK, United States, France, Switzerland and so on. The specific Web sites that we use are somewhat irrelevant: obviously the security implemented by them is a critical issue in many important respects, but let us presume that the highest available levels are used. The process that goes on is something like this: to access a Web site an individual user logs onto the Internet through his or her Internet service provider (ISP) and then goes onto the specific Web site required. Keying in the name of a company to search (just like every other Internet manoeuvre) involves sending a piece of information called a data packet across the Internet. The data packet then jumps from router to router to reach its end destination. You can actually see how this occurs by going to the MS DOS of your PC, and keying 'Tracert' and then the relevant domain name. We tried this with a major US provider of business information, and we got a 17-stage list of how many routers our data packet went through to get to its destination. Then of course, the Web site accessed sends the information back to you. At some stage you key in your credit card details (or alternatively validate details already held by the Web site you are accessing). Those details (in an encrypted form you hope) are sent back across the Internet to the provider of the data. When these details are received at the relevant server, they are then transmitted to the relevant credit card company's computer for validation. Presuming that everything is OK, you get the information you have requested and the details of the financial amount involved ends up on your credit or debit card statement. During this process (of which this explanation is a very simplified form) the possibility for your information being accessed is enormous.

The Digital Age is grounded and advanced by incredibly complex technology which has been made to look and feel very simple to encourage mass acceptance and usage. But it is in this very user friendly concept that many of the axiomatic and recurrent problems concerning crime and abuse are founded.

In August 2001 Howard Schmidt, Microsoft's global security officer, was quoted as commenting that:

> Microsoft built really great things that give you the ability to do really great things and often at times it's almost secondary at the back what someone could do to counter that. The fact is the Melissa virus hit so many of us unprepared because we didn't expect people to do bad things like that. We haven't always paid as (much) attention to security as we should have in many instances. . . I think we as a global economy have paid certain prices on that.

What becomes clearer every day is that both suppliers and users of technology have fatally underestimated the risks in new programs, services and facilities. In most surveys of this problem one key issue is that managers don't understand technology or the risks inherent in it, and thus lack the commitment to improve relevant security. In many instances, individual organizations and their senior managers are still intoxicated by the novelty of cutting edge technology, seeing only the advantages of being the first business to do whatever the new thing is (or is predicted to be), irrespective of any imperfections or security flaws. Digital attackers break into systems by identifying and exploiting holes in the system or relevant applications. In many cases the providers of such systems only learn about such vulnerabilities after a successful attack has occurred – and then create a patch to eradicate the problem. Yet leaving aside the reactive nature of this, there is another logistical flaw in this approach: just because you are running a system or application doesn't necessarily mean that you get to hear about the patch, or incorporate it.

The US Computer Security Institute estimates that only 25 per cent of US businesses that suffer serious computer breaches report them to law enforcement bodies. Which, taking a cynical view, is just as well because even if 100 per cent of the breaches were reported it would be unlikely to improve the detection rate of such incidents. Police resources to tackle digital crime at a national level are woefully inadequate, and at a global level in terms of (at the very least) cooperation are non-existent. We now transact business in a world where information and, more critically, money can flash around the globe at lightning speed. Even if a national police force investigates a digital crime, as soon as it passes over national border any such enquiry is doomed. International law, national law – or the non-existence of either or both – confuse, delay and ultimately halt such work, never mind regional jealousies and grudges. In May 2000 a lobby group and trade association, the Internet Alliance, complained in one of its white papers that 'Law enforcement is trying to catch up with crime in cyberspace and. . . needs more resources to do so, or it will seriously fall behind and may never catch up'. It may well be that the last sentence ought to read 'will never catch up'. Criminals have been exploiting the world of technology from the start – whereas governments have only just realized this, and belatedly attempted to create a suitable law enforcement infrastructure to tackle it. In 1999, for example, Japan set up a national cyber crime centre – primarily as a reactive measure following several large criminal cases in the country that had been facilitated by Internet or phone services and highlighted the ease with which technology could be harnessed by criminals. The FBI Director Louis Freeh has commented that 'Computer crime is one of the most dynamic problems that the FBI faces today'. However it was not until early 2001 that a national initiative was launched to share information on these issues with corporations, universities and other relevant organizations. The National Hi-Tech Crime Unit (NHTCU), the UK's first national law enforcement organization to tackle computer based crime, was belatedly launched in April 2001. These, by the way, are some of the more proactive and advanced attempts at law enforcement action.

But even if law enforcement establishes specific units to deal with cyber crime, there is no guarantee that laws will exist to prosecute digital criminals. Pre-Digital Age there were numerous problems when attempting to investigate and prosecute international fraud. These included the lengthy process involved which seemed to last for eternity (and sometimes did); the problem where an offence in one country was not in another jurisdiction involved; the attempt to 'fit' outdated laws to modern fraud cases as no relevant legislation existed; the difficulties encountered when extradition was attempted; the need for official protocols when attempting to move things forward – with all of these factors being exacerbated with language difficulties, regional jealousies and different working practices. Very little, if anything, has changed at the frontier of electronic crime.

True, virtually every state in the United States now has various computer crime laws and the country as a whole has the Computer Fraud and Misuse Act (Title 18, Section 1030) and the Economic Espionage Act (Title 18, Section Chapter 90) of the Federal Criminal Code. The UK has the Computer Misuse Act (1990), the Data Protection Acts (1994 and 1998), the Telecommunications (Fraud) Act 1997 and the Copyright, Designs and Patents Act (1998). Japan has the Unauthorized Computer Access Law (February 2000) while China has Computer Information Network and Internet Security, Protection and Management Regulations. Simultaneously numerous countries, from Albania through Italy to Zimbabwe, do not appear to have any laws that address the issue of computer crime directly. Have you got the idea? The regulation and legislation of a global marketplace is being dealt with by a patchwork of laws that are outdated, non-compatible or simply non-existent. Even where directly relevant laws do exist, the number of successful prosecutions remains minimal. Moreover the deterrence factor in any of the known laws appears to be limited.

In an attempt to contributing towards sorting this mess out, The Council of Europe has drafted the first ever international treaty to combat electronic crime, which aims to facilitate the harmonization of criminal policy and procedure across all member states and is included in full as an appendix to this book. The explanatory memorandum to the draft treaty spells out the problem:

*These (technological) developments have given rise to an unprec-
edented economic and social change, but they also have a dark side:
the emergence of new types of crime as well as the commission of
traditional crimes by means of new technologies. Moreover, the
consequences of criminal behaviour can be more far reaching than
before because they are not restricted by geographical limitations
or national boundaries. The recent spread of detrimental computer
viruses all over the world has provided proof of this reality. Technical
measures to protect computer systems need to be implemented
concomitantly with legal measures to prevent and deter criminal
behaviour.*

*The new technologies challenge existing legal concepts. Infor-
mation and communications flow more easily around the world.
Borders are no longer boundaries to this flow. Criminals are
increasingly located in places other than where their acts produce
their effects. However, domestic laws are generally confined to a
specific territory. Thus solutions to the problems posed must be
addressed by international law, necessitating the adoption of
adequate international legal instruments. The present Convention
aims to meet this challenge, with due respect to human rights in
the new Information Society.*

Spurred on by the fiasco in the Philippines where the creator of the 'I
Love You' virus could not be prosecuted because the country had no
criminal charge that covered the dissemination of a destructive virus,
the treaty codifies nine relevant criminal offences:

- illegal access;
- illegal interception;
- data interference;
- system interference;
- misuse of devices;
- computer related forgery;
- computer related fraud;
- online child pornography;
- offences related to copyright and similar rights.

The Council wants its members to add criminal codes where no
existing relevant legislation exists in respect of these offences. The
treaty also seeks to extend search and seizure laws. All of this is admir-
able, and the treaty appears to plug a substantial number of current
gaps. Somewhat predictably, right wing freedom of expression groups
have seen this document as a giant advance down the path to a

totalitarian world government. The real drawbacks, though, are at least twofold: firstly this is a treaty that attempts to address the current deficiencies by recommending that individual nations operate adopt a model code. It does not guarantee that this will happen, and if so when. The second drawback is timing: why has it taken so long to implement such a treaty – and might it not be too late?

Ironical though it may be that technology in the Digital Age has broken down barriers only to find that the effective policing of it is restricted and hindered by geographical, political and ideological barriers, this reality brings no comfort or security to the individual or organizational user. To them, security and confidence in the hardware and software they are using on a daily basis is paramount. The only sensible advice to them (which is more correctly us) is that the first line of defence must be self-generated. Users in the Digital Age must protect themselves, because it is unlikely (at least for the moment) that anyone else will.

WHO ARE THEY AND WHAT ARE THEY TO YOU?

Do not open your clothes to embrace the fire.

Traditional Chinese proverb

The profile of a computer criminal? This part is easy, isn't it? All hackers are solitary male teenager computer geeks attacking the very essence of Western civilization from their bedrooms. All computer criminals are hackers so that's the problem solved. . . and if the problem isn't down to teenage hackers then it's an inside job – so which of your staff and co-workers don't you trust? If only life was that simple. . .

In its true sense the term 'hacker' means a skilled computer programmer, engineer or operator who relishes a challenge, especially one that involves accessing and manipulating someone else's computer or system. In the broadest sense of the term a hacker is a knowledge seeker beyond just computer systems. As 'Wired Style: Principles of English usage in the digital age' concludes in its definition of hacker: '*Not* synonymous with "computer criminal" or "security breaker"'. Hackers are spurred on by the intellectual challenge and the sense of adventure. They are willing to bend or break rules to get their fix of information. In its idealized state 'hacking' is viewed as a positive exercise which has led to many and various technological break-throughs that we now take for granted. Of particular importance to more traditional hackers is a sense of ethics, which is either a thief's charter or a code of honor, depending on your point of view. Once upon a time hackers were viewed as paragons of democracy and anti-bureaucracy. There are various versions (and extensions) of the basic set of tenets, which are originally attributed to Steven Levy from his 1984 book 'Hackers: Heroes of the Computer Revolution'. In essence the hacker ethic reads as follows:

- Access to computers (and anything that might teach you something about how everything works) should be unlimited and total.
- All information should be free.
- Mistrust authority – promote decentralization.
- Hackers should be judged by their hacking not bogus criteria such as degrees, age, race or position.
- You can create art and beauty on a computer.
- Computers can change your life for the better.

And if you are of a liberal persuasion, there is very little that you can find offensive or threatening in this ethic. Thus it is entirely logical that traditional hackers are offended by both the activities of modern day 'hackers' and the association between the two groups. This has manifested itself in the wish to disassociate by language and terminology – which has been something of a fruitless exercise because the popular media still perpetuate the theory that hacker equals cyber criminal, come what may. The new 'definitions' attempted are:

Neo hackers

This group has no sense of the true hacker ethic, rather the individual relies on a self-developed code of beliefs. Generally this subset avoids criminal actions, but does venture onto the dark side on occasions.

Crackers

A system intruder – someone who 'cracks' open a computer. The motivation is malicious or criminal intent. One example of crackers' activities is where credit card numbers are obtained illegally and then ransom demands are made of the victim organization. It has been argued (and mostly accepted) that the difference between a hacker and a cracker is their intent. The very elite of this group are sometimes referred to as 'dark side hackers', highly competent and adverse to publicity.

Phreakers

Now taken to mean someone who cracks into long distance telecommunications systems and networks to be able to make free calls. However the origins of these activities are akin to those of the original hackers: people exploring the recesses of phone networks for the fun of it (or the intellectual challenge).

Script kiddies

A derogatory term given to those who merely download a ready made script from the Internet and proceed to try and use it until they get lucky. An example of this is Web site defacement.

Much has been written about the psychology of hacking; in broad terms much of this research and analysis has promoted the view that the majority of hackers are teenage males who live solitary lives. Among the most common traits exhibited by such individuals are:

- having poor social skills;
- appearing as loners;
- speaking too loudly and/or too quickly and/or in an unremitting monotone;
- being unresponsive to humour;
- being easily detracted but able to focus intently on technical problems;
- having an exceptional ability to mentally retain long strings of numbers.

All of this is quite probably true, and certainly available statistics suggest that the biggest criminal group are males between the ages of 16 and 25. However it does seem that the media have convinced both themselves and their readers, viewers and listeners that this is the sole group of concern in relation to high tech crime. Another critical factor has also been ignored in many ways – that online crime is no different in its motives from the terrestrial version. Criminals have different motives to commit any kind of crime, whether it be stealing a car or stealing someone's identity on the Internet. Thus I have great concerns about the apparent differentiation that has occurred between traditional criminals and their online counterparts. In fact, to my mind, the only key variance between the two groups is that in cyberspace there is very little practical deterrent against crime. Leaving aside the separate convoluted topics of the existence and effectiveness of normal deterrents, what is inescapable is that few such deterrents exist in the digital world. Just as lawmakers have struggled to incorporate the rapid changes in the new world order into legislation, law enforcement (in its broadest sense) has immense difficulties with monitoring and policing the online environment. Most – if not all – online crimes are perpetrated by a single person at a computer terminal in the privacy of his or her home or office. This does not presuppose that groups of criminals do not commit such crimes – they patently do – rather that the key perpetrator is an individual. In such an environment it is not necessarily feasible for conscientious and alert fellow citizens to report their suspicions to their local police stations; there are no speed traps for fast or careless driving; there are no regular police or security patrols; there are very few electrified security fences; no guard dogs bark or attack you when you break into a 'secure' site; no patrol cars cruise the block.

Such a low security environment has acted as an electromagnet for criminals of all types, race, creeds and colour. If we accept that some (even the majority) of the crimes that involve computers as a target are carried out by the a group of crackers that fit the psychological profile outlined above, that still leaves an awful lot of other criminal activity, particularly where the computer is a tool of the crime, unaccounted for. The United States Securities and Exchange Commission through their Internet Enforcement Program have brought numerous actions against companies and individuals that are predominantly involved in crimes where the computer (in its broadest sense) is used as target. The individuals and companies that have been accused of such frauds make an interesting bunch:

- A school bus mechanic who peddled false securities industry and stock advice.
- A college student and part-time driver for a car service who inflated the prices of stocks via the Internet.
- An 'international' company selling prime bank guarantees from their palatial global headquarters – someone's front room. The

Web site mainly consisted of material stolen from other Web sites.

■ A former roofer who claimed to have over 14 years of investing experience and a 'proprietary computer trading system'. He didn't have the experience, and his unique IT system could be downloaded from elsewhere on the Internet.

While these and many other cases investigated by the SEC are obviously serious to the extent that investors have lost large amounts of money, such cyber criminals are the lighter side of the digital underworld. Far darker, and deadly serious, is the use of cyberspace by organized criminal groups and terrorists. Organized crime groups, in particular, have exploited the potential offered by technology for a considerable time, through such activities as:

■ The use of cutting edge technology to evade and frustrate official investigations, particularly by creating anonymous and secure methods of communicating. (These techniques are also used to devastating effect by terrorists.)
■ Generating income by cyber attacks.
■ Creating and running Web sites that defraud customers and investors.
■ Making extensive use of international business and banking technological advances and resultant systems to transfer information, funds and goods across the world.

In December 1999 prosecutors and police in Palermo, Sicily, discovered a £330 million scam operated by the Mafia. The funds were moved electronically through New Zealand, the Cayman Islands, Israel, Spain and Switzerland. Effectively the perpetrators had dematerialized their criminal gains and had reformatted them as digital amounts without mass. But such events are merely scratching the surface of the involvement of criminal gangs: Colombian drug cartels are believed to have hired IT 'experts' to install and run a secure communications system; The US Government believes that the IRA and ETA use technology extensively to implement their objectives; Amsterdam based criminal gangs employ crackers to monitor and disrupt the surveillance and communications systems of police surveillance teams. To add to this is the activity in cyberspace by Mexican drug cartels, the Japanese Yakuza, Chinese Triads, Turkish gangs and our friends from West Africa.

One group of criminals has been particularly efficient in their use of advanced technology: the Russian Mafia (for want of a better term). The criminal groupings in the former Soviet Union have been very active in this area, recruiting crackers and targeting US companies. Although no hard evidence is available there are strong suspicions that crime groups recruit crackers by placing advertisements for 'computer programmers' in newspapers in Moscow and St Petersburg and on the Internet. The tasks for the successful applicants include stealing credit card and bank account details, particularly targeting unpatched holes in Windows NT operating systems. One potentially profitable way of using such information is to demand money from the victim organization for the return of the information. In May 2001 Russian police apprehended a gang of suspected crackers who had stolen about 300 credit card numbers from Westerners. The gang was led by a 63-year-old man. In 2000, Maxus, a Russian cyber thief, claimed to have stolen credit card numbers from the CD Universe Internet retailer site. He demanded a US $100,000 ransom, which was not paid. On Christmas Day Maxus posted 25,000 of the numbers on a Web site – Maxus Credit Card Pipeline, the front page of which read:

> *Hello, my name is Maxus. I would like to present to you a credit card datapipe. If you press the button you will get a real credit card directly from the biggest online shop database. No kidding.*
>
> *Hmm, still no reply from the shop! I can't wait anymore! Use the f****** cards guys:*
>
> *Click here for virgin credit card.*

The FBI soon shut down the site, but only after it is believed that thousands of card numbers were downloaded. Maxus told *The New York Times* that he had been stealing credit card details since 1997 and sent a reporter a list of 198 credit cards as proof of his abilities. Maxus has never been caught: but after this provocative episode has been the subject of fierce debate as to whether he was acting on his own or for an organized crime group. What is certain is that Russian crackers are immensely capable – a Web site poll on a hacker/cracker orientated site showed that 82 per cent of respondents considered Russians to be the best hackers in the world. Moreover if organized criminal groups have not yet realized the inherent criminal potential in such skills, they soon will. Somewhat typically though, just as with traditional criminal activity, there is an awful drawback when such criminal conspiracies occur in that it is always far easier to get the front man and far more difficult and complex to identify, apprehend and successfully charge the real people behind any attack.

While 'Russian Mafia attack Western firms through cyber crime' is always good media copy, a far better story is 'Foreign government hacks national confidential information'. Perhaps I've been watching too many James Bond films, but it appears to be entirely logical and totally probable that the greatest threat of all might not come from teenage males, terrorists or Russian crooks but from governments themselves.

Reliable intelligence as to what exactly goes on – even from confidential sources – is hard to get. However, as the intelligence services of governments have been routinely monitoring analogue communications traffic of each other for decades (and before that written communications) it seems safe to assume that monitoring of the digital world takes place. As with Maxus though, the acid test of what happens is not whether a system intrusion is detected but having hard copy evidence of what information is acquired by such an attack. It has often been reported that the French intelligence services spied on foreign companies by wiretapping US businessmen flying on Air France flights between New York and Paris. Such exploits raise a key issue: digital spying by governments is not simply confined to defence and security matters: economic and business information is just as valuable so that foreign states can obtain technological advantages for their domestic companies. The FBI have claimed that Germany's Federal Intelligence Service has had various successes in the field of economic espionage through a top secret computer facility outside Frankfurt. From there data networks and systems of numerous companies and governments have been attacked. Lawrence Gershwin, the head of the CIA's intelligence on technology, commented in 2001 that 'Only government-sponsored programs are developing capabilities with the future prospect of causing widespread, long duration damage to US critical infrastructures'. He also added – with a prediction that would come horribly true later that year – that terrorists are a limited Internet threat as 'Bombs still work better than bytes'.

Earlier in 2001 an example of the real threat of such activity came to light at the US Sandia National Nuclear Laboratory which designs all non-nuclear components for US nuclear weapons together with performing a wide variety of energy research and development projects. Somewhat ironically in the circumstances the laboratory also works on assignments that respond to national military and economic security threats. Reports appeared – which have been denied – that crackers from a foreign government gained access to classified information concerning nuclear weapon design. It has been claimed that the incident was so serious that the CIA issued a report and George W Bush was briefed on the incident. Separately in March 2001 the Defense Science Board (a US federal advisory panel) observed that the Pentagon 'cannot today defend itself from an information operations attack by a sophisticated, nation-state adversary'. Whether an attack can ever be identified as being by a foreign government or a teenager is open to question; moreover the growth of 'cyber mercenaries' means that even if a successful attack on confidential information is made by a teenager as an intellectual challenge, there is no guarantee that he or she will not try and sell what he or she has obtained to the highest bidder.

There still exists a substantial volume of commentary and analysis that propounds the view that the biggest risk to an organization comes from its own staff. I am no longer certain that this is the case – but simultaneously this group should never be underestimated. Disgruntled current staff or ex-staff pose real threats. Never mind temporary staff and staff who are deliberately placed in an organization by a competitor, criminal group, terrorist organization or foreign power. Staff also cause more prosaic problems, such as attempting to gain access to unauthorized areas, distributing offensive junk mail and misusing Internet facilities.

The US Army Space & Military Command, for example, issues specific warnings about long term foreign visitors, quoting an example of a joint venture where a contractor had a number of foreign representatives working on unclassified projects. One of them was caught hacking into an unclassified local area network. He had accessed company proprietary source code information and was promptly expelled from the facility. The attacks subsided, only to restart in a few days: the suspected perpetrators being the remaining foreign representatives. At the time of writing a UK court case is running that vividly demonstrates the hazards inherent in this area. It is claimed that a senior former employee of Barclays Bank tried to blackmail them for £25 million. The ex-employee had been responsible for devising security code patterns for credit and debit cards, but resigned as he felt that his suggestions for improved security were not being implemented. He then sent four letters to Barclay's Chief Executive that contained highly sensitive codes relating to the Bank's plastic cards. In order for security not to be breached he is alleged to have demanded £25 million.

One interesting case which demonstrates the maxim that once one thing has gone wrong everything else will is the BT (British Telecom) hacking episode in 1994. The original story was that thousands of pages of confidential information from BT records were sent across the Internet to a young Scottish journalist, Steve Fleming. The journalist had asked for information on BT and hacking and was sent this information 'anonymously' The apparent hacker also gave the journalist information on how he could access the information by applying for a job as a temporary worker at BT. Fleming did this and gained access to various pieces of sensitive information such as the location of MI6's training centre, information about the bunker in Wiltshire where the government would go in the event of a nuclear war, details of telephone installations at Buckingham Palace, details of telephone installations at 10 Downing Street (including personal lines of the then Prime Minister John Major and his wife). But of course, nothing in life is simple – or as headline grabbing as originally portrayed. The reality of the situation was that Fleming was never sent confidential information across the Internet (well strictly speaking he was – he sent it to himself), but worked as a temp at BT himself for a period of three months and was issued with legitimate access to the BT 'Customer Services System'. Thus the great hack of 1994 was a fiction, and was promptly denounced as such. But that seems to miss the issue – even if the information was not hacked from outside the organization, it was still obtained. This demonstrates, surely, the inherent risks of staff accessing computer based records. Fleming may not have hacked the system, or stolen the required passwords but he was a lowly temporary member of staff who was given access to highly confidential information. Never mind the more important issues of keeping such very sensitive data in the same database as non-confidential information. Perhaps we just thought we lived in more innocent times then: but what if the temporary member of staff who accessed all of this information had been a planted associate of a criminal gang or a terrorist?

Finally, the purpose of this entire chapter is not to persuade you that the Dark Avenger's maxim of not buying a computer or if you do, not turning it on is the logical response to the terminal velocity that has created and sustained the Digital Age. On the other hand, it quite obviously pays to be paranoid about these things.

SYSTEM ERROR

It is a working principle of the Head Bureau that the very possibility of error must be ruled out of account. The ground principle is justified by the consummate organization of the whole authority.

Franz Kafka The Castle

In view of all the deadly computer viruses that have been spreading lately, Weekend Update *would like to remind you: when you link up to another computer, you're linking up to every computer that that computer has ever linked up to.*

Dennis Miller, Weekend Update, *US TV programme*

HACKED AND CRACKED

The hacker threat is often perceived as being one of the major ones of the Digital Age; certainly it is the endless number of hack attacks that grabs the media headlines. However, hackers are just one of the groups that threaten you. One of the key differences with hackers is that the majority of attacks are carried out not for financial gain, but to prove that such an attack can be successful – and thus inherently demonstrate the severe security flaws in the Web site or system being attacked. The term hacker has now gathered a certain amount of controversy in that 'ethical' hackers consider that the term does not apply to cyber criminals who access systems and databases for monetary gain – these should be described as crackers. Moreover one of the key factors in the apparent fear of hackers is that they have a vibrant subculture which is perceived as being alternative to, and at variance with, the 'mainstream'. Like any formal or informal group they share experiences, backgrounds – and values. They have their own heroes, villains, myths, 'in' jokes and 'no go' areas. There are at the very minimum 33,000 underground bulletin boards where hackers chat, trade experiences and technical knowledge. There are now also a substantial number of public Web sites that contain extensive data on both hackers and how to hack; one that I recently visited has a whole range of interesting and lengthy articles such as

Hacking into Citibank

Hack into McDonald's Online

A hacker's account of hacking NASA

It is not my intention here to go down the well trodden route of describing the key figures in hacking history but rather raise what I consider to be some fundamental issues. Firstly, have we not mythologized hackers as bogeymen akin to digital enemy number one, when in reality if every system and Web site had watertight security then hackers (in their true sense) would have a job finding something to do? The US Department of Justice stated in one of its press releases that: 'Unlawful computer hacking imperils the health and welfare of individuals, corporations and government agencies in the United States who rely on computers and telephones to communicate'.

However, other commentators might point out that corporations and government agencies that run systems, databases and Web sites that have major security flaws so that confidential (or classified information) seeps out are also imperilling the health and welfare of the civilized world. It could be argued that hackers (obviously this does not included cyber extortionists) are explorers who think that part of what they are doing is bringing such problems to the public's attention. No one really knows what prompts each and every attack made by a hacker, but various research projects into this issue have consistently discovered the following types of motivation:

- fun;
- profit;
- espionage;
- a need to prove oneself, or prove that hacking can be done;
- extortion;
- exposing system weaknesses;
- problem solving;
- viewing what they are doing as a game or sport.

Looking at the problem from a corporate standpoint (and by that I mean any business entity ranging from a one person firm to the largest global corporations), surely the paramount issue in relation to hackers is not what they can do (which is considerable). Instead it should be what your organization can do to ensure that the digital security that you rely on is sufficiently robust to withstand and repel such attacks. Because if such security isn't up to scratch, I think it's a fairly lame excuse to blame hackers for all of your self-inflicted woes: thieves don't steal items that can't be stolen (or even if they do, such items are only rarely stolen and then only by the very best thieves). In detailing a sample of the dangers posed to business by hackers and the successes they have achieved, it could be more informative to label all that follows as corporate digital security failures:

January 2000: Japanese Government Web sites were hacked: the intruders recorded their presence through insults, criticism of Japan's war record and links to pornography sites.

2000: A hacker broke into the Web site of the Australian Taxation Office and sent 17,000 copies of its bank information out. The hacker claims that he took the information to prove how lax the security on the site was. A subsequent audit of Australian Government Web sites found that most of the 10 examined had serious security flaws, the principal one being the Australian Radiation Protection and Nuclear Safety Agency Site, which had classified security documents ready to be accessed through the Internet.

June 2000: By now hackers have obtained MP4 software, the video equivalent of MP3, which compresses video down to 1 per cent of its original size, thus making it easy to copy and distribute. The *Independent* in the UK reported that *Gladiator, The Matrix* and *Saving Private Ryan* had already been pirated in this way. The hackers are alleged to have stripped the software from Microsoft's Windows Media Player, which was subsequently locked.

June 2000: AOL confirmed that hackers obtained access to 'a small number' of its 23 million account records which contain (among numerous other things) credit card details. A Trojan Horse was used which was attached to e-mails sent to various AOL employees; once opened a connection was created with the computer that sent it, thus giving it access to AOL's system.

October 2000: Hackers successfully broke into the systems at Microsoft's headquarters. There is some subsequent dispute as to what data the hackers were able to access. The attacks appeared to have originated from St Petersburg, thus fuelling claims that they were orchestrated by Russian organized crime groups.

March 2001: The FBI warns that more than 1 million credit card details may have been stolen from e-commerce sites in the preceding 12 months because of security flaws that could have been patched three years earlier; the FBI blames 'organized' hacking groups in Russia and Ukraine.

April 2001: Warner Brothers Online sent an e-mail to its subscribers confirming that 'someone gained unauthorized access to our computer system' which resulted in many of those subscribers receiving an e-mail that claimed that the recipient could 'Make over half a million dollars every 4 to 5 months from your home for an investment of only US $25 US Dollars expense one time THANKS TO THE COMPUTER AGE AND THE INTERNET!' Essentially the mail was asking recipients to send US $5 to five others.

June 2001: Online credit card processing and security provider Anacom Communications databases were illegally accessed, resulting in fraudulent transactions using merchant accounts.

August 2001: The Nasdaq quoted company Eagle Inc's Web site was attacked by a hacker who e-mailed hundreds of press releases containing false financial statements relating to the company. Trading in the stock in the company was halted for two hours. The motive? Very difficult to tell, as no money was stolen and the 'press releases' were riddled with grammatical errors. The company put it down to someone who was simply displaying his expertise.

August 2001: A hacker broke into the Web site of Brass Eagle, a Nasdaq quoted paintball company and – yes, you've guessed it – e-mailed out 'hundreds, if not thousands'(according to the company) of phony financial statements. Trading in the company was halted for two hours.

September 2001: A public service TV programme in Germany hired hackers who proceeded to hack into the online banking servers of

HypoVereinsbank, one of Germany's largest. The TV channel claims that it was in the public interest that such security holes were exposed; the details obtained included names, account numbers, PINS and IP addresses.

October 2001: *The New York Times* Web site was brought down by a denial of service attack which was signified by a massive volume of electronic transmissions that flooded the system. In 1998 the site had been defaced with pornography and expletives.

Defacing a Web site is hardly a great money making opportunity. Usually the motives involved include the ability to show that it can be done, a revenge attack (which may have a range of submotivations) or simply because it is humorous. The list of hacked Web sites is endless, but among notable victims have been:

- The Colombian Government: The site was changed in January 2000 to read 'We demand 25 kiloz of dank chronic herb and a big old pile of coca leaves! WWIII our country is elite and were here to say your box has been owned by the I.D.K. dont fuck with us or we'll nuke you we have twice the power that you do so if your smart you wont talk shit cuz the IDK hackers aint legit we cant say that were the best were just a few kiddies that can RDS USA OWNS YOU!!!' (quoted verbatim, complete with grammatical and spelling errors)
- RSA Data Security's Web site which was hacked in 2000 to read 'RSA Security inc. Hacked. Trust us with your data! Praise Allah!'
- Nasa's Web site was hacked in 1999 with the words 'nasa goddard space flight center.ytcracker is back in space once again, to the us government and military – i have warned you about these security flaws. please secure our military systems to protect us from cyber attack. if the most powerful country in the world is not prepared to defend against its own citizens, how can we trust other countries to show the same grace? this hack is not malicious. i did not poke my nose into any data other than data essential to this defacement. the logs will reflect the same. i want the same thing you do.'
- One of the US Army's Web sites was attacked in 1999, with the front page being replaced by 'Good Evening. Here at hV2k we decided to own this box in memory of all the men and women who lost their lives for us in the wars. R.I.P all who died during those wars. hV2k 0WNS J00.'

- The City of Beverly Hills Web site which was changed to read 'owned by kryptek #cat motd W E L C O M E T O C I T Y O F B E V E R L Y H I L L SUnauthorized access will be recorded andinvestigated by CBH Police Departmentheehee! i owned your site!! =P come find me you stupid fuqers... who the hell coded the html for you guys anyways? really fuqin cheeesy.. Your system wasnt damaged, though you did deserve it. I secured your system, because obviously your overpayed fatass administrator wouldnt have figured it out. (yes, stop eating donuts fatboy, read up on security.) Anyways, bye bye!!shouts to: flipsmile, overdosis, khromy, smoothy, kim, nikleand to all the people @ school missing me =) ill be back s00n.. mwuahah!!'
- The US Senate Web site which has been hacked on various occasions, including in May 1999 when it was changed to read 'wh0 laughs last? we dec1d3d 2 haq the UUS $ sen4te az a b1g 'SKREW U GUYZ! (in the w0rdz of uRea) t0 0ur fr1endz at the FBI.WITH0UT FURTHER DELAY, LAD1EZ AND G3NTL3MEN, B0YZ AND G1RLZ, PLAYERUS $ AND PLAY3R-H4TERZ... WE ANN0UNC3!@ MAST3RZ 0F D0WNL0ADING, GL0B4L D0MIN8T10N '99!The FBI may be all over the other groupz, like those gH and tK queerz, cl00bagz gal0re. M0D make th0se m0ronz l00k like a gr0up of special-ed st00dentz!@# FBI vs. M0D in '99, BR1NG IT 0N FUQRZ! (BTW NIPC IZ ALS0 0WNED) S0METIMEZ U G0TTA G0 WITH A NAME U CAN TRUST. 4 S0ME, REGULAT10N IZ JUST A WAY 0F L1FE.0wned (0wn`3d) : the art of showing how stupid a sysadmin can be, see sekurity.'

Among other notable hacked Web sites have been the Library of Congress, the Electronic Frontier Foundation, the State of California, the California Democratic Assembly, various US Army sites, the Samaritans (UK), Moscow Bank, the Hong Kong Government, the Bureau of Arms Control, the US Army Aeromedical Center, the Minnesota Department of Agriculture, the NY Office of Mental Health, the Texas State Auditors Office, the New Mexico State Library, the Sex Offenders Hotline, the US Department of Agriculture and the US Navy – and these are just a small selection of attacked sites.

Self-made disasters (and a few own goals)

Not all of the risks in the Digital Age involve the deliberate theft of money or information or defacement of Internet material. Some are just nuisances, and nothing more, while others may be malicious but are not apocalyptical. Then there are those events that can cause loss of reputation and money, but are totally and utterly self-inflicted. When I go online to access my phone bill, carry out a financial transaction, buy a CD or even see if my contact details are listed correctly on a third party Web site, I presume that such data is as secure as it is possible to be. In fact I do more than presume, because somewhere there will be a long policy statement assuring me that the Web site I am accessing has a stringent and robust security regime and that the administrators place the security of data as their number one priority. Company X is a typical company that provides e-commerce facilities to its customers, together with the facility for those customers to check financial and buying history online. Company X, like most other similar operations, proudly displays its privacy policy, an extract of which goes something like this:

> Your privacy is very important to us. To better protect your privacy we provide this page explaining our online information practices and the choices you can make about the way your information is collected and used. To make this notice easy to find, we make it available on our homepage and at every point where personally identifiable information may be requested.

DISCLOSURE OF INFORMATION

Company X complies with and is registered under the data protection laws in the United Kingdom and takes all reasonable care to prevent any unauthorized access to your personal data. The staff of Company X and those working for agents or contractors of Company X have a responsibility to keep your information confidential and will only use it to offer products and services on behalf of Company X.

The personal details that we use to provide or promote our products and services (for example your name, telephone number, or details of the services you use), as well as any information taken from you while you are using this Web site, will NOT be passed to ANY organization beyond Company X to be used for marketing purposes. Your details may occasionally be shared with contractors or agents of Company X in order to provide you with our products and services you have requested, but we will make this clear to you in the relevant terms and conditions we give you when you order.

SECURITY

We at Company X are very serious about guarding the security of your personal data and the details of any transactions you make.

Your account number is a sensitive piece of information, which can be used to find out information about your Company X services, if it is used with your password or other identifier. Please be sure to keep this information safe and do not share it with others. For access to some of our online services, extra proof of identity and authorization may be needed.

HOW DOES COMPANY X PROTECT YOUR DATA?

When you register details with us, make an order or access account details, we use a secure server. Any data you give us is encrypted using a Secure Socket Layer (SSL) session. SSL is an industry standard and is one of the best ways to ensure Internet messages are not intercepted. You should be aware, however, that older browsers cannot use SSL. To be sure, you will need Netscape version 4.05 or Microsoft Internet Explorer browsers, version 4 or above.

Over and above what Company X do to safeguard your privacy and security, there are a number of things you can do to protect yourself from Internet fraud:

- Choose a password you can remember but others will not guess, change it regularly, and if you do write it down, keep it somewhere safe and secure.
- When you have finished your session on our Web site, make sure that you prevent your details being seen by anyone that you do not wish to see them. So, if you have registered and

logged in, remember to log off. Clear any 'cache' so there is no record of any transactions left on screen – both Netscape and Internet Explorer let you do this. We also recommend you then close your browser so any history of the session is cleared. As an extra precaution your session on many of our Web sites will 'time out' if you have not used the site for 30 minutes.

GENERAL SECURITY MEASURES

To prevent unauthorized access, maintain data accuracy, and ensure the correct use of information, Company X has put in place appropriate physical, electronic, and managerial procedures to safeguard and secure the information we collect online. All of our users' information, not just the sensitive information mentioned above, is restricted in our offices. Only employees who need the information to perform a specific job (for example, our billing clerk or a customer service representative) are granted access to personally identifiable information. Our employees must use password-protected screensavers when they leave their desk. When they return, they must re-enter their password to re-gain access to your information. Furthermore, ALL employees are kept up to date on our security and privacy practices. Every quarter, as well as any time new policies are added, our employees are notified and/or reminded about the importance we place on privacy, and what they can do to ensure our customers' information is protected. Finally, the servers that we store personally identifiable information on are kept in a secure environment, behind a locked cage.

Ironically Company X's privacy policy is probably far more comprehensive than those of many major e-commerce and e-service Web sites. Which is a bit of a shame, because I made the policy up in about 15 minutes by paraphrasing and cutting then pasting the best bits of a variety of real policies. However, why is it that such Web sites and the organizations that own them, which proudly detail all of these security and privacy measures, on many occasions do not need to put protection against intruders as their number one priority? Rather they need to protect themselves from themselves. The history of the Internet is littered with stories relating to well known companies that manage to cause chaos (and disclose your personal information) without any help from anybody else.

On April 20 2001 BT suspended its Web site for two hours as it became obvious that an upgrade to the site had created some un-planned side effects. When a user logged on to the 'View My Bill' service – the telephone records and costs of their line – they saw not their own billing records but those of the last person to use the service. But such compromising of personal information is nothing remarkable: this BT episode was fairly harmless and even comical, but the accid-ental disclosure of other types of data could have more damaging effects. There have been various controversies of this type in the United States, particularly where the home address details of family doctors have been posted on medical directories. Doctors have long argued that both for privacy reasons and because of personal security concerns their home contact details should not be made public; however, such details have appeared on medical directory Web sites – usually because state medical boards have sold databases of their doctors to private companies, without paying much regard to what details would be made public. The posting of home address details of doctors, in many cases, falls into some kind of black hole between the provider of the information and the host.

In an earlier example of what BT's Web site users witnessed on 20 April 2001, new users of the Moneygator.com Web site got more information than they expected when they registered to use its services. The site (now defunct) provided comparison details of financial products in the UK and then acted as an aggregator of those services. Unfortunately in May 2000 each new user had the privilege of seeing the previous new user's registration form: which included bank details, account numbers, telephone number and mother's maiden name. The situation was not much helped by reports that the CEO of Moneygator told one of the affected customers that 'when breaches like this happen, it makes the Internet safer'. It must be supposed that this was said without any irony: a quality that existed in abundance in relation to events on the US Commerce Department 'Safe Harbor' site. US and EU officials had established this site so that US firms could avoid prosecution under an EU law that prohibits personal data being transferred from the EU to countries that do not meet its standards for privacy safeguards. The United States is one such country: so this site enabled US corporations to sign up and certify that their internal privacy practices met EU standards. To sign up each corporation had to provide information on various detailed issues, including financial and sensitive matters which it was explained 'would not be posted on the Web site'. But if you visited the Web site and clicked through various links you could easily have ended up at set of files containing confidential information such as each firm's revenue, number of employees and the European countries the firm does business with. Even stranger was the fact that not only could the casual searcher read this information but it was possible to modify – and even delete – the data!

The red faces at the US Commerce Department – the main comment being that if the US Government can't get it right, who can? – were matched in June 2001 by those at the UK Consumer Association. The Association has long been a champion on consumers' rights and the publishers of *Which?* magazine, which deals extensively with such issues and provides detailed product reviews on a wide range of articles. In June 1999 the Association set up the Which? Web trader scheme with the aim of reinforcing consumer confidence in the security and integrity on online e-commerce transactions. This code provides guidelines on various key aspects of e-commerce, including a suggested privacy policy which reads as follows:

We are committed to protecting your privacy. We will only use the information that we collect about you lawfully (in accordance with the Data Protection Act 1998) and according to the Which? Web Trader Code of Practice.

We collect information about you for 2 reasons: firstly, to process your order and second, to provide you with the best possible service. We will not e-mail you in the future unless you have given us your consent.

We will give you the chance to refuse any marketing e-mail from us or from another trader in the future.

The type of information we will collect about you includes:

- your name;
- address;
- phone number;
- e-mail address;
- credit/debit card details.

We will never collect sensitive information about you without your explicit consent.

The information we hold will be accurate and up to date. You can check the information that we hold about you by e-mailing us. If you find any inaccuracies we will delete or correct it promptly.

The personal information which we hold will be held securely in accordance with our internal security policy and the law and the Which? Web Trader Code.

If we intend to transfer your information outside the EEA (European Economic Area) we will always obtain your consent first.

We may use technology to track the patterns of behaviour of visitors to our site. This can include using a 'cookie' which would be stored on your browser. You can usually modify your browser to prevent this happening. The information collected in this way can be used to identify you unless you modify your browser settings.

If you have any questions/comments about privacy, you should e-mail us.

This is all extremely sensible and praiseworthy (as is the scheme itself). Unfortunately, as is often the case, things didn't quite go as planned at the CA's own Web site. According to the BBC the flaw related to the CA's TaxCalc Web site from where 2,700 customers had bought this tax self-assessment software program. It was discovered that it was possible to download pages from the site into Microsoft FrontPage which contained details of all of the credit cards used by the purchasers of the software. To their credit, the CA immediately shut down the site and contacted all its relevant customers to ask them to cancel their credit cards. While some commentators and experts found it hard to contain their glee at the irony of this event, it is actually just one of many which include (but certainly are not limited) to the following:

- In April 2001 Accubyte.com (an online computer hardware superstore) admitted that it had a security issue with e-mails confirming orders. The problem appeared to be that such messages (which contained the home address and credit card details of customers) were being sent out in clear text, thus exposing the information on the Internet.
- In August 2001 RegWeb.com, an online registration, e-marketing and attendee management system was reported as having a major security flaw regarding credit card numbers which resulted in a list of credit cards being posted on a hacker chat room, together with a link to access about 300 to 400 credit card records held on the site.
- During 2000 Barclays Bank were probably cursing the very idea of online banking: in July a software upgrade to their system did rather more than expected of it, by enabling customers to see the

details of other customers' accounts. Barclays acted quickly, shutting the online banking system and stating that it 'views this compromise in the security and integrity of its online service as unacceptable'. Nevertheless it was perhaps not totally diplomatic to confirm that customers who saw data that wasn't their own couldn't do anything other than read account summaries of other people. But that wasn't all: just a few days later it became clear that if you logged off the bank's online system, but then hit the 'back' button on your browser you would be back where you started – the account that you have just signed out of. While it smacked of paranoia when this was reported as being a great risk if users accessed their account on a public terminal, it may have proved more interesting to other family members when you accessed your account at home.

- In July 2000 Powergen PLC, a major UK power utilities company, reported that a 'technical error' had meant that names and credit card numbers had been posted on its Web site.
- In August 2000 the Woolworths UK site was shut down for two months after customer credit card details were found online.
- In 1999 the UK Halifax Bank's online share dealing system was closed down after a 'technical fault' made it possible for some customers to trade shares in random accounts.

Many more such errors and omissions could be listed.

If you don't get caught in human errors by Web site operators, then there is now the possibility that the increased sophistication of search engines may throw up some results that weren't quite meant to be there. In November 2001 an article on Cnet news drew attention to an intriguing side effect of Google's efficiency in routing out information. Google had introduced a new file-type search tool that probes for additional file types that have been traditionally ignored by search engines, which normally focus on html files. Google had expanded this and by doing so had perhaps opened up 'non-public' files to search engine robots. The two problems that this highlights is the possible exposure of sensitive, unsecured data such as passwords and credit card numbers; and the use of search engines to identify Web sites that are running programs that have known vulnerabilities (such as CGI – common gateway interface).

The crucial point is that none of these events involved any effort to obtain the so-called 'confidential' data. When a Web site is hacked, some endeavour and expertise is needed by the hackers to succeed –

they are looking for security flaws to exploit. In these cases, you didn't need to look – the information just came at you. Although such occurrences are frequently confused in the media with hack attacks, the two events are completely different. Just two final observations: at the base line, technology does not, *per se* make errors; no program or system is self-generated – it is designed and tested by humans. Thus companies should not hide behind the oft quoted 'technical error' excuse, when the fault is entirely of their own making. Moreover, what confidence should consumers have in the many and various security and privacy policies that each e-commerce Web site proudly displays?

THE THREAT INSIDE

One of the pre-eminent risks that any organization faces is that posed by its own staff (including temporary staff and external consultants). As William Marlowe, the former head of the Computer Operations Division of the Washington DC Police, commented 'The most serious problem will always be the trusted employee with legitimate access to computers'. You can do everything that is possible to guard from outside attack, such as installing firewalls and using encryption, but all such techniques may be useless because an insider can very easily sidestep such defences. Many organizations now take great steps to guard their information, intellectual property and funds from intrusions by outsiders, thus ensuring that such assets are accessible to their own staff, who have no need to break in as they are already there. There are various reports and surveys that seek to show that the threat from outside in the Digital Age has been vastly exaggerated, and the real insidious danger is from within any organization. While I agree that the dangers posed by staff are substantial (and have spoken and written on this issue for a number of years), I am conscious of a type of reverse psychological reaction that can occur if the hazards of staff are overemphasized. Put simply, an organization can begin to consider that the sole source of risk comes from within, and subsequently focuses on that strand, ignoring the dangers without. The control of staff risks can be achieved by adopting some basic principles such as:

- Vet and credit check all your prospective employees, temporary staff, associates and consultants (in fact vet anybody who can access your systems and/or information). Don't forget that when you go home at night, your workspace is invaded by cleaners who can (and have) accessed PCs and data by using the password conveniently written on that 'Post It note' stuck on the front of a monitor. You should also revet your staff while they are employed by you, to identify any financial, legal, criminal or personal problems that have occurred since you employed them.

■ Have a system of control and a set of procedures that are robust – and then make sure that they are followed. Establish authorization and approval limits together with an audit trail which involves the completion and retention of proper and adequate documentation.

■ Monitor what you are doing, and accept that in the instant world in which we live any system and/or control may have been adequate and effective yesterday but may not be so today.

■ Don't forget physical security: you must control physical access to computers and thus to information and systems.

■ Have a written policy covering all aspects of acceptable and unacceptable activities (particularly including Internet usage and e-mail) together with what constitutes fraud and illegal activities. To make this effective you must have a clearly documented (and fair) disciplinary procedure that is followed. All suspected illegal actions must be investigated, and offenders treated in a consistent manner.

DISPENSING CASH

As if to prove that the old ones are the best, even in the Digital Age one should turn to the ATM (cash dispenser networks) that we now take so much for granted. The world's ATMs are a prime example of how small the world has become in the Digital Age. But it should be borne in mind that this is very much old technology. You are now able to use your bank ATM card, or your Visa/Plus/Diners (or whatever) card at virtually any ATM across the world. Individual financial institutions have signed up to become credit/debit card issuers and therefore joined the ATM network of that issuer; financial institutions have also merged, bringing together previously separate ATM networks; financial institutions have made their own ATM sharing arrangements with other financial institutions; and it goes on. . . the net effect is that I can use my ATM card at many ATM machines anywhere. The technology of ATM cards and machines is in essence very simple – your ATM card has a magnetic stripe which contains your account number and perhaps some generic information about the card issuer. You insert your card into an ATM and key in your PIN (personal identification number) – that is relayed through telecommunications links back to your card issuer's home computer, which checks your account number, compares the PIN you have keyed in against the one it holds for you ('user authentication') and then validates that the you have the money in your account that you have requested to withdraw (or an overdraft to cover it). All of this takes place in a few seconds. . . even though you may be using an ATM in Singapore and your card issuer's computer is in Madrid.

However there is a fraudulent catch in all of this. If a criminal can obtain both your card details and your PIN and somehow reproduce your card, then there is nothing to stop that person withdrawing money from your account at will anywhere across the planet. We have all heard of credit cards being copied in the Far East and false transactions then being made, but in those cases innocent customers can almost certainly prove that they did not make the transactions possibly because they were not even in the relevant country at the time. Anonymous ATM transactions are somewhat more difficult to dispute – particularly when financial institutions have, for years, vehemently denied the existence of (and the liability for) 'phantom' ATM withdrawals.

A few years ago a major crisis in the life of an ATM network unfolded before my eyes. It started with numerous seemingly unrelated reports of bank staff opening up ATMs on a Monday morning and finding in the card reject bins various plain white plastic cards. This meant that 'customers' had been trying to use these cards but the machine had 'swallowed' them as some kind of unauthorized act had taken place which triggered the retention of the card. Various branches reported such findings centrally – many more branches didn't report them and simply threw the blank cards away, thinking that some drunken idiot after a Saturday night binge had inserted a wrong card into the ATM.

The white cards were the product of a simple yet simultaneously sophisticated fraud which went something like this (as I later found out when I interviewed a fraudster in prison who had been convicted previously for a very similar scam). At that time the data held on ATM card mag stripes was very primitive. The stripe had three tracks – track one contained generic information common to all cards issued by that financial institution, track two contained the account details and track three was blank. Some card issuers put more information on their mag stripes, but the fraudsters obviously avoided them and targeted the customers who had accounts with the institutions who had scant data on their mag stripes. Mag stripe read/write machines are commonly and cheaply available (because their legitimate uses are many and varied) so that it is totally feasible that if you know the construction of a genuine mag stripe you can replicate it on another card. And the best way to determine the construction is open a genuine account then analyse how the mag stripe is constructed. So all you need now are some genuine account details and corresponding PINs – which should in theory be extremely difficult to obtain as every card issuer incessantly chants the mantra of not keeping your card and PIN together. There is of course one place where it is impossible not to have the card and PIN together... and that's at the ATM itself.

ATM's are busy places – particularly in prime locations in bustling cities such as London. Financial institutions have also tried to make ATMs customer friendly – by producing receipts for example. When this fraud took place most receipts spewed out by ATMs showed the full account number on them – and don't you just know it, some ungrateful customers didn't want another piece of paper in their lives and stuffed the receipt in the litter bin provided next to the machine, threw the receipt onto the ground or walked away without taking their receipt, so it was still sitting there when the next customer arrived. Any of these actions provided rich pickings for criminals.

The acquisition of genuine customers data is almost simplicity itself: place a zoom lens video camera as near as possible to an ATM – ensure that it can record the keying in of PINs. If this fails revert to a far more primitive method: stand behind users of the ATM and remember (or dictate into a hidden tape recorder) what digits they keyed in to compose their PIN. So now you have a few PINs...

As for the account numbers all you have to do is scoop up the discarded receipts and work out which one belongs to which PIN. With this information you can use your mag stripe reader/writer machine with confidence. Obviously there may be some cards that you did not get the correct PIN for and those will be swallowed by the ATM, but for those you did get it right on you can withdraw up to the maximum daily withdrawal limit for as long as the account can stand it or the genuine customers realize that there are numerous withdrawals going on and their money is disappearing fast without their knowledge. The gang who perpetrated this fraud used to stand at a different ATM each night and feed in one card after another obtaining £250 virtually every time.

There is another variation on all of this where a bogus ATM machine is fitted on the front of a real one. The customer inserts his or her card and keys in his or her PIN. The bogus machine grabs the card and records the PIN. The customer goes away annoyed without card or money; and the criminal opens up the bogus ATM and has both card, PIN and very quickly that customer's money.

This tale also raises another spectre: that of financial institutions and their industry bodies repeatedly claiming that criminals have not and cannot compromise the integrity of ATM cards or networks. But all of this is, to a large extent, old news, or so I thought until (in the final stages of research for this book) I can across an article in *The New York Post* that appeared in November 2001. This report concerned a recently discovered major ATM fraud in the United States, which bears an uncanny resemblance to the one I describe above. The key difference being that this fraud was now being referred to as a 'cyberscam' perpetrated by 'cyberthieves' (who also happened – for good measure – to be allegedly connected to the 'Russian Mafia'). The story of what happened is depressingly familiar – as far as is known this criminal group obtained both genuine ATM card details and PINs of the genuine customers. While, at the time of writing, it was not exactly known how this data was acquired it is suspected that 'rigged' ATMs had been installed in various delis and grocery shops in New York which captured the PIN that was keyed in together with the card magnetic strip details. Armed with this information, it is a fairly simple process to replicate cards. Just how much was stolen is still being debated: reports say that the fraudsters struck at least a hundred times in New York city, mostly targeting customers of Chase and Citibank. The attacks reached a peak in New York in mid November 2001: but ATM customers in Florida and California have also been hit. The initial loss figures have been put at £1.5 million; both banks known to have been hit have stated that they are working very hard to ensure that no customers suffer financial loss. This is gratifying: because my educated guess is that across the globe each day there are rather more cases of ATM frauds than any of us realizes. By this I am not talking about stolen cards or cards 'borrowed' by other members of the account holder's family – rather the replication of cards, which can be done as we have shown, by very low tech means. Such financial losses are very rarely reported *en bloc* – one reason being that even if the ATM issuer reimburses the victim customer, many such cases are recorded as unexplained system errors.

Yet stranger still is the fact that as I write this book another variation on the ATM replication theme has hit the big time again. This is very much a variant on the original in that the person behind you in the ATM queue peers over your shoulder and memorizes your PIN as you key it in. You wait for the card to be returned by the machine, but before that happens an attractive young lady taps you on the shoulder to tell you that you have dropped a £10 note on the floor. Miraculously (particularly if the reason you went to the ATM was because you had no money) there is a £10 note on the floor, which you pick up. While you are doing that, the gentleman behind you has quickly pocketed your card as it is returned by the ATM. You are left to presume that the ATM has swallowed it, but presumably you want to leave the scene quickly as you are £10 richer. By the time you phone the card issuer to report that the machine has your card, it has been used to its limit in numerous ATMs – and if it is a credit or debit card probably in a few shops as well. As they say in comedy, the old ones are always the best!

DIGITAL LAUNDERING

The rise of the Digital Age presents valuable opportunities for money launderers. Firstly, and hotly disputed by online banking providers, is how effectively the 'know your customer' policy can be implemented when your customer could be anybody in front of a computer screen anywhere in the world. The security and confidentiality claimed by all banking institutions on line are the very qualities and attributes that money launderers are always seeking in the terrestrial banking world. At the very heart of commerce on the World Wide Web is the international borderless environment in which it is located together with:

- the cost effectiveness of the medium;
- the Internet's breadth of reach;
- the difficulties with authenticating identity – both of the user and the supplier;
- anonymity;
- novelty.

What we are seeing in the field of digital money laundering is the effective use of international delivery and supply channels by organized criminals which should evoke the response of greater and ongoing cooperation between individual countries. Bearing in mind the differing standards, policies and opinions of countries how likely is this?

The opportunities which are being capitalized upon by digital launderers are:

- The use of cutting edge technology to evade and frustrate official investigations particularly by creating anonymous and secure methods of communicating.
- Generating income by cyber crime attacks.
- Using services offered via the Internet by 'genuine' suppliers to aid money laundering operations.
- Advertising their own services (via front companies) on the Internet.
- Making good use of international banking and business technological advances and systems to transfer funds and goods across the world.

While organized crime groups are active in this area then there are also many other methods and subjects of attack that could bring them substantial benefits:

- There have been numerous proven examples of customer details being stolen online, particularly relating to credit cards. In May 1997 Carlos Felipe Salgado was arrested in San Francisco after trying to sell 100,000 credit card data sets to undercover FBI agents for US $200,000. Essentially, then, each customer's details were being sold for US $2!
- Another key target of attack by criminals are government or law enforcement systems – in other words trying to get relevant information on what is being done by the authorities to fight crime and money laundering. There have been millions of attacks on US government and defence agencies in the last few years. Moreover both on these networks and those of defence companies secret military and product data can be obtained – to be sold on to the highest bidder, normally a foreign group or nation.
- The computer networks of multinational and domestic corporations can yield vital information concerning customers, products and anti-crime defence systems.

The use of the World Wide Web as a medium to aid and facilitate money laundering has many facets. Certainly the Internet has been a major factor and facilitator in the growth of obscure and even obscurer offshore financial centres. Five years ago – or even two years ago – to open a 'secret account' you would either have had to travel to a bank that still offered that facility or hunt out a company that provided the service through numerous telephone calls or hunting through the ads in a newspaper. Now all you have to do is click on the button that says 'Order my secret account now'. The same principle applies to offshore banks – click your mouse and you can obtain full details of what is available, compare jurisdictions and order online. More importantly because we now live in a virtual digital world a location that is so obscure that you have difficulty finding it in a world atlas suddenly becomes and feels more real, and far closer, because it has a Web site or is described and pictured on hundreds of others. In various books describing tax havens details are given concerning how to get to them, which hotels to stay at and where to eat. Such helpful details miss the point: to open an international company or offshore bank the nearest that any prospective purchasers have to ever go to the actual location is by remaining seated in front of their computer screen.

Even more amazing is the fact that organized crime uses the World Wide Web as an advertising and information medium for their activities. While I haven't yet found a Web site that has a button marked 'Click here to join the Yakuza (or any other organized crime group of your choice)' there are a few that come perilously close. There used to be (until it was closed down by its owner) a www.gotti.com that was a spirited defence of John Gotti, the head of the New York Gambino crime family. There is a www.yakuza.com ,which I presume is a joke site. Various US gangs have Web sites to promote their activities and simultaneously rubbish each other. However it has also become apparent that organized crime groups are taking an active interest in associated areas of the Internet: traditional Mafia groups are known to be behind various online sports betting sites. Even more audaciously in June 1998 it was disclosed that a New York based Italian mob family had set up a consultancy offering services to help businesses cope with the Year 2000 problem. The consultancy firm – boasting its own Web site and toll free 1 800 number – had devised a remarkable solution to the Y2k bug. The firm's programmers came into the client company and rejigged the financial software so that the company's funds were redirected to other offshore accounts operated by the mob.

The vast array of services, facilities and products now available to everyone is presenting wonderful new opportunities to criminals and simultaneously a new and even more difficult set of problems for regulators and investigators. Just on the Internet itself there is a dazzling choice of:

- Free e-mail programs that mean you can access your mail from any computer anywhere in the world.
- Numerous free e-mail routing programs that send your e-mail to another e-mail address.
- State-of-the-art encryption software.
- 'Anonymizer' programs.

Bolt on to these facilities the other types of services available:

- If you use a free e-mail account then you can access it on the Internet from anywhere in the world – for example a public library, an Internet café, even a friend's computer. Thus one could establish such an e-mail facility and only access it from public terminals – meaning that to track such communication access and usage would be almost impossible.
- The widespread availability of 'pay as you go' telephones is an open invitation to anonymous communication. (These are phones that you buy off the shelf without your identity being known and top up by credit card or, more suitably, cash). As such phones are so cheap – and can be used internationally – a criminal or money launderer could buy one, use it for a day or a week and then throw it away.
- Because of various cases where law enforcement officers have used bugging devices criminals are routinely having their homes, offices and vehicles swept for electronic eavesdropping devices.
- The use of secure digital encryption on mobile phones by organized criminals has already frustrated attempts by law enforcement bodies to track and investigate such criminal activity. (Encryption is a critical tool for all concerned in technology. Legitimate providers need encryption to ensure the authenticity, integrity, privacy and security for legitimate transactions. Criminals on the other hand can communicate freely if all such communication is securely encrypted. The opposite side of this coin is that law enforcement's efforts to prevent, detect, investigate and ultimately prosecute criminals are severely diminished if they are unable to decrypt such messages.)

The irony of all of this is that the various public outcries about the new Digital Age totally removing the privacy of an individual (which we debate later in this book) have been turned inside out and on their head by money launderers and criminals carefully researching what is available and focusing on the facilities that anonymize rather than publicize.

If you consider this to be scare-mongering then reflect very carefully on a report that appeared in the Italian newspaper *Milano Finanza* in December 1999. According to that report, prosecutors and police in Palermo stumbled on a £330 million fraud that is part of a global money laundering operation masterminded by the Italian Mafia. Money was moved between a US company that was in fact registered in New Zealand, the Cayman Islands and accounts in Israel and Spain. Subsequent to those movements the funds were deposited in Switzerland and physically transported to banks in Romania, China, Croatia, Russia and Liberia. Somewhere along the way the money disappeared into cyberspace and reappeared as stocks and shares purchased online. Palermo's prosecutor concluded that their 'Investigations have highlighted an unregulated and borderless financial market open to anyone with the capacity, for whatever reason, to exchange stocks and money'.

One should not however underestimate the potential of the Internet to be used either as a channel to facilitate money laundering or to generate the proceeds of crime that need to be washed. Among the commercial sites available on the Internet the following types present significant opportunities to criminals:

- online gambling;
- pornography;
- online prostitution services;
- sexual exploitation of children;
- various other commercial sites offering illegal services or products (drugs, body parts).

A Web search in March 2000 using the exact phrase 'Virtual Casino' produced 36,000 matches. By picking just one game (blackjack) a list of over 350 virtual casinos appeared – including one that managed to combine playing blackjack with the best in adult entertainment. The total number of virtual casinos must be in the hundreds if not thousands. These sites seek to replicate the inside and experience of playing in a real casino – and just like in the real world aims to take as much money off you as possible. It has now been estimated that by 2002 online gamblers will be losing US $3 billion each year. The real danger of these sites returns us to obscure offshore jurisdictions. A large number of such online casinos (it has been estimated up to 75 per cent of them) are said to have their physical presence in 'Caribbean locations'. Having said that, a couple of sites I went on either had no physical address shown or it was almost impossible to locate. As with anything in the remoter offshore world, just because something has an address there doesn't mean that anything actually exists at that address. The governments of these countries profit handsomely from such registrations: roughly US $75,000 fees per year for sports betting sites and US $100,000 and over for virtual casinos. In 1999 it has been reliably reported that the relevant jurisdictions that licence these enterprises are raking in over US $1.5 million per month thanks to these annual fees. Obviously any one in the world can play on these virtual casinos – with no idea of what regulation (if any) exists in relation to their operation. There are additionally other risks such as credit card details being used fraudulently by the operators of such sites. Just with legitimate gambling there are wonderful opportunities for laundering funds. The FBI has in at least one previous investigation targeted such offshore Web sites and their connections with wire fraud and money laundering. The jurisdictions involved were Curacao, the Netherlands, Antilles, Antigua and the Dominican Republic. One is therefore not certain whether to laugh or cry when one finds something like the following on an online casino site (this is a paraphrase of an actual Web site entry, but its essential meaning has not been altered):

We are one of the most trusted casinos on the Internet. . . we operate under a license granted by (Offshore Jurisdiction named). . . To play for money you first must register credit with our casino. Any funds will be played and paid out in US dollars. You can pay by:

- valid credit card;
- Wire Transfer or bank wire;
- Western Union money orders;
- bankers drafts, cashiers checks or certified checks;
- personal checks.
- cash. However we do not recommend this method because it creates the wrong perception to Government officials. We operate a legitimate business and do not wish to be involved in any money laundering activity. Sending cash should be the method of last resort. We will not accept more than US $5,000 in cash *at any one time* (my emphasis).

The method you use to establish your credit is the method we will send back your winnings or any unused credit. . . they will either be credited back to you by a credit on the credit card used or sent by bank wire or company check.

My advice then is send cash in sums of just less then US $5,000 each time; play a few games (there are about 20 different ones to choose from) and then request online that your remaining credits are returned to you in the form of a cheque.

The proliferation of sex sites of all nature and description (and many that defy description) is obviously a fertile ground for organized crime groups to generate funds through their significant control of sex related industries. It has been stated that the annual growth rate for an Internet pornography site is approximately 400 per cent. While adult pornography on the Internet is a very lucrative business the dissemination of pornography involving children is largely free. There is no widespread evidence of the involvement of organized criminal groups in such activities, but it can only be a matter of time before it happens – additionally raising the threat of blackmail and extortion of the subscribers to such sites by the criminal operators.

The greatest boon to money launderers is the increasing use and promotion of online banking and electronic payment systems. Firstly it is important to distinguish between banks that have promotional Web sites and those that operate transactional services. Increasingly with the dot com explosion the banking industry is piling into sites that offer transactional services. More often than not set up as subsidiaries with Web friendly titles, the banking world sees the Internet bank as the logical extension of telephone banking. Recent research has shown that just as massive call centres were a cheaper alternative than branch networks, the back office staff needed to service a Web based bank are even smaller and cheaper than call centres. Thus new legitimate banks are starting up on the Web offering account opening, direct payments, electronic funds transfers, issue of cheques, securities purchase and closing of accounts. Additionally customers of existing terrestrial banks are being encouraged (or perhaps cajoled is the more correct term) to bank via the Internet: rarely a month goes by without my main bank sending me a circular or computer program to encourage me to do this. The last such circular (with accompanying beautifully packaged CD ROM) informed me that this secure system meant that I could:

- View my account details including my balance and overdraft limit.

- View my current and last statement.
- Print account information or save it on my PC.
- Pay bills.
- Move money between accounts.
- View, amend and cancel standing orders.
- View direct debits.

What more could I possibly need? I need never physically go into my branch again. And therein lies the rub. . .

Like everything else in a virtual world online banking removes any need for physical contact. Any bank has no idea of knowing whether the person at the other end of the telephone line is their customer. As with e-mail, the bank's customer has the ability to access his or her account from anywhere in the world using a wide variety of ISPs, none of which can verify who it is that is accessing the account. By taking the provision of online banking services to their logical conclusion Know Your Customer (KYC) procedures are thrown out of the window. This claim has been vehemently denied by online banking providers. In Japan it has been stated that online transactions can only be conducted on accounts that have been opened in a traditional face-to-face manner. In Belgium there is no distinction whatsoever between the medium by which any account is opened and thus money laundering KYC regulations are applicable to all of them. In the United States accounts can be opened online but the customer must supply official identification numbers that are verified by the bank. Yet all of this seems to miss the point by a long way: I have just been on the Internet and many of the solely Internet based banks are promising prospective customers immediate decisions online. Moreover even if KYC procedures are followed then if the account is Internet based there will be absolutely no physical contact whatsoever with the customer. Let's imagine for a minute that a launderer can produce or have access either to genuine individual's details and documents or counterfeit ID documents. The launderer can then open up as many accounts as he of she wants, access them from anywhere in the world and wash money and spin it dry to his or her heart's content. Once again the question of jurisdictional control enters the equation: just which country is responsible for the regulation of such online service providers? The official response (I think) is that online financial service providers are subject to the same regulations in any particular jurisdiction as the terrestrial providers there. This sounds fine – until one compares it to the reality of the situation which immediately renders such a view redundant. Take the European Union Bank in Antigua (well registered there at least): the Bank of England warned potential customers of the risks of investing money in it but in reality could do nothing about it. The whole point about the Internet is that wherever you are based you can tout for business from anyone anywhere.

MY ELECTRONIC WALLET

The logical extrapolation of doing business on the Internet is the creation of some universally acceptable and negotiable form of cyber currency. For the last 15 years the financial environment has been leading us to a situation where the vast majority of money is virtual: your salary is paid into your bank account and all you see is the written representation of it on your bank statement or on the screen of an ATM; you pay for most goods by credit or debit card; when the credit card bill arrives you write out a cheque; you go on the Internet and pay for goods or services anywhere in the world with your universally acceptable piece of plastic. The next obvious step is the establishment of some mechanism that facilitates the transfer of financial value without the need for cash. Such a system has been termed a variety of things: cyberpayments, digital currency, e-cash, e-money – in essence all the same animal. There are a variety of different systems and techniques that are bracketed under the term electronic payment technologies. According to FinCEN (the US Government's Financial Crimes Enforcement Network):

> The common element is that these systems are designed to provide the transacting party with immediate, convenient, secure and potentially anonymous means by which to transfer financial value. When fully implemented this technology will impact users worldwide and provide readily apparent benefits to legitimate commerce, however, may also have the potential to facilitate the international movement of illicit funds.

A range of different companies is trying to sell a system as the one that will become the standard; additionally there are different types of systems being promoted. There are almost a hundred forms of electronic cash already available to use the facilities of Web sites; if, for example, you go onto various news sites you set up an electronic purse or wallet through credit card payment and then the costs of your searches and article retrievals are deducted from this digital money storage facility. The concerns regarding the use of these systems by digital criminals include:

- From a regulatory point of view banks and financial institutions have been increasingly relied upon both to report suspicious transactions and control money laundering attempts. If banks are no longer part of the loop this fundamental control point will be eradicated.
- At present the types of EPT systems are diverse so it may be difficult to create and install common reporting principles together with common fraud prevention controls.
- The other 'old chestnut' is the international jurisdictional issue together with the mandatory need for extensive and enhanced international cooperation. As FinCEN puts it without pulling any punches: 'The apparent and immediate erosion of international financial borders resulting from Cyberpayment transactions mandates enhanced co-operation and efforts among international entities to ensure that there are consistent policies and standards. It will not deter financial crime if one country has extensive links and regulations and another has none. The illicit money will merely move to the weakest link.'

The UK's NCIS states the obvious fears in its 'Crime on the International Highways Report':

> It is conceivable that criminal organizations will take time to recognize and exploit new technology. Yet, historical precedent provides a contrary view. Following the introduction of various anti-money laundering obligations in the UK during 1993–95, criminal use of less regulated sectors (where risk of disclosure was less) accelerated sharply. It is reasonable to expect that new payment systems will be similarly exploited if the opportunities are sufficient.

One fundamental point that has been simultaneously ignored and highlighted is this: to obtain electronic money the criminal has to convert real money; to cash-in digital money he or she has to convert it back to real money. In fact while the first part of that argument is correct the second is not: while not suggesting that electronic money will completely replace and supersede real money it will presumably be possible to buy high value items with electronic money (such as cars): in this way criminal funds will be laundered and there will be no need to convert electronic money back into real money. The risks inherent in electronic money are that it is incredibly mobile and can be anonymous. The situation at the moment with no predominant system or product is very attractive to digital criminals: a plurality of approaches and systems means no common controls, standards or regulation.

Another form of electronic cash is smart cards. These have been trialled in various parts of the world, most commonly by Mondex (now part of Mastercard International) who to my knowledge have run experiments in the UK, Australia and New Zealand. At the time of writing there are a large number of franchise holders across the world waiting to launch this technology. Essentially these cards are similar to an electronic wallet in that you credit the card with funds and then use it like a credit/debit card to make purchases with the funds available on the card. Certainly in the trial in Swindon, UK, the impression gained was that it was not particularly successful as the Mondex card gave no great advantage over a credit/debit card and in fact was more troublesome because you had to make sure that it was loaded with funds. However in Australia and New Zealand it was possible to have a non-attributable card, which could be charged by transfers from other cards but not by debiting and crediting bank accounts. Transfers to these type of cards could be made by telephone, online and by a special wallet that moved amounts from one card to the other. As Stanley Morris, the director of FinCEN, observed, such cards have deep inherent money laundering risks:

> Suppose an Internet user is a narcotics trafficker or an agent for a gang of sophisticated criminals of any other sort. Consider the invoices the trafficker might pay, the supplies he might order and the transactions he might accomplish if, for instance, he could download an unlimited amount of cash from a smart card to a computer and then transmit those funds to another smart card in locations around the world – all anonymously, all without an audit trail, and all without the need to resort to a traditional financial institution.

Everything that digital criminals need to launder money is now available online: they can open a bank account, order an international company, enrol in a multitude of stock trading schemes, communicate by anonymous e-mail, trade using electronic cash systems that are already available, funnel money through online casinos and betting shops, buy houses online, funnel money through online auctions, open their own offshore or online bank: you name it, it can be done. And whatever the authorities say there are no country boundaries, no face-to-face meetings required, no professional advisors asking awkward questions, there is very little if anything at all that presently can halt or restrict this aspect of digital crime. Just one final thought: it is entirely probable that criminals who make extensive use of electronic systems to hide, wash and distribute their funds, acquired such riches through digital crime.

VIRUS ATTACKS

I am never quite sure that I understand the point of computer viruses. Perhaps I am not alone in that it is frequently presumed that hackers hold virus writers in low regard due to the perceived lack of skills that the latter have and the indiscriminate damage caused by viruses. Perhaps the very *raison d'être* of viruses is where I miss the point: presumably the attraction in writing and unleashing viruses is the very fact that you (as the writer) can do it, and then sit back and watch the trail of havoc you have created. Some such trails are very long indeed. Research has shown (surprise, surprise) that the majority of virus writers are intelligent males between 15 and 23 years old who are probably bored, curious, intent on testing what can be done or simply vindictive. The main psychological buzz that viruses bring to their writers is either the intellectual satisfaction of completing the challenge they have set themselves or the fact that they are fighting the 'system'. The word 'virus' has itself mutated into more of a generic term which is now used to cover a multitude of computer vermin (also known as malicious software).

A virus, *per se*, is a manmade, independent program or piece of code that is loaded onto your computer or system without your knowledge, and runs in the same manner. Viruses usually spread by 'infected' files that are passed between computers. Five years ago the largest risk was probably users inserting floppy disks that were infected into their PC. Now the infinitely more critical risk is viruses originating via the Internet. Viruses can reproduce themselves, attach themselves to other programs, create copies of themselves. Viruses normally damage or corrupt data, use available memory, clutter up disk space and bring the system to an abrupt halt. The most dangerous types of viruses transmit across networks, exploiting security flaws. Running a anti-virus program that isn't up to date is almost worse than useless; even the best fully up-to-date anti-virus programs cannot protect against all viruses. Somewhat ironically, there is also a thriving market in hoax viruses, mostly through e-mails that claim to have latest information and demand that you pass them on.

Then there are worms. The use of the word in this sense was originated in a 1982 research paper by John Shoch and Jon Hupp of the Xerox Palo Alto Research Center. However, this paper derived the term from 'The Shockwave Rider' by John Brunner, published in the early 1970s and now promoted as 'a cyberpunk story from the days before cyberpunk was a concept'. Normally a worm propagates/replicates itself across a computer network causing malicious damage such as using up resources (storage, processing time) and shutting the system down. The worm may copy itself from one disk drive to another or via e-mail. Worms appear to be the computer infection of choice, accounting for approximately half of the computer infections in 2000. Whereas in the past some technical knowledge would have been required to create worms, now worm generators can be downloaded from the Internet. A typical transmission mechanism for worms is an 'interesting e-mail attachment'; other worms need no human intervention and infect computers with specific security flaws and then seek out other computers that have the same flaw. Because of the power to replicate it is now being argued that worms have in effect caused denial of service attacks on the Internet because of the bandwidth consumed by them. In the roll call of infamous worms are:

- The Anna Kournikova virus – which was, in strict terms, not a virus but a worm (2001).
- The Christmas Tree virus – possibly the first worm on a worldwide network that spread across BITNET in December 1987.
- The Cornell Internet Worm – which exploited computer security flaws in 1988 and infected about 5 per cent of those users connected to the prototype Internet.

The key difference between a virus and a worm is the method by which each replicates and spreads: a virus is dependent on a host file or computer's boot sector while a worm can run completely independently and spread by itself through network connections.

Just like in Homer's *Iliad* a Trojan horse is something that is apparently harmless (or even beneficial) but once inside the gates turns out to be something else entirely. Trojan horses do not replicate like viruses and worms, but can still be extremely destructive. Trojan horses rely on users to install them, or they can be installed by intruders who have gained unauthorized access by other means. Then, an intruder attempting to subvert a system using a Trojan horse relies on other users running the Trojan horse to be successful. Among various Trojan horses that are common are anti-virus programs that actually install viruses and software upgrades that are nothing of the kind, but when loaded proceed to modify files and contact other remote systems.

A logic bomb will lay dormant in a system until triggered by some event or specific system condition. When set off, the bomb will carry out a malicious act, or set of acts such as changing random data or making the disk unreadable, The trigger mechanism can be anything – among favourites are a specific date, a specific event or the number of times a certain thing is done (even the number of boot-ups). A logic bomb does not replicate itself.

These various forms of malicious software are no joke: in September 2001 the Reuters news agency reported that the total global cost of viruses was US $ 17.1 billion in 2000 and US $ 12.1 billion in 1999. The main reasons for such phenomenal costs were:

- The Code Red Worm, which by September 2001 had already cost US $2.6 billion, comprising US $1.5 billion in lost productivity costs and US $1.1 billion in cleaning up computer systems.
- The Sircam virus, which cost US$1.04 billion in total including US $575 million in lost productivity and US $460 in clean-up costs
- The Love Bug virus, which still remains the most financially damaging virus ever, costing US $8.7 billion in lost productivity and clean-up costs.

The Code Red worm itself is a fascinating example as to how the digital world, once again, is really a very small place: its major inherent risks are ever present in its fundamental global interconnectivity. This worm is not aimed at Windows 3.1, Windows 95, Windows 98 or Windows ME systems but attacks Windows NT 4.0 and Windows 2000 computers and Web sites that use that technology. The world of viruses holds a certain academic interest combined with curiosity value to see what fascinating damage can be caused – useless beauty indeed. Examples include:

■ CIH or the Chernobyl virus. This was created by a student in Taiwan in 1998 and struck up to a million PCs on April 26 1999 as well as cropping up at various times after that date until now. This virus only attacks Windows 95 and 98 systems and is triggered when the date is 26 April (or if you have a PC that shows the wrong date it strikes when your system states it is this date). The virus overwrites critical information on your hard disk, and in some cases deletes information stored in the PC's bios memory, which then makes it impossible to boot the PC. Just to confuse the situation some variants of this virus trigger on the 26th day of other months.

■ The FunLove virus. To their embarrassment in April 2001 Microsoft e-mailed their key support customers to inform them that they may have been infected with the FunLove virus. The reason for the infection? One of Microsoft's Servers did not have anti-virus software installed – the server that provides updates and bug fixes to Microsoft's premier customers.

■ The Sircam worm. This can potentially create more damage than wrecking your system by random mailings of documents on the users' hard drive. Sircam arrives by mass e-mailing using Outlook Express to distribute itself. The e-mail arrives with a fairly innocuous attachment, reading something along the lines of 'Hi how are you? I send you this file in order to have your advice. See you later! Thanks'. This message is helpfully also available in Spanish. Once the attachment is opened Sircam gathers files from the user's hard drive and all the e-mail addresses in Windows address book. The virus then sends copies of itself to all of the addresses it has obtained – together with a randomly chosen file. Additionally Sircam computes a random number that has a 1 in 33 chance of triggering the PC to fill up all of the remaining space on the hard disk by adding text at each start up to a system file that the worm has installed in the recycle bin. The choice of Windows Recycle Bin for the location of this file was interesting, as most virus checkers did not check the Recycle Bin. Then the worm checks to see if the date is October 16; if it is and the PC is using the European date format the worm will generate another random number – this time it has a 1 in 20 probability of success. Success being a relative term: as victory for the worm will result in the machine deleting all of the files on its hard drive.

The wonderful world of viruses is further complicated by hoax viruses together with various e-mail security bulletins which purport to alert the user to new viruses but in fact contain a virus themselves. One such e-mail tells users that their PC contains a virus called sulfnbk.exe, which should be deleted – the drawback being that this is a perfectly legitimate file in Windows, which is a utility that restores long file names. The Web site www.vmyths.com contains many more examples of similar incidents.

The best response towards viruses is to adopt common sense policies and procedures regarding the following key topics:

- Don't use illegal or counterfeit software, and never run an unknown disk without virus checking it.
- Always back up your files.
- Delete e-mail attachments, specifically where the sender is unknown to you.
- Do not let others borrow program disks – if you do virus check them before you use them again.
- Always run an anti-virus program, and just as importantly make sure that it is updated frequently.
- If you download software from the Internet always do it to a diskette, not directly to your hard drive (for further security you can write protect your hard drive during this operation).
- Disable Word Macros and ensure that, depending which version of Word you are using, macro virus protection (if present) is running.
- Be aware of strange occurrences on your system (although most systems appear to have such events on a daily basis without it necessarily indicating that a virus is present!). Watch out for:
  - your system slowing down;
  - files that disappear (although by its very nature this is easier said than done);
  - attempts to access the hard disk to read or write when there should be no such activity;
  - strange display corruption and/or unusual visual occurrences;
  - unusually large program file;
  - decreases in memory or reduced disk space.
- Educate users about computer viruses, what they do, how to recognize them, how they can be prevented and what actions to take immediately one is discovered.

WIDE OPEN TO ABUSE.COM

The safest way to double your money is to fold it over once and put it in your wallet.

Variously attributed

There is no reason for any individual to have a computer in his home.

Ken Olsen, President of Digital Equipment (1977)

THE MEDIUM IS THE MESSAGE

A once in a lifetime chance to cash in on the Millennium Bug. By the year 2000 you could triple your money.

So who is MBI?
MBI was founded in 1997 by three Swiss business leaders... the company was set up for the sole purpose of providing blue chip companies and governments with insurance against Millennium Bug problems. After its huge success in Europe and the United States MBI is coming to Australia. MBI is establishing offices in Canberra, Sydney and Melbourne by the end of May 1999.

Guaranteed profits
It is confidently expected that investors will triple their money between the time of the investment and September 30 2000, after which time the insurance policies become null and void.
Yes, you should expect to make a return of 200 per cent on your investment in just over 15 months. . .

How does this investment work?
The explanation is simple. Because of the lack of competition in this category, and our unique expertise, MBI and its investors can achieve extra ordinary levels of profit. . .

So how exactly does it work?
It all sounds too easy.
MBI has a group of IT experts with leading edge knowledge of the Millennium Bug. With detailed analysis of computer systems and operations we are able to classify corporations and government departments into five separate risk categories. We can then target the corporations and departments that fall into the two lowest risk categories. We make approaches to them at the highest level offering our underwriting services. These insurance premiums are heavily loaded beyond normal underwriting criteria because of lack of competition in this market.
You can receive GUARANTEED RETURNS for your INVESTMENT OUTLAY.

Eleven people complained that this Web site, set up on 1 April 1999, was a fraud. More than 10,000 potential investors visited the site and 1,212 potential investors asked for more information. Investments were pledged by 233 people and totalled in excess of A $4 million.

In May 1999 the Australian Securities and Investments Commission admitted it had all been an elaborate April Fool's Day joke to highlight the danger of fraudulent investment scams on the Internet. ASIC chairman Alan Cameron hit the nail on the head when he commented that 'Investors should be wary of fraud and not believe that the Internet offers some sense of instant authority'. The only saving grace of the MBI Web site was that ASIC revealed it was a fraud – and collected no money from 'investors' (who, it had to be said, were very keen to pour money into this venture). The same does not apply to hundreds of other Web sites that are equally fraudulent but are not discovered to be so by surfers until it is too late. Leaving aside the issues of how both information and money can be obtained on the Internet by digital attacks, the Internet is a wonderful mechanism for criminals, because in cyberspace everyone is equal – if a Web page says that the company behind it is a well regarded, long established concern who are you to doubt them? If they want money up front why should you question it? There are many enthusiastic Internet users who are only too willing to be convinced by the flashy Web sites detailing cyber shopping, chain letters, pyramid schemes, work at home plans, phony investments and fake off shore banks (to name but a few frauds). These avid prospective customers would do as well to visit the Fraud Watch site first and dwell on its motto borrowed from P T Barnum: 'There's a sucker born every minute.' Across the globe there are probably thousands, rather than one, born every minute. Such frauds are nothing new – but what the Digital Age has provided to fraudsters is a mechanism whereby they can advertise their services and products very cheaply – if not for free – to a global audience.

Fraudulent cyber banks are a particularly popular scam: anybody can launch a Web site claiming to be a bank and solicit deposits. You can make up a false history, non-existent directors and claim ridiculous returns on investments; if you are vaguely clever you will probably give your 'bank' a name, which sounds remarkably similar to a genuine (and financially stable) financial institution. Your scam bank has various distinct advantages (for you) over its terrestrial equivalents: no regulation, no financial standards and no insurance to protect investors. In 1998 the Freedom Star National Bank in Phoenix offered certificates of deposit with an 18 per cent return before regulators closed it down. Its owner somewhat perversely commented that he 'didn't want to apply for a charter because I didn't want to kiss the government's butt. Our deposits were backed up by a gold mine I own in Alaska'. The role of dishonour of such scam banks is already a long one, with one bank still at its pinnacle: European Union Bank. One would however think that as this phony financial institution imploded in 1997, with a large amount of media coverage attached to it, potential investors may have realized the risks of investing with a bank that they have never heard of. . .

European Union Bank was founded in 1994 by two émigré Russians. The rumour from the beginning was that it was used by Russian Mafia to launder money. The bank was incorporated in Antigua, which has 57 or so offshore banks registered there for its 60,000 inhabitants and is a constant cause of extreme concern for both regulators and law enforcers. Claiming to be the world's first offshore bank on the Internet, its main advertising was done, naturally, via its Web site and included at various times:

- Offering a one year US $1 million certificate of deposit that paid interest of 9.91 per cent – sometimes its interest rates were 10 times that of its competitors.
- Stating that 'EUB provides clients with total privacy and. . . strict confidentiality. . . under Antiguan law no person shall disclose any information relating to the business affairs of a customer. . . except pursuant to an order of a court in Antigua. The court can only issue such an order in connection with an alleged criminal offence. There is no exchange of information treaty between Antigua and any other country.'
- Pointing out that 'The ultimate incentive to clients is an internationally attractive interest rate offered in the milieu of a tax-free jurisdiction.'

I'm sure you get the picture. . . and can predict the outcome. A bank nobody had heard off in an obscure offshore location? Too good to be true financial returns promised? In October 1996 the Bank of England drew attention to EUB's activities and warned that prospective depositors should carry out due diligence on it. Still the money poured in. . . until August 1997, when the bank was shut by Antiguan authorities after an investor had tried unsuccessfully to withdraw his investment of US $128,000. While it may or may not have been the first offshore bank to be established on the Internet it certainly was the first failed fraudulent offshore bank there. There was no sign of the Bank's founders. . . or of funds. Of course as it was an offshore private bank depositors went to it for discretion: thus it may be difficult to identify customers who will admit depositing money, never mind tracking down what funds were stolen. Press reports at the time commented on 'wealthy investors' and 'heavy losses'.

In fact, rather than being scared off by such frauds perpetrated in cyberspace, the willingness to be taken in by such schemes has increased – but why stop at a bank when you can create your own nation in cyberspace and confer on it all of the attributes of a real country. The fraudulent offshore 'cyber nation', the Dominion of Melchizedek, also known as DOM, has been a notable feature on the Internet for a number of years. DOM is an entirely fictitious nation dreamt up by convicted Californian conman David Korean aka Mark Pedley aka Ambassador Korem. In 2000, in just one of its many adventures, DOM was linked with a real Polynesian island, Rotuma (part of Fiji). 'Agents' of DOM had been selling stock on the Internet in non-existent Rotuman corporations such as the 'Rotuma National Copra Corporation' 'Pacific Paradise Citrus Corporation' and the 'Rotuma National Fishing Corporation'. Even stranger, Melchizedek has, it is claimed, its own stock exchange; so watch out for the following companies, which are listed there:

Rotuman Dominion National Airlines.
Rotuman National Copra Corporation.
Rotuman National Fishing Corporation.
John Hassan Inc.
Airline Transportation & Leasing Services Ltd.
Bank of Salem.
FBHC, Ltd.
Hong Kong Private Bankers.
Pacific Paradise Citrus Corporation.
The International Monetary Reserve.
Taongi Import Trading Company.
Movieland Development USA, Inc.
Equitable Suisse Bank, AG.
Dominion Productions, Inc.

At the risk of restating the obvious:

- The Dominion of Melchizedek (DOM) does not exist, in any accepted physical or legal sense.
- Thus any documents which make any reference to the Dominion of Melchizedek must be considered to be suspect. The US Department of State has warned that the Dominion of Melchizedek is 'fraudulent in intent and practice'.
- Any individual or company that claims to live or operate from the Dominion of Melchizedek must also be considered to be totally suspect.
- A Dominion of Melchizedek passport or company incorporation certificate is not a valid legal document.

It may come as a surprise to realize that there are many more 'micro-nations' with equally dubious claims to nationhood. The US Department of State confirms that there are 191 countries in the world, but none of the following 'nations' appear in their list. The Internet has facilitated the growth of numerous new 'micro-nations', many of which are the creation of conmen who offer false passports, fraudulent financial documents and bogus companies.

There are of course a few 'micro-nations' that have been set up purely for fun, such as the Principality of Outer Baldonia that was founded on a tiny rock off Nova Scotia in 1949. Its government charter was based on swearing, drinking and lying about the size of fish caught. The Principality gained some sort of notoriety when it declared war on the Soviet Union.

However, many of the 'micro-nations' have more dubious and devious agendas. Our own research has shown that each of the following 'nations' has issued passports, or has had passports issued in its name, which could be used for fraudulent purposes. None of these passports is legitimate:

Colonia.
Conch Republic.
Corterra (Republic of).
Empire Washitaw de Dugdahmoundyah.
Hutt River Province.
Khalistan.
Koneuwe (Republic of) – actually somebody's back garden in Zurich!
Oceanus.
Paisos Catalans Calalunya.
Palmerya (Principality of).
San Christobel (Republic of).
Trust Territory of the Pacific Islands.
Vera Cruz (Free and Independent State of).
Vikingland Furstentum Wikingland.

Additionally there are numerous sham organizations that issue passports, which once again are totally fraudulent. Our list of these quasi-organizations is amazing long: among the more plausible sounding bodies are:

Association D'Entrade Humanitaire International.
UNO (United Nations Office, Inc.).
Centre d'Information Corps Diplomatique et Consulaire.

Among the more notable 'micro-nations' are the Conch Republic, Redonda, The Kingdom of Talossa and the Hutt River Province.

The Conch Republic does actually exist in a physical form (well, kind of!). It was 'formed' on 23 April 1982 in response to the United States' border blockade of Florida Keys. As the Web site (www.conchrepublic. com) explains 'Since the United States Government insisted on treating the Keys like a foreign country, Key West Mayor Dennis Wardlow seceded from the Union, declared war, surrendered, and demanded foreign aid. During the intervening years the United States never reacted to the secession, thereby establishing sovereignty for the Conch Republic under International Law'. While the Conch Republic does issue passports, the aims of this country appear to be rather more spiritual as it 'aspires only to bring more warmth, humor and respect to a planet we find in sore need of all three'. However, holders of passports from the Conch Republic may not put those documents to such altruistic purposes.

Redonda and Talossa, two separate 'micro nations', appear to be at the more lunatic end of the spectrum. The Island of Redonda, according to its comprehensive Web site (www.redonda.org) 'lies in the Caribbean Sea. . . thirty four miles WSW of Antigua and approximately fifteen miles NW of Montserrat. It is about one mile long by one third of a mile wide. . . and is a rocky and uninhabitable remnant of an extinct volcanic cove'. Perhaps a clue to its authenticity is given by the contact details for this 'nation': which are care of a PO Box number in Norwich, England. The Kingdom of Talossa was formed by a 13-year-old high school student who is now King Robert I; it has existed on the Internet since 1995 and once again the contact details for this 'country' – in Milwaukee – perhaps give the game away.

The Hutt River Province perhaps ought to be taken more seriously – or at least the fraud risks posed by it should be. This entity originally claimed to be an independent American Indian nation in Canada, but now claims to be an independent state in South West Australia. The Hutt River Province Trade Bureau Corporations Register 'provides facilities and services to any persons of good character wishing to establish a Business Name, Corporation or Company'. Currently the following business names and corporations are 'registered' in this way:

Carvalue.
Take Control.
Graphic Lane.
Asia Corp.
Buttler.
Asiapacific Network Corp.

Cars.net.au Corp.
Apacnet Corp.
Guatemala Trading Corp.
Trade Force One Corp.
Drug Aid Corp.
David Ross Holdings Corp.

Also watch out for similar non-existent 'nations' such as. . .

The Knights of Malta.
The Kingdom of Enio Kio.
New Utopia.

In April 1999 the United States Securities and Exchange Commission was granted an emergency restraining order against 'Prince' Lazarus Long (also known by the more prosaic name of Howard Turney) who was offering what the SEC claimed to be bogus bonds on his New Utopia Web site – which at the time of the complaint by the SEC had received over 100,000 hits. Believe it or not New Utopia is a country which will appear out of the Caribbean on giant concrete platforms built on a land mass 115 miles west of the Caymans Islands. I really wanted to believe this (?) but the clincher were the details of the Prince's partner, Princess Maureen! The serious side to this is that the Web site offered:

- Unregistered 5-year New Utopian government bonds promising a 9.5 per cent return – which were promoted by e-mail by the Prince.
- Up to a 200 per cent return on New Utopian currency investments.
- The opportunity for investors to become charter citizens of the new country.

Recently, more by accident than design, I have visited at least 10 different Web sites that are almost certainly fraudulent. Three of them, for example, have soundalike names to real institutions – a bank, a European chamber of commerce and (almost unbelievably) what appears at first sight to be a governmental department. All three sites are offering business loans – for incredibly large amounts – if you enroll by paying an annual subscription by credit card. Thus the innocent investor is not only being ripped off with a phony annual subscription but also hands over his or her credit card details.

Internet 'banks' and other related Web sites cannot only defraud the innocent but also be a front for organized crime – so who does have jurisdiction and regulatory powers in cyberspace? The awful truth is that a 'virtual' fraudulent bank (or any other type of virtual company which defrauds gullible customers) if done with style and a modicum of intelligence is virtually untraceable and unprosecutable – and the funds it has taken in are unrecoverable.

Yet all such frauds inherently have built into them the possibility of being discovered as such; the really clever digital financial frauds are those which as far as possible resemble a legitimate Web site, business transaction or service. As with every type of fraud, the more realistic it sounds the more likely it is to succeed totally. Which is presumably the principle that Mark Jakob worked on when he sent an e-mail on 20 August 2000 purporting to be from a public relations company, with an attached press release that stated that the chief executive of Emulex had resigned and its earnings estimates were overstated. Emulex is a high tech storage supplier, in which Jakob (aged 23) had stock. Jakob had previously worked at Internet Wire, an online distributor of company press releases. The details contained in Jakob's press release were totally false – but that didn't stop both Internet Wire and Bloombergs reporting them as fact. The effects were immediate: within less than half an hour of these reports appearing Emulex's stock fell US $61 as 2.3 million shares were sold. This resulted in the company losing US $2.2 million in market capitalization, which suited Jakob just fine as the whole purpose of his scheme was to recoup the US $97,000 he had lost a week earlier by short selling 3,000 of Emulex's stock. As the stock price went into freefall Jakob covered his short position, pocketing US $54,000 and then made a profit three days later of US $186,000 on shares he had bought on the fateful day. Emulex, being based in California, were three hours behind what was happening in New York; they managed to get a press release out by 12.51 pm and salvage the situation by the end of the day. Jakob was arrested on August 31 and subsequently sentenced to almost four years in prison. The fact that the perpetrator of this fraud was caught and imprisoned though is not the real point. As Arthur Levitt, the then Chairman of the US Securities and Exchange Commission was to comment later 'The Internet, with its low cost, anonymity and large number of innocent investors, makes it ripe for out-and-out fraud. Be wary of illusions of easy money or fancy Web sites promising that you'll make a fortune with one quick gamble. Be wary of hot press releases'.

There are also Internet frauds that are so outrageous that they must be jokes (they are aren't they?) and some which are unintentionally comical. One of my particular joke Web sites – or at least I hope it is – is this one:

ABSOLUTE MONEY LAUNDERING

Money laundering and tax evasion. Reliable money laundering schemes. We are professional money launderers. Clients and partners from any country are welcome.

Search terms: money laundering, tax evasion, dirty money, cash, offshore, front companies, offshore bank, offshore accounts, money laundering, cash cleaning, tax evasion, money laundering.

E-mail: (address given on Web site, but excluded here)

But not all fraudulent Web sites are comical in content such as this one; rather their claims are ludicrous:

(Name Given). . . Offshore Trade is a group of experienced traders who trade in Offshore High-Yield Investments. The traders have extensive knowledge in this area and consistently make a profit for their clients. They are bringing you this unique opportunity to share in the wealth that they have created. As a member of. . . Offshore Trade, you can receive weekly payments into your e-gold account without any effort at all.

The names and photos of the entire staff on the site, along with their mailing address. Also, a telephone conference call for December 3 will soon be announced.

Invest from US $20–1,000 for 7 days receive 185 per cent
Invest US $2,000 for 7 days receive 186 per cent
Invest US $3,000 for 7 days receive 187 per cent
Invest US $4,000 for 7 days receive 188 per cent
Invest US $5,000 for 7 days receive 189 per cent

The launch for Program 2 will be at 9 am US Eastern Standard Time on December 1st. You may join in the program now but all investments will be recorded as a December 1st transaction.

Although this is a passive investment, you may promote Program 2 and make 10 per cent of every investment made under your referrals.

Simply have the people you sponsor use your e-gold account number as their referrer when they fill out the Confirmation Form.
(Hyperlink to Web site of offshore trading company Web site – just one slight drawback – the link takes you to a site that tells you that 'The page or file you have requested was not found on this server' and this site is from Belize!)

DECEMBER 1ST – LAST DAY TO GET INTO THE 2500 PER CENT CHRISTMAS PROGRAM
Other 2 programs continue to operate.
Here is a program that is looking real good. I CONTINUE TO GET PAID. Read their forum and I think you may want to get in on this. It is worth a look!

They have 3 programs to join
125 per cent in 3 days
250 per cent in 5–7 days
2500 per cent is a special Christmas program
They even tell how they make the money on the Web site.

This site's claims may be ludicrous – but an example quoted by *The Sunday Times* made fools of the 'subscribers', who didn't know that they were. Crescent Publishing agreed to refund US $30 million to thousands of customers who had their credit card charged for visiting the sites operated by the company. The sites included Playgirl.com and HighSociety.com – but the clever thing was that visitors were told that their credit card details were only needed to prove that they were not minors, and if they gave details they would get a 'free' tour of 64 gambling and pornography sites. The free tour actually cost up to £65 a month, which is what was charged to the user's credit card. But there was a double 'Catch 22' for investigators of the fraud – not only do victims have a natural reluctance to admit they have been taken in, but in this case many victims were just too embarrassed to complain. Such frauds are big business; it has been estimated that Crescent alone generated up to £130 million by this fraud between 1997 and 1999.

If you want an example of completely pointless digital manipulation, then come on down John Zuccarini of Andalusia, Pennsylvania, who was allegedly behind thousands of Web sites shut down by the US Federal Trade Commission in October 2001. The scam, the FTC allege, went like this: Zuccarini registered numerous domain names which were slight misspellings of popular ones or inverted names of popular legitimate domains, together with 41 variations of the name 'Britney Spears'. When surfers misspelt the genuine domain name they would end up at one of Zuccarini's sites which would proceed to bombard them with numerous rapidly opening windows – an FTC demonstration showed that in their case 29 such windows opened. Just to really confuse things further in some instances the genuine Web site opened, thus implying that the other almost subliminal windows were associated with it. The windows that opened in front of your very eyes were solicitations for various useful services such as online gambling to hardcore pornography, and if you tried to get out of the eternal maze that you had been deposited in, even more problems occurred. Pages were programmed so that if you hit the 'Back' button or attempted to close the windows that were hitting you, more windows opened: a good example of a 'mousetrap'. Zuccarini has something of a history: he has been sued numerous times over the domain names that he has registered (and lost at least 53 such cases). Even stranger is that he is reported to have registered various company names under which he does business, of which more than 20 contain the term 'Cupcake' in their title!

THE WHEELS OF FORTUNE

There are many and various lists and surveys of the main types of frauds perpetrated on the Internet (many such frauds are also marketed by spam mailings, and are detailed later in Section 5), however, the following are constantly reported as being the most prevalent scams:

- Credit repair: particularly popular in the United States – you pay an upfront fee to have your bad credit record repaired or to get a new US Employee Identification Number. Just two problems here – no one can erase a bad credit record if it is an accurate reflection of your financial history and it is illegal to set up a new credit identity using an Employee Identification Number.
- Guaranteed loans: the loans are not guaranteed, and probably are to be granted by non-existent lenders. These two factors don't stop many people paying over 'arrangement fees'.
- Investment opportunities: more of what we've already discovered, usually offering high rates of 'no risk' returns or interest.
- Free products: there are hundreds of Web sites that offer free high value products (such as computers). A few are genuine – in that,

for example, you can get a 'free' printer if you buy various ink or toner items. Many are out and out advance fee frauds some of which then mutate into a pyramid scheme (what a combination!): subscribers don't qualify for the 'free' gift until, and unless, they recruit other 'members'.

- Get rich quick offers: which is a fairly unique marketing message, as neither claim applies and the entire point of such Web sites is to get money out of unwary consumers. Just one thought: if it was as easy to get rich as it was claimed, wouldn't we all be millionaires?
- Health, diet and medical scam Web sites: preying on surfers with medical or self-image problems, these Web sites offer 'miracle cures', 'secret formulas' 'ancient recipes'. While we may simply laugh at such recipes for things like weight loss, the sites that offer 'cures' for cancer and HIV/AIDS are despicable – and are preying on very ill (and probably extremely desperate) people.
- Business opportunity scams: everything that applies to all the other scam Web sites applies to these sites in spades. Almost all of them are advance fee fraud scams crossed with pyramid schemes.

The US National Consumers League Internet Fraud Watch Site (www. fraud.org) has some fascinating statistics on the complaints they receive. In the year 2000 the Top 10 Internet frauds that they recorded were:

- online auctions – 78 per cent;
- general merchandise sales – 10 per cent;
- Internet access services – 3 per cent;
- work at home – 3 per cent;
- advance free loans – 2 per cent;
- computer equipment/software – 1 per cent;
- Nigerian money offers – 1 per cent;
- information adult services – 1 per cent;
- credit card issuing – 0.5 per cent;
- travel/vacations – 0.5 per cent.

In the period of January–October 2001 the same 10 categories reappeared, with online auctions still in top spot with 63 per cent of the total. This decrease is not necessarily as good as it sounds, because the primary reason for it was the rise in the number of complaints relating to Nigerian frauds, at 9 per cent of the total. Thus, as shown by many other surveys, the type of Web site that is head and shoulders above all others in terms of complaints is the online auction site. The attraction of these sites completely passes me by – but obviously I am a bit of an oddball in this respect, as an estimated 1.5 million transactions take place in relation to online auctions every day. And if you want to join in the fun, there are various simple steps that you can follow:

- Register an auction domain name, either with a free service or, as it's so cheap now, register a 'proper' domain name.
- Set up all e-mails so that they end up at an untraceable e-mail address.
- Open a bank account – preferably somewhere offshore so that disclosure of ownership and tracing of funds will prove difficult.
- Become a credit card merchant.
- Start the Web site and collect a substantial amount of money from eager consumers.
- Oh I almost forgot... while you don't actually need to have anything that you are supposedly auctioning, if you feel duty bound to send your customers something, fake a few pictures or get a few counterfeit watches.

Cynicism aside, it doesn't take a genius to work out that online auctions are fraught with dangers. How can you possibly know the provenance of any antique or piece of fine art that you are purchasing online? How can you even know that what you are bidding for exists? For example, a recent search I did on one of the most popular auction sites to dig up what autographs they had for sale produced a list of almost 18,000 entries. While I am not suggesting that all of these sellers are less than honest, the possibility of fraud with something like an autograph is immense. Some of the frauds that come out of online auctions are simply comical, but others involve innocent people losing their life savings, or even worse. One story that has elements of both farce and tragedy involves a Rolex watch. Disabled Tom Shead, from Peterlee in County Durham, England, paid £4,700 for a lady's Rolex that he had found on an auction site. The watch would have cost £25,000 new: thus Tom thought that it was worth paying over his life savings to buy the gold diamond watch as a birthday present for his wife. The money was wired to the seller – a US student, who promptly sent Tom a photograph of the watch. This was followed up with an e-mail in which the seller confirmed that Tom had bid for a photograph of the watch, not the Rolex itself. An FBI investigation followed which resulted in a 21-year-old student from Seattle, Jeffrey Chastain, being identified as the seller. The FBI were just about to arrest him when Chastain jumped off the Aurora Bridge and killed himself.

Online auctions offer a diversity of fraud opportunities:

- Merchandise misrepresentation – it isn't what is claimed.
- Failure to supply merchandise bought – presumably because it doesn't exist.
- The fencing of stolen goods.
- Advertising counterfeit goods.
- Shell auctions – not only does the merchandise not exist, but the point of the transaction, as well as to rip the buyer off, is to get his or her credit card details for further fraudulent use.
- False bidding – aka Shilling – getting a friend to bid against a genuine buyer, thus increasing the price of the item (or if you don't trust your friends, doing it yourself).

In the realm of Internet auctions, the maxim *caveat emptor* (buyer beware) applies more than ever. Although the following guidelines may sound like simple common sense, it is fairly obvious that they are not being followed by eager buyers:

- Establish how the particular auction site that you are using works and understand the terminology used on the site.
- Research what you are bidding for: find out what it's worth; whether there is a warranty; keep records of what is promised by the seller.
- Check out the seller: many auction sites have feedback pages where buyers can offer opinions on the site's regular sellers. Obviously don't buy anything from a seller with a poor track record, but also realize that such comments can be (and have been) manipulated by the fraudsters themselves to give the appearance that they will be canonized for services to humanity.
- Pay attention to the seller's contact information. Check (as far as you can) that the details are correct: look the seller up on the relevant online White Pages, for example. Don't deal with sellers who quote PO Boxes. Be sceptical.
- Use a credit card: it may well offer you financial protection, and simultaneously it offers a genuine seller some guarantees against non-payment.

- Report fraud: you won't get anywhere unless you report it to both the auction site and law enforcement agencies.
- And finally (but probably most importantly): if it sounds or looks too good to be true, that's because it is.

IMAGES OF INNOCENCE

At various times in this book I have quoted the number of pages generated by search engines to demonstrate the popularity of a particular topic on the Internet. Perhaps most unbelievably, a search for 'bestiality' on Google in December 2001 gave 87,200 hits. The Web sites that you got served up were not, it must be added, scientific and medical studies of this topic. The first site (and only one that I could stomach visiting) had a free sample section which included three full size pictures which defy description, but helpfully could be e-mailed as 'a postcard to a friend'. It is now generally accepted that the Polaroid camera, video player and video camera have all been decisive factors in the growth of domestic pornography. The Internet should of course be added to the list: it has been claimed that 22 minutes out of every hour that is spent on the Internet in Britain is used for viewing or downloading pornography. Nobody knows the true financial turnover generated by the digital porn industry; what can be said however is that it was undoubtedly the first profitable industry sector on the Internet and remains an incredibly lucrative one. To start up an Internet porn site requires very little start-up capital: you just enroll with a free 'adult services' Web hosting services, steal images from existing sites and you are up and away. Image theft is predominant in online pornography – everybody is ripping off everybody else and continually searching for new 'content'.

While a liberal person may agree that it is perfectly right that one should be able to see pictures of naked women and men on the Internet in soft core poses, that is far from being the limit of what is freely available to view or download. While you may think it humorous, or sexy, or vindictive to post a picture of yourself, or your partner (or ex-partner) or co-worker in various stages of undress on one of the many sites that cater for such pictures, but this is just the tip of the iceberg. Even sites such as these raise substantial issues regarding national obscenity, privacy and censorship issues which effectively are rendered useless by the global reach of the Internet. However, the most concerning issue of this topic is the way that the Internet has become a magnet for child pornography. The Internet did not create this problem, but what it has done is provide a virtual meeting ground for those unfortunates who are sexually turned on by children; it has also facilitated the spread of such material over a wide geographical area. This is not the place to debate the ramifications of such hideous, offensive and illegal images and discussions – but the threats posed by this insidious problem to both individuals and organizations should not be underestimated. If you are still unconvinced of the scale of these activities, pause awhile and consider the Wonderland Club. The 'club' was an international ring of 180 paedophiles that eventually had over 750,000 images of children (including babies) and 1,800 computerized videos of children suffering sexual abuse seized by police. At the UK trial of seven of those involved, the prosecuting QC told the court that 'All of the children involved were under the age of 16 and in one case the child was only three months. In many cases the children were aged 2 or 3 years and the vast majority were under 10'. There were 1,263 children involved whose images were traded electronically using encryption in a club that saw itself as 'the cream of paedophiles'. The main criteria for membership were that each new member had to have at least 10,000 images of pre-teens and had to agree to share those images with other members. Leaving aside all of the feelings of disgust and despair at this awful episode, if you are responsible (and culpable) for an organization and its staff just consider the ramifications if your facilities had been used for such activities, and somewhere on a staff member's PC is a file full of 10,000 such images.

IDENTITY THEFT

It is very easy to lose oneself on the Internet: but it is now equally possible to lose one's identity. Identity theft has become one of the boom fraud types of the last few years, and substantial media hype has ensued directly equating this with the Internet and Digital Age. The simple fact, however, is that identity theft existed long before the Internet. What the Internet has done is to facilitate both the ease with which other people's information can be obtained and then used. Identity theft is a blissfully simple concept: the fraudster illegally acquires and uses an innocent person's personal details, credit or account information to obtain money, credit goods, services and anything else of value. All such spending or goods ultimately end up being recorded on the innocent victim's credit record (as the criminal is hardly likely to pay for the goods he or she has acquired in this way). A note of caution, though: such a scheme will only work if the victim has a good credit record – one large case of identity theft that I investigated actually involved the theft of the details of various people with very poor genuine credit records.

There have always been numerous ways of acquiring the required personal information to commit identity theft including:

■ Mail theft – credit cards being a good option.
■ Theft of rubbish – you'll be amazed at what people throw away without it being shredded.
■ Insider access – the staff of an organization steal personal details of customers and then use them illegally.
■ Straight theft – steal a purse or wallet and you will usually get all the details you need to commit identity theft.

The Internet provides interesting further opportunities for criminals to collect the information that they need. One such method is through spam – the crook sends an unsolicited e-mail and amazingly the potential victim is attracted by the offer made in the e-mail, and proceeds to send his or her identifying data. Another twist on this is when false job advertisements are placed on the Internet, and the information from submitted CVs is used. The abundance of personal information that is available on the Internet (particularly in relation to US citizens) means that it is fairly easy to obtain key details in this manner. I have lost count of the number of US Web sites that I visit which have a pop-up window offering the facility of obtaining a free copy of my own credit report. It doesn't take much imagination to see how a fraudster could use such offers to his or her advantage, and obtain the credit reports of other individuals. According to the Privacy Rights Clearinghouse there are over 400,000 thefts of identity each year in the United States with annual losses of more than US $2 billion. Identity theft is expanding at a rate of 50 per cent per year through such techniques as what follows (which is a paraphrased extract from a real e-mail that I recently received):

(Name) has several financial accounts, some of which are managed and utilized online. (Name) unfortunately used the same member name and password for all of his accounts including his Internet Service provider and bank accounts. The fraudster had obtained a considerable amount of information on (Name) and proceeded to carry out numerous transaction on (Name)'s online accounts.

Which is akin to what it is alleged that 32-year-old Abraham Abdallah, a restaurant dishwasher, did. In March 2001 *The New York Post* broke the story of this unlikely identity thief – and his even more improbable victims. The story goes that Abdallah used a hi-tech tool kit to steal the identities of 200 celebrities. Well, OK I'm being slightly sarcastic: it is alleged that he used the PC at his local library that had Internet access and a moth-eaten copy of *Forbes* magazine 'Richest People in America' list. Among the celebrities named in press report who had their identities stolen are Oprah Winfrey, Steven Spielberg, George Soros, Ross Perot and Ralph Ellison. The fraud began, it is believed, by Abdallah writing to credit agencies requesting confidential information on individuals using letterhead paper from a brokerage house. The information that was returned appears to have been enough for Abdallah to obtain access to the stars' credit cards and bank accounts. The *Forbes* magazine was helpful as a notepad as well – it was reported that he listed on there the stars' home addresses, mobile phone numbers, social security numbers, account numbers and that old favorite, mother's maiden name. There were some hi-tech elements to this extensive identity theft episode: there was an elaborate network of post office boxes together with a voicemail system that fooled banks and credit card companies. The messages left there were picked up via Abdallah's WAP phone.

The beauty of using the Internet for identity theft is not only that relevant source details can be obtained online, but when the scam artist has sufficient information to assume the identity of an innocent victim the Internet is the ideal place to spend someone else's money.

FOUR

INFORMATION WARFARE

Shrimps may attack dragons in shallow water.

Traditional Chinese saying

Although we have not experienced the electronic equivalent of a Pearl Harbor or Oklahoma City as some have foretold, the statistics and our cases demonstrate our dangerous vulnerabilities to cyber attacks.

Michael Vatis, Head of the FBI National infrastructure Protection Center (March 1998)

When one has been hurt by new technology, when the private person or the corporate body finds its entire identity endangered by physical or psychic change, it lashes back in a fury of self-defence.

Marshall McLuhan War and Peace in the Global Village

ORIGINS AND DEFINITIONS

On Monday September 30 1996 I was in New York and as usual bought *The New York Times*. On the front page of the 'Business Day' section of the newspaper was a lead story (which occupied most of the page) about a new concept – information warfare (IW) – that was headed

'Ready, Aim, Zap: National Security Experts Plan for Wars Whose Targets and Weapons Are All Digital'. I found it a fascinating, thought provoking analysis of where modern warfare was heading: so much so that I have kept the article to this day. Over the years, I have added to this article numerous other press cuttings that essentially repeat and echo the original observations. I have accessed numerous Web sites on the subject: in November 2001 for example a search on Google with the term 'information warfare' produced 'about 62,900' results. I have seen (but not necessarily read) numerous books on the subject. And after all of this, I remain unconvinced. The final proof to me happened in New York just less than five years after the original article. On September 11 2001, like most of the world's population, I watched in horror as the unbelievable events at the World Trade Center (WTC), and then the Pentagon and then near Pittsburgh unfolded. At first it was suspected that one small plane had accidentally collided with one of the twin towers; then the desolate truth slowly became clear – two passenger aircrafts had been hijacked and deliberately crashed into the WTC. These awful events depended not on digital terrorism but kinetic energy caused by the most basic of tools: converting four aircraft into flying bombs which detonated with appalling human consequences. None of the scare stories that had previously been run about the electron being the ultimate precision guided missile could match this atrocity.

In many ways as well, the September 11 2001 attacks showed both numerous flaws in the digital infrastructure and how it could end up being used in many previously unthought of ways. IW as a unified military strategy has a long way to go before it can match the carnage and destruction achieved by the imaginative (an unfortunate but still correct term) use of far more traditional and basic materials and tools. These terrorist attacks were also not an exception: much of modern warfare at a ground floor level is conducted in a distinctly low-tech manner. Small arms technology has not really progressed much since the Second World War (or even the First World War, for that matter). Weapons may have got smaller, but their firing rate is very little different to weapons of a hundred years ago. The Kalshnikov AK47 rifle is used (officially) by more than 50 armies around the world, and hundreds if not thousands of terrorist, militia and organized crime groups. Yet it was developed in 1974. Just imagine still using a computer that was built in the same year. Grenades are, in many cases, homemade and primitive: the kind of thing that you can build in your garden shed; and if you don't believe me just try searching on the

Internet – within about five minutes you can probably knock up a launcher and something to propel from it. Road mines, for all their awful power, are basically chunks of explosive, which can also be home made. Car bombs are more of the same – if they are so technologically advanced (which they aren't) how come so many bombers manage to accidentally blow themselves up when planting them? Bombs in aircraft may have catastrophic results, but are no more than small charges of Semtex that have a timing delay. The 'bomb' that caused the Lockerbie disaster had probably been hidden in a radio cassette player.

All of that being said, numerous commentators saw the events of September 11 2001 in a diametrically opposite way: that what happened should convince everyone that the threats of IW were even more real than before. The arguments put forward went something like this: that the next deadly attack by terrorists would involve some kind of cyber terrorism. To support this doomsday scenario various examples were quoted, including:

- The vandalizing of various Indian government Web sites by a group of hackers calling itself the al Qaeda Alliance and posting messages of support for Osama Bin Laden.
- Historical attacks such as those perpetrated by Palestinian hackers during 2000 when they got into the Web sites of the Israeli Parliament, Foreign Ministry and military. These attacks also succeeded in getting into the sites of the Bank of Israel and the country's stock exchange.
- The arrest of a hacker in Texas in 2000 who had intended to plant a worm with the aim of shutting down the 911 telephone service of a wide area by flooding it with calls from infected computers. The estimate was that the worm could have infected 250,000 computers in about three days.

The crystallization of this school of thought was provided by Richard Clarke, the Chairman of the US President's Critical Infrastructure Protection Board, who in early November 2001 spelt it out by commenting that 'Freedom isn't free, and security isn't free either. . . cyber attacks can cause catastrophic damage to the economy. . . being the functional equivalent of 767s crashing into buildings'. My problem with all of this is not that I don't believe it could happen (because I do) rather that the WTC attack was, in many ways, one heavy with symbolism. Even a prolonged IW attack (which may cause significant economic damage) would not possess such a philosophical punch – neither would it kill so many people. Moreover it also became clear that IW could be achieved rather like the terrorist attacks on September 11 2001: in a very low tech fashion. Want to cut power lines? Don't bother hacking the power provider's system – just blow up a few power pylons on the main grid (much more visual). Want to stop the flow of oil or gas? Sabotage the actual pipelines. Want to cause chaos in telephone networks? Cut a few wires or blow up an exchange – don't bother with high tech hacking. Moreover, is not the theory of IW rather one sided? Let us imagine that a terrorist group staged a series of unified attacks on the critical infrastructures of the United States and the UK. These unnamed terrorists succeeded in taking down the power grids of both nations; disrupting emergency response systems; making sophisticated weapons implode *in situ*; together with ensuring that the financial infrastructures ground to a complete halt. Would the US response to such actions be to launch some type of cyber attack as a response? I think not: the natural reply would be in an old-fashioned military way.

Equally, one of the most fundamental difficulties concerning IW is that no one can agree on what exactly it is. Emmet Paige, the Assistant Secretary of US Defense for Command and Control, Communications and Computers, commented in 1995 that IW comprised 'actions taken to achieve information superiority in support of national military strategy by affecting adversary information and information systems while leveraging and defending our information and systems'. While the US Air Force defines the concept as 'any action to deny, exploit, corrupt or destroy the enemy's information and its functions; protecting ourselves against those actions; exploiting our own military information functions'. Both of these functions appear to promote the view that IW is merely an extension of military intelligence in that, in very basic terms, it is a traditional war fought with more extensive and focused military intelligence. However, my understanding of the origins of the IW concept is that it was being promoted as an alternative to traditional war – in future all our battles would be fought in cyber-space using technical weapons and attacks. Certainly the definitions of this concept emanating from the world of technology (as opposed to the military) usually stress the notions of attacks on vital computer systems that control security, transportation, communication and suchlike. Yet such attacks could easily be achieved by traditional methods – warfare through information if you will. Such military orientated definitions could, in effect, apply to any war at any time:

as the vast majority of victories will always have been achieved through the application of intelligence in both the military sense and the broader one (think of the original Trojan horse). This narrow traditional definition has also led to various logical arguments being advanced that recent wars (particularly the Gulf War) have been very good examples of this concept.

Sun Tzu's quotation that 'attaining one hundred victories [in] battle is not the pinnacle of excellence. Subjugating the enemy's army without fighting is the true pinnacle of excellence' is an excellent summary of what IW in its truest sense seeks to achieve. The Joint Chief of Staff Instruction No 3210.01 (issued in 1996) seems to take the concept out of a pure military basis by defining IW as 'actions taken to achieve information superiority by affecting an adversary's information, information based processes, information systems, and computer based networks while defending one's own information, information based processes, information systems, and computer based networks'. The French Ministry of Defence have amplified this type of definition by outlining three types of IW:

- Guerre pour l'information (war for information) which is the obtaining of information about the enemy's means, capabilities and strategies in order to defend oneself.
- Guerre contre l'information (war against information) which involves the protection of one's own information systems together with disrupting or destroying similar systems of the enemy.
- Guerre par l'information (war through information). This process is based around actioning operations using misinformation against your enemy to deceive them as to your intentions and operations.

Yet even these definitions are limited, as what has become clear is that IW does not apply solely to nation versus nation battles, but also those that involve terrorists, organized criminals, individuals and commercial organizations. In a connected world, organizations at the cutting edge (particularly where research is involved) would view their enemies as being any of their rivals. The importance of the interconnectivity of all of these users and issues was underscored by the Executive Order of President Bush issued on October 16 2001 on 'Critical Infrastructure Protection' which began with the following paragraph:

> The information technology revolution has changed the way business is transacted, government operates and national defense is conducted. Those three functions now depend on an interdependent

network of critical information infrastructures. The protection program authorized by this order shall consist of continuous efforts to secure information systems for critical infrastructure, including emergency preparedness communications, and the physical assets that support such systems. Protection of these systems is essential to the telecommunications, energy, financial services, manufacturing, water, transportation, health care, and emergency service sectors.

At some stage, presumably in an effort to simplify matters, another phrase seeped into the language: information operations (IO). In essence this is the use of IW techniques at any time and in any environment. This definition in turn focuses on critical infrastructure systems and networks. Whatever phrase is used, the concept of IW/IO hinges on high tech attacks on critical targets such as:

- Electric utilities. Power grids and associated facilities could be brought down by logic bombs or worms. This would cause local, regional or even national power blackouts. Another alternative would be to cause voltage oscillations.
- Water supplies. In most Western countries the process of collecting and distributing water is highly technology reliant. Attacks could disrupt or cut off water supplies. At the other end of the cycle, cyber attacks could (and have already) disturb, divert or destroy sewage systems, thus facilitating the spread of disease.
- Trains. Logic bombs or hacking of traffic control systems could cause crashes and consequent loss of life together with paralyzing logistics and transport networks.
- Air Traffic. Both planes and air traffic control can be attacked. On board systems could be made to malfunction; air traffic control systems could be brought down or made to continue operating but give false information to operators.
- Telecommunications. These systems can be easily attacked causing malfunctions or shutdowns. Additionally it is vital to remember that we are not just talking of civil networks, but military ones as well.
- Civil administration. Civil records and law enforcement systems are prime targets for attack which could result in chaos and disruption.
- Hospitals and associated emergency services. Like most aspects of life in the Digital Age many medical and administrative support functions are heavily IT dependent.

- Financial institutions. Sniffer programs can monitor and track the transfer of funds together with other confidential information; hackers can crack systems to steal money or cause endless chaos by transferring funds and assets to incorrect locations and recipients. Logic bombs and denial of service attacks can cause pandemonium either within one institution or on the market as a whole – and ultimately in the global marketplace.
- Weapons. Ironically one of the most potent effects of an IW/IO attack would be to hack into the sophisticated control systems of high tech weaponry such as missiles, surveillance aircraft and satellites – in fact any piece of hardware that could be used for offensive purposes.

Rather contradicting my own argument is the fact that in isolation many – if not all – of these types of attacks have at the very least been attempted, if not successfully executed. The perpetrators of IO would typically be a foreign government, terrorist group or extremist cell. Additionally – and a very real threat – is the use of IO solely in the business world. But when does a hack attack or denial of service threat become an IW/IO event? So as to differentiate between IO attacks/ events and more 'typical' digital crimes the Canadian Security Intelligence Service, as an example, defines three conditions for an incident to be considered as an IO attack. These are:

- It must be a computer based attack.
- It must, within reason, appear to be orchestrated by a foreign government, terrorist group or politically motivated extremists.
- It must be done for a purpose of espionage, sabotage, foreign influence or politically motivated violence.

Again, though, these defining factors do have limitations: is a hack attack on a commercial organization by unknown perpetrators to steal confidential material on the latest missile guidance system a IW/IO attack or not?

The attractions of IO are virtually a repeat of all of the factors that make digital crime so appealing in all of its guises:

- It is easy to achieve (relatively speaking): to successfully carry out many of the attacks detailed above would only require some basic IT knowledge and the patience to find comprehensive instructions on how to do it on the Internet. The low entry cost for such activities is a major facilitator.

- The globally wired Digital Age makes it easy to carry out an international attack with little chance of quick detection. Thus it can be viewed as a secure, risk free and anonymous pastime. For terrorists who do not necessarily seek recognition for their actions (or wish to taken responsibility for them) this may be particularly appealing. Moreover the blurring of responsibility for attacks severely complicates any response to them, and further back in the process makes the collection of relevant intelligence on the 'enemy' very difficult. This factor is probably the most dangerous feature of IW/IO – you do not have to be physically close to the object of attack.
- As the United States is the most wired country (and thus the most at risk for this reason, not even taking into account ideological ones) the two factors above have an interesting cascade effect. No sane government (or even an insane one) would seriously consider taking on the United States in a traditional war because of the sheer size and might of US military power. But IW exists in an almost level political and economic playing field. Just as importantly many of the critical infrastructures at risk in the United States (and other developed countries) are not under public control, and thus even if the relevant government was hell-bent on robust industrial standards of security it would have difficulty to implement, control and monitor them in the private sector. Moreover the geographical isolation that has provided psychological security to the United States is immediately removed in cyberspace. Pearl Harbor and the events of September 11 2001 may have dented (to varying degrees) this concept: a determined IW attack would demolish it altogether.

Equally, the reasons these threats exist are a repetition of the usual suspects:

- Government and business leaders/policy makers don't understand the technology – never mind the threats inherent in it.
- Investments in digital security, whether it be by governments or organizations, are not seen as a priority – and in some cases are viewed as a waste of money.
- In many countries there is no central agency that controls, regulates and investigates these issues and events. One knock-on effect is that these issues are not raised at the highest national levels. And of course, forget any hope whatsoever of having some kind of international body with teeth.

■ Issues relating to IO are typically treated as operational ones (and then mostly after the event) rather than strategic ones.

Perhaps the most frightening aspect of this topic is that it is now accepted that even governments in advanced and highly digitally literate countries have severe difficulties in dealing with the threats posed. In June 2001 Lawrence K Gershwin, the CIA's top adviser on top technology, told the US Congress Joint Economic Committee that he didn't feel very good about computer attacks on US systems as 'we end up detecting it after it's happened'. While at the time of the Love Bug attack in 2000 Jim Comeau, the Head of the economic and information security unit at the Canadian Security Intelligence Service in Ottawa, observed that 'What if somebody, for political reasons, decides to put out viruses that are targeted at specific types of information? The types of attacks we see are only limited by the imagination. What if a dedicated group of extremists bent on pursuing their cause targeted some very large companies that are dependent on the Internet?'

The media hype surrounding the IW/IO debate has reached far and wide with the Chinese official *People's Liberation Daily* observing that 'An adversary wishing to destroy the United States only has to mess up with the computer systems of its banks by high-tech means'. Propaganda or fact? In truth no one knows. These topics are shrouded in mystery (and probable exaggeration) because very few verifiable statistics are available, either from the public or private sector. The overriding concerns of customer confidence, market reputation and shareholder value ensure that most private corporations will never admit to being the victim of a successful attack. The FBI estimates that electronic intrusions cause losses of over US $10 billion in the United States alone each year (but this estimate is just that, as the FBI has no real way of establishing a true figure if no one is reporting such crimes to it). Other information from the private sector tends to be from consulting firms selling their services or software suppliers hawking their wares. Added to this are the ever recurring problems of hoaxes particularly regarding viruses. However, the opposing view is that the media coverage given to fairly inconsequential events (the prime ones being Web site defacement and denial of service attacks) make us become distracted from the more serious underlying risks. Perversely, while we are disturbed by low level attacks, the very existence of such events makes us more secure as we believe that this is the worst that can happen. Whether such events are the pinnacle of what the enemy can achieve, or merely the first step in a campaign, is very difficult to judge; nevertheless such instances do happen, with what appears to be amazing regularity.

The attacks against the Pentagon number thousands each year, and a percentage of these attacks are thought to achieve breakdown of some type of service. The Pentagon itself continues to insist that no classified networks have been breached, but admits that some attacks have been aimed at sensitive information (which would appear to be the entire point of such occurrences). Much of the US media coverage of this topic has zeroed in on the possibility (or probability, depending on your viewpoint) that such attacks emanate from the Russian Federation. To achieve some kind of equality in this respect, the Kremlin has made various statements that foreign intelligence agencies were regularly penetrating its own computer networks. In February 1998 (at the time of possible military operations against Iraq) Pentagon systems were attacked in what was known as 'Solar Sunrise' which was described by the US Department of Defense as 'the most organized and systematic threat to date'. US Senator John Kyl, Chairman of the Senate Judiciary Subcommittee on Terrorism, later commented that 'For four days, our government did not know who was attacking key defense computers essential to deploying forces to the Persian Gulf. Fortunately, this time, the hackers were teenagers, not Iraqi forces. But what about next time?' This thought was echoed in another context by a Defense Department official at a press conference in June 2001 when he highlighted:

> 'the risk that we run by taking twenty years to develop programs to meet threats that evolve every two or three years, particularly in the area of information warfare. The point has been made that the first hacking tools were posted on the Internet, I think, in 1999. And then there were three generations of new tools posted in the subsequent two years, and we go through one major budget cycle in two years. We're not inside the turning radius of a lot of the threats that we face out there'.

Solar Sunrise was the work of two 16-year-old high school students in California and a teenager in Israel. But the critical issue is that when the attacks were in full flow the US administration did not know this. Because of this uncertainty of who was responsible, the Deputy Defense Secretary notified President Clinton that the intrusions could be the opening of a genuine cyber war, most probably by Iraq as it anticipated renewed US air strikes.

At around the same time various other claims (or predictions) were made by US officials testifying to the Joint Economic Committee of Congress. Lawrence Gershwin, the national intelligence officer for science and technology, made various observations including the fact that Russia, China and some other nations were developing active IW programs aimed at the United States, confirming that 'we watch them very intensely'. Gershwin also observed that such nation programs were unique in posing a threat along the entire spectrum of objectives that might harm US interests – primarily long duration damage to US critical infrastructures. Interestingly, Gershwin also predicted that computer viruses were likely to become more controllable, precise and predictable 'making them more suitable for weaponisation'. The truth of these statements had been manifested two years earlier in 1997 (prior to Solar Sunrise!) when an exercise was run by the Pentagon's Joint Staff. To their horror, teams from the National Security Agency proceeded to demonstrate the blindingly obvious. Using standard off-the-shelf PCs (available from any good computer retailer) and hacker programs that are widely available – predominantly now from the Internet – they demonstrated their ability to disrupt operations at major military commands and disturb electrical power services and emergency telephone facilities in several US cities. What was that about the low entry cost of such activities?

Various denial of service attacks and Web defacement episodes appear to be politically motivated. In October 1998 China unveiled a new Web site that publicized the country's efforts in the field of human rights. Within a few days, hackers had replaced the home page with a message that condemned China's administration for its appalling human rights records. In May 2001 the boot transferred to the other foot when the White House Web site appeared to have been taken for just over two hours by Chinese hackers. The hackers had already defaced many hundreds of Web sites in that time period: their declared intention was to mount a digital offensive against US Web sites to tie in with Labor Day in China on May 1 and as a reminder of the US bombing of the Chinese embassy in Belgrade on May 7 1999. Leaving aside the fact that the US administration commented that the hackers had unsuccessfully tried to deface the Whitehouse Web site for over a week, they also targeted other government sites including the CIA, the Pentagon, the US Navy and the National Security Agency. Commercial sites on their hit list included CNN, *The Army Times* and *The New York Times*.

A slightly more perplexing episode was reported by the New Zealand news service NZOOM in August 2001. The essential elements of this story was that Philip Whitmore, a security consultant with PriceWaterhouseCoopers, claimed that a major hacking incident that he had dealt with originated from a Japanese government agency. The unsuccessful attack was on a private sector medical research institute where a server contained sensitive information. Whitmore confirmed that he was on site at the institute when the attacks were taking place, but questions were still raised about the ability to categorically confirm the exact origin of such attacks, which were presumed to be a Japanese research institute similar to the one in New Zealand that was under attack. Two suggestions made involved the use by the attackers of 'spoofing' or a 'zombie' agent. Spoofing masks the actual IP address of the computer being used by the attacker, substituting another one. Through this method it would be possible to implicate another user or user organization. A zombie agent is a piece of software that takes control of another computer – predominantly to use the second computer to attack another one. Zombie agents are usually delivered by computer viruses, such as version three of the Code Red virus. The report – whether totally accurate or not – stirred up a hornet's nest of scare stories. Various experts concluded that numerous research breakthroughs by companies in the country had made them a prime target for digital attacks, particularly as the country as a whole was lax in its attitude to, and implementation of, network security. And the Japanese? An embassy spokesman rather predictably denied any involvement of the Japanese Government.

As if to illustrate the level playing field established by the Internet, where military strength is no longer the deciding factor between two warring nations, one only has to look towards East Timor. On December 7 1975 East Timor, an island a few hundred miles north of Australia, was brutally invaded by Indonesia, which claimed that its invasion of East Timor, a Portuguese colony until a year before, was necessary to restore peace and security. These altruistic actions proceeded to cost the lives of over 200,000 people in East Timor, according to Amnesty International, in the years since 1975. In late 1997 Connect-Ireland, a Dublin based Internet Service provider, registered .tp as a top level Internet domain for East Timor in a gesture of support. In many ways this simple registration gave East Timor autonomy and independence in cyberspace which it was sadly lacking in reality. This 'virtual nation' became the subject of a massive concerted attack in 1999 when its server was hacked from almost 20 different locations including Australia, Japan, the United States, Canada and the Netherlands. Connect-Ireland suspended its services

– which predominantly comprised 3,000 users in Ireland – and lodged a formal protest with the Indonesian embassy, which of course described such accusations as baseless. A spokesman for the company said at the time that 'We are not calling these people hackers or cyber terrorists, but E-Nazis, because anybody who behaves in such a way is jackbooting on people's right to free communications. Whether they are an individual, a company or a government doesn't matter' and then observed that it was highly unlikely that such a concentrated and planned campaign was the work of a spotty teenager. Connect-Ireland rebuilt its systems – and the East Timor project still lives at www.freedom.tp

OLD WINE IN NEW BOTTLES

But do such attacks necessarily justify the apparent threat known as IW or IO? NATO has referred to some observers believing that this concept is 'old wine in new bottles' – though it must be said that this reference was used without NATO necessarily agreeing with it. Some of the justifications for such an evaluation include official governmental reports outlining the threats of IW/IO making references to hoax viruses, without realizing that they are hoaxes; the fact that the Pentagon, for example, is under constant 'attack' may be a vast exaggeration of the problem. Computer scientist Kevin Ziese has described such events as the virtual equivalent of 'a kid walking into the Pentagon cafeteria'. Then we have the ongoing dilemma of who is responsible for any (and every attack): enemy government, hacker or bored teenager? In truth, as these examples show, we can never be sure. However, this uncertainty should at least convince countries, organizations and individuals of one basic fact: irrespective of who may be engineering such attacks, security of information systems is vital. In the end it is almost immaterial who is attacking you, rather the critical problem remains that you are being attacked. There is no way of getting around this fact, although there have been some brave attempts, the most prominent one being that the real risk to your data and information is not from hackers but your own staff, so forget about the former and solely concentrate on the latter. This concept (for want of a better term) has led to various faintly ridiculous claims being made, such as hackers/digital intruders get far more media attention than their activities warrant because companies do not disclose attacks by insiders. The reality is that both insiders and outsiders are a real threat to any organization, thus security and preventative actions need to be focused in both directions simultaneously.

In the commercial world the concept of information operations may, in many ways, be the repackaging of industrial espionage, or at the very least commercial information operations may encompass both industrial espionage and industrial terrorism for financial gain. Industrial espionage, commercial spying, corporate espionage – call it what you will – has been with us since humans started competing against others in business. Some commentators argue that in the main hacking is fairly harmless, but corporate espionage in the Digital Age is the real problem. But once again it is very hard to obtain reliable figures and analysis on the scale of this problem. The primary reason for this (as always) is that much of such activity goes unreported. The United Kingdom National High Tech Crime Unit which was formed in 2001 admitted this when it concluded that many businesses are often reluctant to report digital crime. So in the absence of hard fact, all that is left is surveys. In 1999 the American Society for Industrial Security conducted a survey which showed that Fortune 1000 companies sustained losses of more than US $45 billion from thefts of confidential information. Another survey by the Computer Security Institute showed that of the 600 companies surveyed, over half felt that their competitors were a likely source of cyber attack. By 2001 186 poll respondents to the same organization estimated losses from security violations at US $377.8 million (and that total is just for the first six months of the year). And such figures do not take into account the possibility of government sponsored agencies conducting industrial espionage on behalf of commercial activities. In March 2000 the US Government had to formally deny (to the European Parliament) that its much touted Echelon surveillance system had been used to illegally obtain commercial secrets. While industrial espionage has traditionally been associated with competitors unlawfully obtaining information, an equal danger is that information will be obtained by outsiders and then used to blackmail the victim organization. There are some real horror stories already that should sufficiently concern any organization (of any type) that is concerned about its reputation, customer confidentiality, financial well-being and, ultimately perhaps, very existence. The roll call of horror includes:

- Hackers broke into egghead.com and apparently stole 3.7 million credit card numbers, together with the address and shipping address of each company. Or at least that is what was reported in December 2000, with minor variations as to the numbers: you were able to choose between 3.7 million, 3.5 million or 2.5 million. The company alerted both customers and credit card issuers – and then subsequently confirmed in early January that after lengthy investigations it had confirmed that no credit card information had been stolen. While not questioning this statement the damage had already been done: media reports faithfully reported the security breach; an anti-egghead site eggheadsucks. com was launched and presumably customer confidence hit rock bottom, with a resultant effect on sales. Not to mention the thousands of dollars that it cost credit card companies to reissue cards and pay their staff overtime to do so. I am not drawing a straight line between these events and subsequent ones, but it is still interesting to observe how the company described its status on its Web site in November 2001:

> *Dear Egghead Customers,*
>
> *As many of you know, since August 15 2001 Egghead has been operating as a debtor-in-possession under Chapter 11 bankruptcy protection. Our plan had been to sell the assets of the business as a going concern and continue providing Egghead customers with great value and selection. Unfortunately, we have reached a point where we are unable to continue operations. As a result, as of 5:00 pm PST on October 25 2001 we have ceased active operations and suspended all commercial activity until further notice.*

■ At the same time as the original Egghead debacle the FBI revealed that it was investigating a case involving the theft of a credit card database from the Web site of Los Angeles based merchant processing firm Creditcards.com. In fact 55,000 credit card numbers had been stolen – and their details then posted online. The company reported that hackers had contacted the company three months previously and had threatened to post the numbers on the Internet if a 'fee' wasn't forthcoming. The fee was not paid and the threat was fulfilled.

■ In 1999 the online music retailer CD Universe was the victim of a hacker who stole around 300,000 credit card numbers and posted them online when the fee he requested was not paid.

■ In November 2000 Charles Schwab Corp said that a flaw in its system gave the potential for a hacker to steal individual customers' stock trading accounts; E*trade, another online brokerage firm, had discovered a similar weakness a couple of months earlier.

None of these attacks events would traditionally fall under the heading of industrial espionage – but they vividly demonstrate what is possible, and if individual hackers can do it, just think what your competitors can achieve if they put their mind to it. Even such episodes as these can have catastrophic knock on effects for the victim company:

- Decreased customer confidence.
- The possibility of legal action, particularly if confidential information is damaging to a third party.
- The real costs of putting the security loophole right.
- In the United States (and increasingly elsewhere) there is also the issue of downstream liability: what if your systems are penetrated and they lead the attacker into the systems of partners of suppliers? You as the originating party can be held liable.

Perversely though, all these events are played out, to some extent, in the public domain: if you receive an extortion threat, you know that you (or your company) have been attacked. A competitor (in the broadest sense) will very rarely let you know that it has stolen your client database, research data, business data – or anything else that is on one of your systems somewhere which could be of commercial value. In a cut throat market some organizations will go to any length to gain a competitive advantage. Just consider what a determined attacker could obtain from you:

- Customer lists.
- Supplier and partner lists – and how much you are paying for what.
- Trade secrets: formulae, details of manufacturing processes, product patent details.
- Expansion plans (or closure and 'downsizing' plans which are just as important).
- Marketing plans on a company wide basis or for a specific product.
- Details of advertising campaigns.
- Budgetary and financial details of any and all types.

■ Corporate personnel records – which will invariably contain personal details of each employee, salary details, medical history, disciplinary issues, addresses.

Just before we enter the world of corporate nightmares when all the above information is stolen 'lock stock and barrel' by a competitor it is also worthwhile remarking that there are some very simple ways for a competitor to obtain your digital information. Every executive worth his or her position must have a personal digital organizer and laptop and the latest all singing and ringing mobile phone will be *de rigueur*. Just consider the data that any of these devices would yield to a competitor – which is why they are stolen to order. In the United States over 1,000 computers are stolen each and every day; an amazing 1 out of 14 laptops is stolen every year. Obviously, much of this is simple theft of equipment – but in July 2001 the FBI reported that 184 of their laptops had been stolen or reported missing. One of these machines contained classified information from two closed investigations. In 2000 CNN reported that the US State Department had 15 missing computers. It is open to conjecture whether such laptops are stolen for the machines themselves or the information they contain. Nevertheless, even if one does not subscribe to the paranoia theory of life, even if a minute percentage of such thefts were carried out to obtain the data on the laptop then this is still a serious concern. There are also various other basic pieces of hardware that can yield commercial information; never mind laptops, if a serious intruder wants to get your data by physical means then he or she can steal your desktop PC. As various well publicized events have demonstrated, some companies do not effectively clear their hard disks when PCs are disposed of. Records of numbers dialled by mobiles are recorded (and thoughtfully provided on your bill); additionally your mobile probably records in its memory the last 10 or 20 numbers dialled – and numbers that have called you. It is not impossible for these details to be obtained by third parties. There are 'traditional' means of doing this, and obviously another route to this data is to hack into the systems of the mobile phone provider. One example of how traditional methods can be just as effective as high tech ones (and equally strange) concerns the mysterious disappearance and subsequent reappearance of two computer hard drives containing extensive details of US and foreign nuclear warheads. The US Energy Department had 'lost' the hard drives on May 7 2000 when a severe forest fire was fast approaching the secret facility at Los Alamos, New Mexico. But it took three weeks for this loss to be reported, and when it was 50 FBI agents descended on the facility. The hard drives eventually turned up behind a photocopier (where else?) in the secure vault of the laboratory. The only problem was that this area had apparently previously been searched – which led to the informed guess that they had been stolen and returned. This explanation, if correct, was even more embarrassing as if they had been returned by a would-be thief, it had been done when the area was under extensive surveillance.

As referred to in the Preface to this book software is now widely available to monitor keystrokes on keyboards, so that every single action that you take on your PC can be recorded. One commercially available package is sold by proclaiming that it can 'monitor, protect and see everything that your children, spouse, employees, anyone. . . is doing on the computer and Internet'. The sales literature then goes on to describe what the software does:

> Runs secretly – cannot be detected!
> Reports can be viewed from a remote computer anywhere in the world
> The software records keystrokes, Web sites visited and window title and captions
> Works on multiple computers
> Works with any Web browser
> Records details of window titles.

And if this was not enough, the deeply ironical fact about such software packages is that they offer complete security for the user (read intruder). Typically the data captured is encrypted before transfer to the intruder and remains encrypted while stored; and naturally this data can only be accessed by password. Wait, there's more. . . these packages also grab everything that the unaware user types into any instant messenger/chat service. For example:

- AOL Instant Messenger: user name, password, conversations and chat room entries are recorded.
- Yahoo! Instant Messenger: screen name, password and instant messages are all recorded.
- MSN Messenger: user name, password and instant messages are recorded.

What is clear is that such software is already in use by various governments and their intelligence agencies – starting with the FBI. Nicodemo

Scarfo Jr, a New Jersey bookie and son of a jailed mob boss, was on trial in 2001 for alleged loan sharking and running an illegal gambling operation. The FBI suspected that he was committing criminal offences and seized his computer records, which proved to be somewhat pointless, as they had been encrypted. The FBI, obviously, could glean nothing from the encrypted files without a password. The FBI then obtained the permission of a judge to enter Scarfo's office and while there installed keystroke monitoring software on his computer. The software quickly discovered his password – together with every other keystroke on Mr Scarfo's computer. Somewhat understandably this case, at the time of writing, had taken on another life regarding the issues of personal privacy, civil liberties and whether what the FBI did was legal. We will return to all these important general issues in Chapter 5.

A WAR FOUGHT BY TERRORISTS

If modern warfare of the 21st century will be defined by battles with terrorists, then an immediate analogy becomes visible in the sphere of commercial IW/IO. For the last five or so years, media articles have appeared sporadically claiming that banks (in particular) have paid ransom demands to 'cyber terrorists' and/or are under constant attack from such intruders. The article that started this debate appeared in *The Sunday Times* on June 2 1996. It is probable that this report, in turn, was inspired by the activities of a Russian graduate in St Petersburg. The sentencing of Vladimir Levin on February 24 1998 brought to a conclusion the most high profile case of cyber crime to date. The saga – which almost resembles a Hollywood blockbuster – began in July 1994 when customers complained of US $400,000 mysteriously 'disappearing' from two Citibank accounts. It ended with Levin being tried in the Southern District of New York and pleading guilty to stealing US $3.7 million from Citibank (the actual amount was far higher – the original charge specified over US $10 million but Levin made a plea bargain). Levin, a graduate of the St Petersburg Tekhnologichesky University, who worked for AO Saturn, a trading company based in St. Petersburg, was jailed for three years and ordered to pay back US $240,015.

Reports at the time and documents filed in court accused Levin of stealing US $400,000 and illegally transferring US $11.6 million more between June and August 1994 by accessing the Citibank system and breaking user identification codes and customers' passwords. The stolen funds were transferred to accounts in Finland, the United States, Germany and the Netherlands. Levin was arrested in March 1995 at Heathrow Airport as he stepped off an incoming flight from Moscow. Six months later he was extradited to New York – the extradition and the actual charges underscore the legal problems encountered with the multijurisdictional nature of cyber crime. In the UK at the extradition hearing Levin's lawyer claimed that no computers in the US were used to access Citicorp's accounts and thus extradition was unwarranted. When that ploy failed Levin's US attorney argued that none of the transactions technically passed through New York (where Levin was being tried) as Citibank's computer is over the river in New Jersey.

Levin was found guilty of routing wire transfers through Citibank's Cash Manager computer system, which enables Citibank's customers to transfer their own funds in and out. Electronic transfers of money are simultaneously one of the most secure areas of bank operations (because so much money is at risk) and thus one of the prime targets for hackers. Correct and current telephone numbers to access such systems are regularly posted on hacker electronic bulletin boards.

This case was not only a serious embarrassment for the perceived integrity of global banking systems but more pertinently for Citicorp itself. It is the largest bank in the US with a presence in more than 90 countries, which electronically transfers about US $500 billion daily and has a marketing strategy stressing it technological competence which facilitates its global 24-hour service 'The City never sleeps'. Citicorp said it was the first time its payment system had been successfully compromised – but the organization deserves praise for the way in which it both reported the problem to the authorities and took the resultant adverse publicity on the chin. Turning potentially damaging publicity to its advantage Citicorp said the only reason US $12 million was transferred from the New York accounts was because the bank cooperated with US authorities investigating the scheme. After the first $400,000 was stolen, the bank said, other illegal transactions were allowed to occur so an electronic trail could be laid that would identify all of the conspirators.

Yet there was a critical gap in security procedures at Citicorp that also helped allow the crimes to be committed. Before a corporate transaction is finally approved, most banks require users to swipe a smart card through a terminal. The card is encoded with an electronic signature unique to the user and if the signature isn't present the transaction is voided (bearing in mind the ATM story earlier this system is probably not as secure as promoted). Citicorp didn't make these cards available to clients before Mr Levin penetrated the bank's network, although it said it has done so since the crime was discovered. Citicorp said that no current or former employees of the bank were involved in the scheme, but some bankers speculated that someone with inside knowledge of Citicorp's security procedures helped perpetrate the crime.

Levin did not ask for a ransom – he simply stole the money. The development of this topic lead to claims that banks, insurance companies, investment houses and brokerage houses on both sides of the Atlantic have paid off criminals who threatened to attack their systems. *The Sunday Times* report claimed that up to £400 million had already been paid to such 'terrorists' who in return promised that they would not destroy the systems of the victim organizations. Specific cases that have been quoted in various sources are:

January 6 1993: A computer crash stopped trading at a UK brokerage house. A £10 million ransom was subsequently paid by the victim organization into a bank account in Zurich.

January 14 1993: A UK bank paid a ransom of £12.5 million.

January 29 1993: £10 million was paid by another UK brokerage house after threats of doom and destruction were made against it.

March 17 1995: A British defence firm paid a ransom of £10 million.

It has been claimed that way back in 1996 there were already 40 such known cases. What took such threats beyond simple hacking was the apparent threat by the terrorists to use weaponry such as electromagnetic pulses (EMP) and HERF (high energy radio frequency) guns. EMP is a wave similar to radio waves which has a similar effect to the electrical signal from lightning – apart from the small fact that it is a hundred times faster. While EMP is not known to damage humans, it can induce large voltages and currents in power lines, communication cables, antennas and wiring. It can also heat up to melting point semiconductors (so bang go your computers). US $500 can build you a HERF gun which essentially consists of nothing more than radio transmitters that shoot out a concentrated radio signal. The damage caused by these weapons can range from temporarily closing the system down to frying it.

Without resorting to frying the system but in a continuation of the trend that *The Sunday Times* reported on all those years ago, in August

2001 Webcertificates.com admitted that an intruder had successfully stolen some personal data of its customers. The data included names, addresses and e-mail addresses, but not credit card details. The intruder turned extortionist when he demanded US $45,000 from the company – who refused to pay and instead publicized what had happened, telling customers that their Web Certificate numbers would be reissued and predicting that the attacker would start contacting them, which is exactly what happened. 'zilterio' e-mailed a number of the company's customers stated that 'I hate to inform you that your account has been hacked on webcertificate.com and ecount.com'. The e-mail then went on to feed back to the customers their own account details such as home address and e-mail address. One interesting effect of Webcertificates' stance is that they stated that the company had got positive responses from their customers for standing up to hackers.

A USEFUL BUSINESS TOOL?

IW, cyber terrorism, and digital extortion – all of these strands can hit any organization, but obviously it is only worth the criminal's time and effort if you have valuable data, which can be used against you, or will substantially benefit your competitors. Thus the type of companies, organizations and business sectors that will be specifically targeted include:

- Advanced materials.
- Aerospace.
- Arms manufacturers – particularly high tech ones. The inherent attackers are many: competitors, terrorists, foreign governments, extortionists.
- Banks and financial institutions.
- Biotechnology.
- Computer hardware.
- Computer software.
- Credit card companies.
- Energy research.
- Engine technology.
- Financial market research companies.
- Insurance companies.
- Human and genetic engineering.
- Molecular technology and associated fields.

- Pharmaceutical companies. Their research is invaluable (both to the companies themselves and their competitors).
- Robotics.
- Semiconductors.
- Stock/share trading companies and associated firms.
- Synthetic materials.
- Telecommunications.

And these are just the more obvious ones. . .

Perhaps the majority of critical issues in the IW/IO debate are crystallized in two events that befell Bloomberg's – although as we will see it is now open to question as to what actually happened in one of these episodes. On August 14 2000 the United States Attorney of the Southern District of New York issued a press release which stated that:

> OLEG ZEZOV, a/k/a 'Oleg Zezev,' a/k/a 'Oleg Dzezev,' a/k/a 'Alex,' and IGOR YARIMAKA, who are citizens of Kazakhstan, were arrested on August 10, 2000 in London, England, for allegedly breaking into Bloomberg L.P.'s ('Bloomberg') computer system in Manhattan in an attempt to extort money from Bloomberg.
>
> ZEZOV and YARIMAKA are charged in separate three-count Complaints unsealed today. They are each charged with one count of interfering with commerce by using extortion; one count of extortion of a corporation using threatening communications; and one count of unauthorized computer intrusion.
>
> According to the Complaints, ZEZOV gained unauthorized access to the internal Bloomberg Computer System from computers located in Almaty, Kazakhstan. In or about the spring of 1999, Bloomberg provided database services, via a system known as the 'Open Bloomberg,' to Kazkommerts Securities ('Kazkommerts') located in Almaty, Kazakhstan. ZEZOV is employed by Kazkommerts and is one of four individuals at Kazkommerts associated with Kazkommert's contract with Bloomberg.
>
> In addition, according to the Complaints, ZEZOV sent a number of e-mails to Michael Bloomberg, the founder and owner of Bloomberg, using the name 'Alex,' demanding that Bloomberg pay him US $200,000 in exchange for providing information to Bloomberg concerning how ZEZOV was able to infiltrate Bloomberg's computer system.
>
> As described in the Complaints, Michael Bloomberg sent an e-mail to ZEZOV suggesting that they meet. ZEZOV allegedly demanded that Michael Bloomberg deposit US $200,000 into an

offshore account. Bloomberg established an account at Deutsche Bank in London and deposited US $200,000 into the account. According to the Complaint, Michael Bloomberg suggested that they resolve the matter in London and ZEZOV agreed.

As described in the Complaint against YARIMAKA, on August 6, 2000, YARIMAKA and ZEZOV flew from Kazakhstan to London. On August 10, 2000, YARIMAKA and ZEZOV met with officials from Bloomberg L.P., including Michael Bloomberg, and two London Metropolitan police officers, one posing as a Bloomberg L.P. executive and the other serving as a translator. At the meeting, YARIMAKA allegedly claimed that he was a former Kazakhstan prosecutor and explained that he represented 'Alex' and would handle the terms of payment. According to the Complaint, YARIMAKA and ZEZOV reiterated their demands at the meeting. Shortly after the meeting YARIMAKA and ZEZOV were arrested.

On August 11, 2000, YARIMAKA and ZEZOV were presented to a British Magistrate in Magistrate's Court in London, where they were held without bail. The United States will seek their extradition.

But stranger things had already happened to Bloomberg, or at least that is what the press reported when high profile stories in 1998 splashed allegations of commercial IW against the company. The allegations were that a US subsidiary of Reuters had commissioned another company to action electronic attacks on Bloomberg, which resulted in confidential data being obtained. Reuters and Bloomberg are strong competitors in various marketplaces. Reuters Analytics Inc based in Stamford, Connecticut, was accused of obtaining information from Reuters' operating code. The story was big news and allegations were made that the Reuters subsidiary had sent memos to an outside consultant requesting information about technical programs for investment analysis. The story then goes that the outside consulting firm broke into Bloomberg's computers and got what was requested – and ultimately this information was passed to Reuter's head office in London. It was a good story, while it lasted – which was up to July 15 1999 when the US attorney's Office for the Southern District of New York confirmed that the investigation had been closed and no charges of legal violations had been filed. Reuters issued a press statement which commented that:

As Reuters has previously stated, the investigation was primarily focused on Reuters Analytics' relationship with a New York-based

consultant who entered into a subscription agreement with Bloomberg LP and thereafter provided Bloomberg information to Reuters.
As Reuters has also previously said, the investigation was not focused on attempts to break into Bloomberg's central computer to extract proprietary code – as had been incorrectly asserted in some public media reports in early 1998.

Michael Bloomberg, quoted in *Global Custodian* at the time, was rather less convinced when he said that 'We put out a press release saying the fact that it took the US Attorney two years to investigate shows how serious the charge is. We believe that the data was misappropriated. Short of that in terms of other things that might take place, or what we might do, we had no comment. I'm not going to say any more'. Commercial IW or old-style industrial espionage? We shall never know.

When record companies want to shift more units of their ageing artists' music they usually digitally remaster classic albums or release digitally remastered greatest hits packages. The hope is that avid fans will fork out to buy something that they have already got, believing that they are buying into something new, sexy and shiny. In my view IW, or IO, or whatever else one wishes to call it, is akin to this marketing ploy. In many ways the commercial risks posed by these problems are nothing new (relatively speaking): all that has happened is that the old risks have been repackaged in a new way, like old wine in new bottles or old music tracks in a new cover. That is not to say that the fundamental problems are not serious ones – they are, and they should not be underestimated. Yet in the end a theft is a theft, blackmail is blackmail and whatever weapons are used in a physical attack – whether it is on a person, or a piece of hardware, the consequences are very much the same.

PRIVACY LOST

Civilization is the progress toward a society of privacy. The savage's whole existence is public, ruled by laws of his tribe. Civilization is the process of setting a man free from men.

Ayn Rand (1905–82)

WE'VE GOT A LINE ON YOU

At the beginning of the 21st century the populations of most Western-ized countries were hooked on a new type of television programme – *Big Brother*. The programme, a phenomenal success across the world, consists of a group of mostly young, mixed sex people being locked in a house together for a period of time. Almost every move that any one of them makes is recorded and then shown on TV; simultaneously various Webcams transmit their behaviour on a 24/7 basis to the Internet. When the first series of *Big Brother* was shown in the UK it was reported that the show's Web site was the most popular in the country. Gradually, as the days pass by, the viewing public vote on various occasions to evict one of the 'residents' from the house, so in the end only the winner remains. Speaking as someone who is totally non plussed by both this show and those similar to it, I have great difficulties in appreciating why anyone would find this almost inter-minable drivel at all interesting, never mind worth changing your entire schedule for so that you can watch every single episode. But in many ways, the *Big Brother* experience is merely a metaphor or emblem as to the strange journey that the Digital Age has taken us all on. . .

The UK has become, it is thought, the number one user of closed circuit TV (CCTV). The country now has an estimated 1.5 million cameras. Pressure group Privacy International suggests that if you live in a UK city then you will be caught on camera about 100–300 times a day. Have you ever actually taken any notice as to just how many of these cameras are in existence? Go into a bank, supermarket, newsagent – the camera will be focusing on you. Fill your car up with petrol, stand on a train station, go to a football match, walk down a street – 'Smile, you're on *Candid Camera*!' Supporters of such schemes (and there are many) point to higher police arrest rates, lower crime rates and improved crime detection rates. Add to the CCTVs the increased use of speed cameras on numerous roads, then don't think that you can escape by driving away. But bear in mind the UK is also the country where there is no national identification card, and until recently your driving licence didn't show your photograph (and the vast majority being older types still do not). The next obvious step for the CCTV is the incorporation of face recognition technology, which will match the faces captured on video with photographic records of known wanted people, criminals or anyone else the operators fancy.

If you're not on CCTV, you are most probably making an appearance on a Webcam. A November 2001 search on Google using the term 'Webcams' gave 833,000 search results – encompassing a few sublime images to the totally ridiculous. Quite why any organization would want to put out a live Webcam of the interior of their offices defeats me; similarly why do you want to sit at your PC watching someone else sitting at their PC? I think it best to move quickly past the idea of watching some bored suburban housewife performing sexual acrobatics in her living room.

One stage further along (but not that much) are devices that keep tabs on the locations of individuals. These are already in use in various environments: in November 1998 *The Wall Street Journal Europe* reported on a system such as this one that was already in operation at two Chicago hospitals. Nurses are required to wear digital badges that emit electronic pulses which are monitored by scanners in the ceiling. The ostensible reason for such monitoring is so that human resources in the hospitals can be used more effectively. But simultaneously, should you want to know how long Nurse A spends in the bathroom each day, then go ahead. Events in 2001 have heightened the calls for a smart card as a national identity mechanism: such a card could contain both your fingerprints and detailed information about you. According to the research firm Morgan Keegan & Co, the US biometrics industry is expected to grow from US $200 million in 2001 to something like US $2 billion in 2004.

All these uses of digital technology, and the apparent lack of public outcry against them, raises the fundamental issue of whether we have any moral or legal rights to expect privacy. Whatever the legal position is in a particular country, the reality is that we leave a constant digital trail of our activities, likes, dislikes, expenditure, contacts, friends and much more besides. Deeply ironic, though, is the fact that the most organized criminals leave a minimal trail – and the all embracing surveillance society has, particularly in relation to recent events, singularly failed to provide intelligence or data that would warn of upcoming attacks or outrages. Similarly, the use of such monitoring by law enforcement agencies in respect of fraud and money laundering has so far been generally non-productive. For these reasons I consider that the key factor in relation to digital surveillance is not presently what crime can be prevented through its use, but what steps you can take to prevent you becoming a victim because of it. Thus for both the organization and individual the digital privacy issue is still a key one: bearing in mind that every security breach invariably involves the seepage of personal information, and consequently becomes (among other things) a privacy issue.

This is a double edged sword – the Internet has given access to millions, probably now billions, of documents relating to every subject and research topic that can be imagined. You can legitimately find substantial volumes of information about both organizations and individuals by using the Internet. If you want to know what kind of information is available about individuals on the Internet, just do the following.

As an example, try and find information about UK residents: you can check to see whether they have a registered phone number, which if they have will also give you their address; you can check to see if they are registered on the voters' roll; you can research to establish whether they are a director of any UK registered company (and companies in many other countries with a so-called 'global' search); you can action a fairly comprehensive media search on them; if they post messages to newsgroups they will probably have an e-mail profile – together with all of the postings that an individual has made; some people have personal Web sites containing full details and photographs.

Try the same exercise on a US citizen and you can be overwhelmed by the public information available (and if you believe some Web sites, the not-so-public data that can be bought).

Paradoxically though, such research on the Web can – and does – leave a trail of your interests and activities. As will be seen in the next section, such surveillance can be legitimate (as in the case of an employer monitoring the corporate e-mail system) or it can be something else entirely. Much of the information that can be collected about you is voluntarily self-provided. If you are a typical Internet user, you will have at the very least signed up to mail services, information providers and bought goods online from various sites. Each of these actions requires you to register, and even if you do not have to hand over your credit card details then you will have provided a substantial volume of intelligence (not ignoring the fact that the actual Web site service that you sign up to also says a lot about your interests and ultimately your personality). Typically you will be giving details of:

- your name;
- your address;
- your phone number;
- your e-mail address;
- your fax number;
- your sex;
- your marital status;
- your interests.

You will also give a vast variety of other facts about yourself if you answer all the numerous voluntary questions posed. Somewhere on the registration page will be a box that states something along the lines of 'On occasions, we may want to notify you of our own special deals or those from carefully selected partners. Tick here if you do NOT wish to be informed of these wonderful opportunities'. If you miss the box, or chose not to opt out, your details will be fairly easily available to anyone who is willing to buy that particular mail list. Even more worrying is the fact that we are presuming that the Internet service that you have just given all these details to is operated by an honest, ethical and legitimate company. There are many that aren't – and there are also quite a few that are out and out frauds.

Every Web site that offers online services or goods will have a privacy policy: which invariably you accept by visiting that particular site. Irrespective as to whether that particular Web site company actually follows its own privacy policy, there are some strange and concerning elements in such policies as they stand:

- Most Web sites say that they receive and store information you enter on the Web site or *'give us in any other way'*. These other ways can include: searching on the site; completing a question-naire or competition entry form; participating in discussion/ message boards; providing reviews of products or rating them; setting up reminders of key dates such as birthdays and anniv-ersaries.
- Many such Web sites collect the IP address used to connect to them; your browser type and version; operating system and platform; your purchase history and a whole lot more.
- Most Web sites that sell you something online use cookies (see more on this below).
- Depending on the Web site provider, the company may not sell your information – but obviously uses it itself and probably provides it to subsidiaries, affiliated companies and/or partners. Amazon.com also states in its privacy policy that 'In the unlikely event that Amazon.com Inc., or substantially all of its assets are acquired, customer information will of course be one of the transferred assets'. This raises key questions about, among other issues, what happens to the customer databases of the many and varied failed dot com companies – a customer database can be a fairly valuable commodity, so how can anyone really know whether such information was sold on by failed companies or taken to pastures new by departing employees and management?

I hold no great store by national legislation in relation to data protection and its misuse, for two key reasons. Firstly much of the regulation regarding data protection predates the Internet, and secondly it is on a national level, which is totally at variance with the concept and practical operation of the Internet. If, for example, you are involved in any type of research (which will almost certainly necessitate registering at various relevant sites) the major joy of the Internet is that you can easily access documents across the world, which prev-iously would have involved a visit to the location where the documents or information were, or a lot of postage charges (and resultant delays). In the UK the Data Protection Act has eight principles of 'good information handling', which are all totally logical and sensible:

- Data must be fairly and lawfully processed.
- Data must be processed for limited purposes.
- Data must be relevant, adequate and not excessive.
- Data must be accurate.
- Data must not be stored for longer than is necessary.
- Data must be processed in line with your rights.
- Data must be secure.
- Data must not be transferred to countries without adequate protection.

As a UK citizen I have a right to see what data is kept about me (including CCTV footage) by any data controller in the UK, and therein lies the obvious problem. If I register with a UK based e-commerce company and buy a book or record from them I can request all the data that they hold on me. But if I register with an online information provider in, for example, Russia what can I do to get a complete extract of the information that such a company stores in relation to me? Moreover what guarantees have I got as to the way that company processes, stores and distributes such information?

Cookies, Carnivore and Echelon

The cookie issue is one of the more misunderstood ones of the Internet. A cookie is a small text file stored on your hard drive by a Web site that you have visited (or a banner ad that has come up). The file records your preferences such as language choice and log on details. According to the US Electronic Privacy Center 87 per cent of all US e-commerce sites use cookies. So what's the problem? A cookie eradicates various time wasting tasks that the user would have to carry out each time he or she accessed a specific Web site, thus they can only be good news, right? Not entirely – cookies have been described as cyber wiretaps – although this description, containing an element of truth, may be an over exaggeration. Cookies are a unique identifier that can then be used to retrieve your information from a Web site's database when you visit that site again. However it is not only Web sites that you visit that place cookies on your hard drive: banner ad companies send out cookies in their millions. It is entirely feasible that if you register on a site which places a cookie on your hard drive it can be linked to the cookie from that Web site on your computer. The next step is to exchange that data with the banner ad company that also has a cookie on your hard drive and thus monitor your Internet activity. If that's the downside there is an upside: cookies can't scan your hard drive, check out what software you are using or grab your credit card details (as they are text files not code). Best of all is the fact that even though you may be passing on a unique, personalized browsing experience, you can refuse to accept cookies on your PC and if they are already there, you can delete them.

The two words that send shivers down the spine of digital privacy advocates are Echelon and Carnivore. The latter is a piece of online detection software used by the FBI. In the spirit of transparency and accountability, the FBI's own Web site gives an explanation of Carnivore. The description stresses the controls under which this 'diagnostic tool' works but makes the critical point that:

> *The ability of law enforcement agencies to conduct lawful electronic surveillance of the communications of its criminal subjects represents one of the most important capabilities for acquiring evidence to prevent serious criminal behaviour. Unlike evidence that can be subject to being discredited or impeached through allegations of misunderstanding or bias, electronic surveillance evidence provides jurors an opportunity to determine factual issues based upon a defendant's own words.*

So what then does the FBI tell us that Carnivore does and how does it do it? The FBI describes the facilities that Carnivore has as being 'surgical' in that it intercepts and collects digital communications that are the subject of a lawful order but it ignores everything else – ie all the communications that the FBI has no legal right to intercept. The operation of Carnivore is compared by the FBI to 'commercial sniffers and other network diagnostic tools used by ISPs every day'. In fact Carnivore may ironically be a lesser risk to privacy than more mainstream events and legislation. In Britain the Regulation of Investigatory Powers Act allows authorities to monitor e-mail and Internet traffic at ISPs and gives the police power to force individuals who have encrypted their e-mails to hand over the keys. Anyone who refuses faces a penalty of up to two years in prison. In the United States ISPs are now allowed to voluntarily give all 'non-content' information of their users to law enforcement agencies with no need for a court order or subpoena. This issue has caused controversy, such as in November 2001 when the UK National Crime Squad made a substantial number of arrests (and seized thousands of files containing images) concerning the sexual abuse of children. While such progress in this hideous area is to be praised, unfortunately a police spokesperson commented that they had 'imaged' the servers of Demon Internet, a UK ISP, for the duration of the enquiry. Demon held newsgroups on which many suspects traded information and files: but the use of the word 'imaged' implied (in its correct technological context) that the police had obtained an entire copy of Demon's server, including all software and traffic logs held on it. And obviously this would mean all traffic logs – including those of thousands of innocent users. To complicate (or probably simplify) matters, Demon is fairly unique in that it gives each of its customers a static IP address, as opposed to a variable one. Various corrections followed the initial comment; these confirmed that the police had the same level of access to the relevant information as a member of the public in that they had a direct connection with the newsgroup servers and Demon retained the message base longer than they would normally do. The phrase 'imaging' appears to have been a word that was misused in this case.

With Carnivore, a simple subpoena can obtain details of all users' online activity can be obtained (such as what Web sites they visit, credit card details and everything else that they key in). Much is made, in the FBI's description, of the controls that exist in relation to Carnivore and the fact that it can focus in on what it is legal to examine. While not disagreeing with the sentiments behind Carnivore, the dilemma is that the description given is not quite the whole story in relation to this piece of equipment. As far as anyone knows (or can guess) Carnivore is apparently the third generation of such software used by the FBI, and is the immediate successor to Omnivore which it replaced at the end of 1999. Carnivore itself is one third of a suite of programs known as Dragonware (which may, in retrospect have been an unfortunate term).The three parts of this suite are:

- Carnivore (aka DCS1000): which is a Windows NT/2000 based system that captures the raw data.
- Packeteer: this processes the raw output of Carnivore, turning the Internet data into more meaningful information about the communication that is being targeted.
- Coolminer: provides statistical analysis and summaries of the information together with displaying to and from information, or shows the full content of the message.

So, in very basic terms, the FBI sets up Carnivore at the ISP of the suspect (for whom they have obtained a content wiretap authority from the court). Carnivore is configured so that data packets will only be captured from this particular location, and will not impede or interfere with the general data flow of the network. The captured data is then filtered to obtain the exact information that the FBI can legally obtain in relation to this specific suspect. The data is then processed using Packeteer and Coolminer. Again, this sounds perfectly reasonable – in fact that is very much the conclusion that a team from the Illinois Institute of Technology Research Institute came to when it reviewed the system for the Department of Justice in November 2000. Essentially the team confirmed that the system does what it says it does. The big but, however, was not that the system could spy on everybody's e-mail (it couldn't for technical reasons) rather that the number of safeguards inherent in the system were limited. According to the report (which was purged of sensitive material) the system had various key security faults:

- The system has no audit log – who accessed it and when cannot be determined.
- Every operator had the same username – the particularly unimaginative 'administrator'.
- There is no feature for confirming that the wiretap had been ordered by a court.
- If it is incorrectly figured Carnivore can record any traffic that it monitors.

Such criticisms obviously fuel the various concerns that have been strongly propounded by critics of the system. The major criticism is that Carnivore is a severe violation of privacy; this does not appear to be so, but even if there are privacy infringements, could it not be argued that this is a small price to pay for obtaining critical data on the activities and plans of terrorists, child pornographers and abusers, fraudsters, organized criminals, terrorists and money launderers? A second objection is that Carnivore is such a massive system that it can monitor, control and regulate the entire Internet. Logically, such a scenario is not feasible – because to do so would involve having a Carnivore system at every ISP in the world. So even if such a system was in place at every ISP in the United States, and it captured every bit, byte and moment of the Internet and e-mail traffic of every single user, it would be fairly useless as the rest of the world could carry on regardless. Never mind the massive systems that would be required to achieve any of this. The other key consideration is that of free speech:

the suggestion is that Carnivore can be programmed to monitor all content flowing through an ISP, and filter out any communications that contain keywords or terms (the obvious ones are always cited: bomb, terrorist, assassination). The simple fact is that any packet sniffer can be programmed to search out patterns of characters or data. As far as anyone can tell, Carnivore does not have the physical power or the ability to do this. One does however think that the FBI may have caused itself fewer problems if it had called the system something bland and technical, rather than the somewhat confrontational Carnivore. Moreover, in the public psyche Carnivore has perhaps become confused and inextricably linked with the rather different Echelon.

The Echelon system is the subject of conjecture, fantasy, paranoia, controversy, misinformation and hundreds of Web sites. Finally, in May 2001 a leaked European Parliament report confirmed the existence of such a system. The report 'on the existence of a global system for the interception of private and commercial communications (Echelon system) 'concluded that Echelon was a reality. However, the report also observes that the system cannot be as extensive as feared, as it is based on worldwide interception of satellite communications. From other sources, Echelon is run by the intelligence bodies of the United States, UK, Canada, Australia and New Zealand, as follows:

- The National Security Agency (USA).
- Government Communications Headquarters – GCHQ (UK).
- Communications Security Establishment – CSE (Canada).
- Defence Signals Directorate – DSD (Australia).
- Government Communications Security Bureau (New Zealand).

It is thought to date back to a secret treaty signed in 1947; the first system being built in 1971. The system is thought to capture data traffic and then analyse it for keywords. Just what communications traffic is intercepted is just one of the many areas of dispute: the European Parliament report thinks that it is limited; other observers think that it can not only intercept satellite transmissions (which carry only a small proportion of global data traffic) but also tap into wire communications; phone calls; fax transmissions; sniff into data packets through Internet routing centres; tap into undersea fibre optic cables. This is achieved through a network of ground stations and about 120 US satellites in geostationary orbit. The ground stations that are normally named as being part of the Echelon system are:

- Menwith Hill, Yorkshire (UK).
- Morwenstow, Cornwall (UK).
- Bad Aibling, Bayern (Germany).
- Geraldton Station (Australia).
- Shoal Bay (Australia).
- Misawa (Japan).
- Waihopai (New Zealand).
- Yakima Firing Center, Washington State (United States).
- Leitrim (Canada).
- Sugar Grove, West Virginia (United States).

Whatever data the system does capture is then analysed by a large supercomputer network which is presumed to search for keywords, phrases, addresses and names. Various claims have been made as to how powerful such a network is – there have been numerous references to 'collecting millions of phone calls, faxes and e-mails every minute' and the NSA computer system being able to store up to 5 trillion pages of text. However, such claims can lead to total exaggeration, such as the Web site that claims that the system is the source of 'psychotronic attacks' (whatever they may be). The truth may just be much more prosaic: it is fairly obvious that all nations monitor communications to identify any such data traffic that contains information relating to, and more importantly, threatening national security. Various observers have propounded the view that the Echelon system is basically this, and anything more than this is a fiction. Certainly there is some logic for this – imagine for example how much processing power would be required to do what is claimed, how much equipment, the level of cooperation required with the private sector (particularly with telecommunications and IT companies) and finally just how many people would be needed to build, install, maintain and run such a system. Cynics have also pointed out that governments are probably the last people who would be able to effectively run such a system – and even if they could analyse all of the planet's data traffic, what would they look for? Certainly there is no great evidence to suggest that, if Echelon does exist in the massive way that it is suggested, it is working particularly well! However, the conspiracy theory is somewhat aided by reports such as the one that surfaced in 1998 that the US National Security Agency had 1,056 pages of classified information on the late Princess Diana. This was in response to a Freedom of Information request, which was denied; unfortunately no one knows what information was contained in those 1,056 sheets of paper. NSA denied that Princess Diana was a target and thus it is highly likely that many of the references could be incidental. Such disclosures can be viewed as evidence of the existence of a sinister all knowing and all seeing Echelon system – or they could simply confirm what we already know that the US and other governments collect electronic data and then analyse it. The questions that remain unanswered is how much data, from what sources and how are they analysed. Perhaps we have been watching too many reruns of *The X files*, alternatively the truth may well be out there somewhere...

One of the interesting facets of the continuing and ever present Echelon debate is that it is widely presumed that the system works by searching for keywords and phrases (although this is open to wide debate). It has been suggested that each of the five countries supplies dictionaries to the other four of keywords, phrases, people and places to look for in the data that country has collected, and then such intercepted data is forwarded to the requesting nation. This concept has led to an interesting event: the Block Echelon Day (aka Jam Echelon Day). The premise was a very simple one: if the Echelon system ran on keywords then if those phrases were known (or an educated guess made of them) and as many people as possible fired off e-mails or postings containing them, the system would be overloaded – a kind of Echelon denial of service attack. The first Block Echelon Day was October 21 1999 and it was repeated on October 21 2001. The result was somewhat variable – and obviously no one this side of the fence can ever know whether it succeeded. Complaints soon surfaced that mail lists were being clogged up with obscure rantings about drugs, bombs, terrorism and numerous other key phrases. Obviously another major problem was what comprised the Echelon dictionaries – the words or phrases that triggered things off. There are now various lists posted on the Internet which claim to contain these keywords. However, while not wishing to appear cynical, some of the lists I have seen border on the comical – one contained the word 'Mum'; another suggested that both 'Bill Clinton' and 'Hilary Clinton' had pride of place on the list; Both 'Mulder' and 'Scully' came up on various lists. But, if we suppose that Echelon does exist, in some form akin to the worst case scenario propounded, then it is useful (for a variety of reasons) to have at least some idea of the type of keywords that may be targeted. Thus, later in this chapter are some examples of what appear to be the more plausible Web postings of Echelon keywords. I make no claims about the list's accuracy, but it is, at the very least, interesting to view what are perceived as being some of the most damaging and inflammatory terms in the Digital Age.

Depending on your level of digital paranoia there are numerous steps that you can take to minimize leakage of personal information, such as the following:

- Use anti-virus software (low level paranoia – an essential for every user).
- Use firewall software (low level paranoia – another essential for every user).
- Regularly delete cookies, either manually or using one of the many cleaning programs available (low level paranoia – very sensible for not only security reasons but also to ensure that your system does not get cluttered up with junk) Additionally you should clear your Internet Browser temporary files and such facilities as 'AutoComplete' (in Internet Explorer) as both of these could be used to reconstitute Web sites that you have visited previously.
- Configure your Internet browser on the maximum security settings, which can be done easily and disables cookies (slightly more paranoid, and has practical problems as some Web sites don't work properly, which is particularly annoying when you can't sign in but don't realize that the reason is that you must have cookies enabled to access that particular Web site).
- Don't set up user profiles: Internet chat sites, and many Web sites encourage you to set up user profiles for a more personalized experience – ignore them and only file in the information that you have to. If you are not likely to order anything by credit card or mail, the address of Beverley Hills 90210 or London WC1 is good to know (fairly low level paranoia, but sometimes you have to give more information than you want to so that you can register on a site, alternatively you can just walk away).
- Encrypt your e-mails if you can do it, but it has certain drawbacks as the whole point of encryption is that the recipient has a key to unlock the message, which is fine if you know the person you are writing to (and have already given them the key), but has fatal drawbacks if this is not the case. Have you ever thought of faxing, phoning or writing on paper instead?
- Use a PC solely dedicated to Internet access. This is actually not quite as crazy as it sounds – the most effective firewall is a

physical one. By using a totally separate PC for the Internet you completely remove the risk of any intruder gaining access to any other files on your PC – because there shouldn't be any. Just one obvious word of warning: a PC solely to access the Internet cannot be part of a network, for obvious reasons. The only other drawbacks – which are fairly considerable in their own right – are the expense involved and the lack of practicality. (Originally I thought that this was high level paranoia, but now consider it to be medium level).

▪ Access the Internet through a public computer only. For criminals only I think, and even then there are some reverse drawbacks. Using a public computer for Internet access gives complete personal anonymity, but perversely can leave more of what you did in the public domain. I do a considerable amount of travelling and over the last two years have used a variety of public access Internet terminals – including one mounted in a wall in a Vienna U-Bahn station, public library machines in New York and numerous Internet cafés in Amsterdam, Geneva, London and Spain. If you use such machines, try something before you start broadcasting to the world: open the history folder and see what is in there. My experience is that in many cases you will be able to see exactly which Web sites numerous previous users have accessed. There are some honourable exceptions to this, where the PC reboots and cleans after every user, but if this is not the case then unless you clean and delete the PC after your use, the next user will be able to see exactly where you have been (high state of paranoia).

But all of this may be to no avail whatsoever, as your privacy may be being invaded in digital ways that you never imagined. In October 2001 *The Times* reported that Cambridge University had suspended a member of staff after a Webcam was found in a women's lavatory and shower unit. The camera was discovered by workmen and was found to be linked to a computer in the university of a male member of staff, who subsequently resigned. It was reported that he would escape prosecution as there was no evidence that he had recorded any of the images or that they had been transmitted on the Internet. While referring to the civil liberty issues that this episode had raised, a female spokesperson for Cambridge police remarked that 'Watching a naked woman is not necessarily an offence, even in these circumstances'.

POSSIBLE ECHELON KEYWORDS

There are numerous lists posted on the Internet that claim to contain Echelon keywords – to see what is *de rigeur* at any one time try a search on Google with the term 'Echelon keywords'. That should give you a few thousand references to be going on with. Having waded through many of the lists, one is left with the impression that many of them border on the gibberish, with a few personal references thrown in by the compiler(s). Acronyms abound, together with a preponderance of female Christian names laced with various names of corporations (are we really to believe that Cable & Wireless, Lexis-Nexis and AOL are trigger words?) An example of such a list goes something like this:

Explosives, guns, assassination, conspiracy, primers, detonators, initiators, main charge, nuclear charges, ambush, sniping, motorcade, hostages, munitions, weapons, TNT, amfo, hmtd, picric acid, silver nitrite, mercury fulminate, presidential motorcade, salt peter, charcoal, sulfur, amatol, petn, lead azide, lead styphante, ddnp, tetryl, nitrocellulose, nitrostarch, mines, grenades, rockets, fuses, delay mechanism, mortars, propellants, incendiaries, incendiary device, thermite, security forces, intelligence, agencies, hrt, resistance, psyops, infiltration, assault team, defensive elements, evasion, detection, mission, communications, timing devices, boobytraps, Air Force One, special forces, INFOSEC, ASPIC, Information Security, SAI, Information Warfare, IW, IS, Privacy, Information Terrorism, Terrorism Defensive Information, Defense Information Warfare, Offensive Information, Offensive Information Warfare, Computer Terrorism, Military, White House, Corporate Security, Police, sniper, Security Consulting, M-x spook, Z-150T, High Security, Security Evaluation, Electronic Surveillance Fax encryption, white noise, Fernspah, MYK

To which you can mix in as many acronyms as you want:

USDOJ, NSA, CIA, S/Key, SSL, FBI, USSS, NCCS, Mayfly, PGP, SALDV, PEM, RSA, Perl-RSA, MSNBC, AOL, AOL TOS, CIS, CBOT, AIMSX, STARLAN, 3B2, BITNET, SAMU, COSMOS, DATTA, E911, FCIC, HTCIA, IACIS, UT/RUS, JANET, ram, JICC, ReMOB, LEETAC, UTU, VNET, BRLO, SADCC, NSLEP, SACLANTCEN, FALN, 877, NAVELEXSYSSECENGCEN, BZ, CANSLO, CBNRC, CIDA, JAVA, , RDI, BIOL, AMME, ANDVT, Type I, Type II, VFCT, VGPL, WHCA,

WSA, WSP, WWABNCP, ZNI1, FSK, FTS2000, GOSIP, GOTS, SACS STU-III, PRF, PMSP, PCMT, I&A, JRSC, ITSDN, Keyer, KG-84C, KWT-46, KWR-46, KY-75, KYV-5, LHR, PARKHILL, LDMX, LEASAT, SNS, SVN, TACSAT, TRANSEC, DONCAF, EAM, DSCS, DSNET1, DSNET2, DSNET3, ECCM, EIP, EKMS, EKMC, DDN, DDP

Among the more outlandish suggestions for keywords are:

Firewalls, Secure Internet Connections, Passwords, Hackers, Encryption – which would mean that Echelon must pull every e-mail or communication sent out by companies which specialize in digital security.

The same type of conclusion goes for the suggested keywords fax, import, bank, credit card, press release, sex – but I particularly like the keyword which is 'keyword'.

Bugs Bunny, Daffy Duck, Scully (as in Mulder and Scully), garbage, Elvis, quiche, pornstars as keywords seem to stretch one's credulity somewhat – but I do advise the lists of keywords that include references to the compiler's own Web site!

Interestingly none of the keyword lists that I have seen contain any real names of criminals, terrorists or wanted individuals; neither do they contain the names of drug/organized crime groups, terrorist cells or what may be presumed to be 'front companies' of crime or terrorist groups. All of this having been said, the fact that the keyword lists appear to be somewhat contrived does not mean that the basic premise is false.

SPAM, GLORIOUS SPAM

When I opened my e-mail inbox yesterday morning I was gratified to see that I had 'won' a voucher for free petrol that could be used at any petrol station of major oil companies. Or to be strictly correct, I could claim my free US $10 worth of petrol at any gas station in the United States within the next seven days. This might prove to be a problem, as I am based in the UK. Welcome to the world of spam – but I probably don't need to welcome you, as I am certain that you are already knee deep in it already (and if you're not, and use e-mail, please tell me how you've managed to avoid it). I try to do everything that I can to limit spam, and am very conscious of the dangers that lurk in the attachments of unsolicited e-mails, but that hasn't stopped the following wonderful missives being received by me in the last few days:

- Powerpoint productivity tips.
- A circular on .info domain names.
- A circular on a credit management newsletter.
- A message about free fax services.
- 'Only two weeks to get one month free and no setup fee'.
- 'Access your PC from anywhere – free download'.
- 'Up to US $150 free at xyzonlinecasino.com'.
- 'Win $100 in domain names'.
- 'Increase sales and revenues'.
- 'Get up to 2 per cent cash back on your purchases'.
- 'Solutions for buying or selling your business'.
- 'Free printer, scanner or digital camera'.

Thankfully I have not had any e-mails offering me free pornography, but somewhat ironically I have had one headed 'Mail pile getting you down?'. Spam is also known as unsolicited commercial e-mail (UCE), unsolicited bulk mail (UBE) or make money fast (MMF). While spam is now a universally used term which has been taken to cover each of these different types of e-mail abuse, in fact each of these terms has, strictly speaking, a different meaning. The exact reason for the use of the term spam has never been entirely clear, but obviously it refers to the tinned luncheon meat of the same name that was made a cult item by the famous Spam song from *Monty Python's Flying Circus*. Originally spam was used to describe a particular type of Usenet posting, but has now been accepted as a generic term to describe a whole range of inappropriate Web events, predominantly related to e-mail. The term encompasses the following:

- Unsolicited bulk e-mail (UBE): messages with the same (or almost the same) content sent to many addresses that did not ask to receive it. Before e-mail if a company or individual wished to carry out a bulk mail shot they had to compile or buy a mail list, print leaflets or circulars, stuff them in envelopes, mail frank the envelopes (or lick thousands of stamps) then post them. This was a laborious and time consuming task – not to mention the most important factor – the expense involved. E-mail removed all of these problems – as long as you had an e-mail circulation list, all you have to do is write something and press the 'send' button. Best of all it's free! Well kind of: in fact it may be free for the sender but bulk spammers actually can cause horrendous band-width problems when automated e-mail programs can send millions of messages each day. Then there are the consequent costs such as the time (and money) wasted in the workplace by dealing with such e-mails – and also, it must be said, on occasions, replying to them and sending money! UBE, by its very title, implies large numbers of messages.

- Unsolicited commercial e-mail (UCE) is virtually the same as UBE but can be a single e-mail to one user.
- Make money fast (MMF): In essence messages that guarantee immediate (and ludicrous) profits. Such communications are in the most part illegal, but more importantly (to use a technical term) bull****. Just as with both UBE and UCE there is nothing new in these communications as they have been sent by post for decades, but once again the Internet gives the sender the ability to dispatch thousands if not millions of these at the click of a mouse. The obvious advantage to the sender is that a percentage of recipients are always taken in by the ludicrous promises made and send money: so the more e-mails that are sent out then the higher number of people taken in, and thus the larger the illegal profit for the criminals behind the scheme. There is some semantic dispute as to whether multi-level marketing schemes fall into this category, but as I prefer to refer to such offers as pyramid schemes – with all the connotations that such a phrase implies, then I think that they well and truly belong here.

In very simple terms, the usual technique used to compile mail lists for such exercises involve the use of e-mail sniffers, which roam the Internet searching for and then recording e-mail addresses posted on Web sites, mailing list postings or anywhere else that e-mail addresses can be found. Such programs can be downloaded very easily from the Internet: at the moment I have on screen the details of a shareware program (costing US $10) that 'will extract valid e-mail addresses from almost any type of file including HTML, ASCII and binary files, handling up to 30,000 addresses per address list'.

Initially I thought that it would not be relevant to include details of e-mail spam that was essentially fraudulent, as there was very little (if any) possibility that anyone of a sane disposition would be taken in by it. However, all the research into this subject and logic suggest that people are taken in by it – otherwise what would be the point in it being sent in such large numbers? Nevertheless, it is important to distinguish between two types of spam. First is honest spam, which, for want of a better term, is bulk mailing that does relate to a legitimate product or service, but was not requested by the recipient. Then there's fraudulent spam: at the worst end of the make money fast syndrome, which perhaps ought to be rebranded LMF – lose money fast.

And what better place to start with than Nigeria. Here is not the place to discuss at length the vast and panoramic background of Nigerian fraud: I have written at length on this subject in the past and a White Paper on the many facets of this problem is on my firm's Web site at www.proximalconsulting.com. In essence, Nigerian fraudsters have, for many years, been sending out letters by post offering recipients the chance to be involved in a large financial transaction. The numbers of letters sent in the traditional way have been enormous – on average the US authorities receive at least 100 calls per day from victims or potential victims of this fraud and 300 related pieces of correspondence (per day!). In 1998 a UK police squad collected 150,000 Nigerian letters in the first four months of the year. But here's the rub: typically for each 100 letters sent, one recipient responds and another sends money: usually thousands of pounds. If there was ever a 'service' that begged for bulk e-mail distribution, this was it. Thus it came with very little surprise that in the last couple of months I have received a variety of these unrepeatable offers, such as:

REQUEST FOR ASSISTANCE IN A FINANCIAL TRANSACTION

I am contacting you based on information and esteem recommendation I received of you from a high ranking official in the commercial section of the Nigerian Chambers of Commerce and Industry who guaranteed your reliability and trustworthyness in business dealings. This business proposal I wish to intimate you with is of mutual benefit and it's success is entirely based on mutual trust, cooperation and a high level of confidentiality as regard this transaction.

I am the Chairman of the contract Advisory Committee (CAC) of the Nigerian Federal Ministry of Works and Housing (FMWH). I am seeking your assistance to enable me transfer the sum of US $16,500,000.00 (Sixteen Million, Five Hundred Thousand United States Dollars) into your private/company account.

The fund came about as a result of a contract awarded and executed on behalf of my Ministry the Federal Ministry of Works and Housing. The contract was supposed to be awarded to two foreign contractors to the tune of US $60,000,000.00 (Sixty Million United States Dollars). But in the course of negotiation, the contract was awarded to a Bulgarian contractor at the cost of US $43,500,000.00 (Forty-Three Million, Five Hundred Thousand United States Dollars) to my benefit unknown to the contractor. This contract has been satisfactorily executed and inspected as the Bulgarian firm is presently securing payment from my Ministry, where I am the Executive Director in-charge of all foreign contract payment approval.

As a civil servant still in active government service, I am forbidden by law to operate an account outside the shores of Nigeria. Hence this message to you seeking your assistance so as to enable me present your private/company account details as a beneficiary of contractual claims alongside that of the Bulgarian contractor, to enable me transfer the difference of US $16,500,000.00 (Sixteen Million, Five Hundred Thousand United States Dollars) into your provided account.

On actualization, the fund will be disbursed as stated below:

- 30 per cent of the fund will be for you as beneficiary.
- 10 per cent for reimbursement to both parties for incidental expenses that may be incurred during the course of the transaction.
- 60 per cent of the fund will be for me which I intend to invest in your country with you as my partner.

All logistics are in place and all modalities worked out for a smooth actualisation of the transaction within the next few working days of commencement. For further details as to the workability of this transaction, please respond by return mail on my confidential e-mail address: fmwhbakare@yahoo.com.or by fax .+234-1759-7154.

Thank you and God bless as I await your urgent response.

Yours sincerely,
Ali Bakare (Engr).

On almost the same day as we received our e-mail (actually we received it twice – presumably just in case we ignored it first time around), another Nigerian fraud came to light in Canada. Three Toronto residents have been arrested as a result of a joint investigation run by the Canadian Federal Bureau of Investigation and US Secret Service. The three men are alleged to have taken part in a global fraud involving more than 300 victims, who lost sums ranging from tens of thousands to millions of dollars.

One of our contacts has also recently received another variant of the Nigerian letter, this time from Mr Albert Sankarah in the Congo, who quotes a South African telephone and fax number. His letter reads as follows:

I am Mr Albert Sankarah from the Democratic Republic of Congo and the special adviser to the late President Laurent Kabila.

On the first week of this year the late President assigned me to the Republic of South Africa to conclude the Arms and Ammunitions procurement negotiation with an arm dealing company right here in South Africa as was a call of urgency. Before I left Congo, the President and I were made aware of the plans of the opposition to topple the government.

On the 15th of January 2001, I arrive to South Africa with the sum of US $23 Million (Twenty Three Million United States Dollars) through diplomatic means. To proceed on my mission I heard the most shocking news of my life; the assassination of the President who sent me on this mission. Having a thought of his death, I saw it as a golden opportunity to enrich and reward myself for my loyalty to him towards the overthrow of the late President Mobutu Sese Seko. I decided to deposit the funds with a reputable Security Company here in Johannesburg.

Knowing that since I am currently seeking asylum here in South Africa, I have got a lot of financial limitations. Coupled with the way in which this money was acquired, I cannot invest or use this money in South Africa. That is why I thus decided to seek for a God fearing person who can assist me in transferring these funds into his company or personal account.

In anticipation of your assistance I have agreed to offer you:

- 25 per cent of the total funds for your assistance
- 5 per cent to be set aside for every reasonable expenses incurred by both parties
- and the remaining 70 per cent will be for my investment in your company.

I have done everything necessary that will lead to the success of this transaction before contacting you, so all I want from your side is sincerity. Remember that the keyword to this transaction is confidentiality and I assure you that this transaction is 100 per cent risk free. If you are interested in assisting me please notify me on the above telephone and fax numbers. In case you cannot assist, do keep it confidential.

Best regards.

The contents of this letter confirm additional information that suggests that South Africa is becoming a centre of Nigerian activity, with many fraudsters operating out of the country, trying to lure innocent 'investors' there. Another variation on the dead statesman theme is the following letter, which is currently being sent by e-mail:

Dear Sir,

I am Mr. Varsadi Mobutu, the son of the late President Mobutu Sese Seko of former Zaire now Democratic Republic of Congo. My family and I now live in exile, in Morocco. Due to seizures/confiscation of my late father's properties as well as the frozen of all his bank accounts including that of the family members and the recent confiscation/seizure of his choice property châteaux in South of France, which were all carried by the International Press, made us not to make any meaningful investment without a sincere and trusted front. In this line, therefore, it is the wish of my family to solicit for a trustworthy and sincere person who will invest these funds under trusteeship for the family. We have US \$500m to put in any meaningful investment that will yield good dividend.

Source of fund

Before the death of my father he deposited the above stated funds with a Security Firm here in Morocco. Hence I am in asylum here in Morocco therefore, I intend to have a front who will manage this fund and invest it into property development, buying of shares/stocks in multinational companies and engage in non-speculative investments, and other related ventures.

As soon as I hear from you I will then arrange a face-to-face meeting for us to deliberate on this investment. It will also, give me the opportunity to assess your capability of handling this investment. Please I will like you to send me your private telephone/fax numbers, to allow us discuss privately and establish a voice contact. Meanwhile reach me on the above stated e-mail. Please treat this matter with utmost confidentiality.

Best Regards,
Varsadi Mobutu.

While the Nigerian 419 letter by e-mail is an important strand of fraudulent e-mail spam, it is merely one of many types that hit both individuals and businesses. Among other notable offers of instant wealth are:

- Chain letters – the classic 'get rich quick' schemes that promise unbridled wealth. The high tech variant of this perennial chestnut is no different to its paper mail counterpart. Typically the e-mail includes the details of several individuals; you are instructed to send US $5 to the person at the top of the list, cross that name off and add your name to the bottom. You are then told to e-mail this communication to other individuals, who will repeat the process so that you name comes to the top of the list and you will not be able to get to your post box because of the influx of plain brown envelopes stuffed with cash.
- Free prize schemes – telling you that you have won a valuable free prize, all you have to do is contact a phone number (usually costing a premium rate) and then pay for the shipping of your prize. It is not unusual for victims to be charged hundreds of pounds or dollars for the shipping of a free car or other seemingly valuable item. Of course, the prize never materializes.
- Free holidays – 'Yes, you have won a completely free one week holiday which can be taken at any time of the year (including school holidays) at any location in the world'. All you have to do is join a travel club, which may cost anything up to £300. When you come to book your holiday, mysteriously the flights you want will be fully booked, or if they're OK the hotel you choose will not be available, or if everything is available there will be some obscure clause that can be invoked so that you pay a hefty surcharge. And all of this actually presumes that you get this far: many such free holiday offers by e-mail result in victims joining 'travel clubs' that mysteriously disappear completely before any holidays can be booked.
- Advance fee frauds – the old favourite much favoured by Nigerian fraudsters but well used by every other criminal. In its simplest form the applicant pays a fee for a 'guaranteed' loan. This raises the obvious question, in these days of cheap and readily available finance, as to why anyone would need to pay a fee to borrow money. The obvious answer is that such spam is aimed at those who find it difficult to get credit and/or want to borrow more than they can afford. Thus these groups are hit with

a double whammy – no loan and handing over money that they can't afford.

■ Investment fraud schemes – we could be here all day listing the various types of such scams. However, beware in particular of investment stock tips by e-mail (which involve investing that capital) and anything at all that promises way above average financial returns.

■ The rest – and there are many. Junk any e-mails that you get which are about distributorships and franchises; job opportunities; work at home schemes; oil and gas investments; schemes that charge money for services that your government or other state bodies provide free (such as training, unclaimed tax refunds); life saving medical products. For organizations one particular type of spam can be particularly costly – e-mails that appear to be invoices that a staff member might think are real and proceed to pay. One particularly prevalent example relates to apparently pre-agreed entries in business directories in print or Web site format.

Just because someone has your e-mail address doesn't mean that you have somehow been magically chosen to be the only person on the planet to receive this wonderful offer! At the risk of stating the obvious, the often stated guidelines (equally applicable to normal mail) apply to any such spam:

■ When you are approached by any unknown person and/or organization to establish any new business relationship you must validate that person's or organization's claims and history. The best advice (which means that you don't have to read the rest of this warning list) is that if you have never heard of the person/ company sending you the e-mail, delete it without even bothering to read it – never vary from this dictum, even if your curiosity tries to persuade you otherwise.

■ Never forget: if any deal or offer appears to be too good to be true, turn it down – because it is.

■ There are no such things as 'once in a lifetime opportunities' 'guaranteed returns on investments' – when the figures guaranteed are astronomical.

■ Be suspicious.

■ Question all transactions.

- Jealously guard all your personal and/or business information such as bank account details, credit card numbers.
- Don't sign any document before you have had it checked out.
- Find out if the individual or company exists, and is registered with the necessary regulators or licensing authority.
- How long has the individual/company been trading – who are the principals?
- Check out the filings of the subject company – it might be registered somewhere, but is it trading? If so does its financial status in any way reflect the deal being offered?
- Check out addresses and contact details of those approaching you (it still surprise me how many of these people use dead lines or business centres).
- Validate any documents presented for authenticity.
- Ask for references – but don't take them at face value.
- Ask for a prospectus and brochure.
- Carry out a media and Internet search on the individuals.
- Don't pay for anything upfront unless you have dealt with the person/company before and know that the person/company is reputable.
- Don't be afraid to say 'No'.
- Don't be rushed – one key factor in many of these frauds is that the criminals try to rush you, usually saying that you must act quickly to take advantage of the unique opportunity.
- The Internet may be a great medium to promote fraud, but it is also a brilliantly effective way to search for information and detail on fraudsters. You may be surprised by what you find by searching – details of earlier investors who have lost money, for example, or investigations that are going on into the company/individual that is offering you the wonderful investment opportunity. I recommend searching on Dogpile, Google and Northern Light at the very least.
- If you have any doubt whatsoever, walk away – even if you are continually pressured to sign on the dotted line (in fact, particularly if you are pressured to sign on the dotted line).

In many US states the issues relating to even 'normal' spam (ie circulars offering legitimate services) have been the subject of legislation. In Washington a law enacted in 1988 allows state residents to sue for damages of up to US $500 for each unsolicited e-mail message received. While such legislation is very worthy and well meaning it is, in practical terms, useless. If the sender is outside that state, or outside of the US, how can it possibly be enforced? ISPs in virtually all cases have clauses regarding e-mail abuse in your agreement with them. Which is all very fine, but numerous and varied complaints have surfaced over the years regarding the lack of response from ISPs over spam. The argument is that as combating spam is not a revenue generator then ISPs are not particularly quick or efficient in dealing with the problem. There is also and inevitably the other side of the argument, that bulk e-mailing gives small businesses (in particular) a valuable marketing tool, and thus any ISPs that try to control and eradicate it are effectively anti-business. There are also various attempts to make search engines prohibit the inclusion of sites that offer services and software relating to spam. This has practical problems: at the very least the kind of search terms that would have to be monitored would include the following – and searches would need to allow for variations in spelling (for example e-mail and email) and case sensitivity:

- spam;
- bulk mail/bulk e-mail;
- direct e-mail;
- unsolicited bulk e-mail;
- unsolicited commercial e-mail;
- UBE and UCE (which is a bit of a shame if your legitimate company or organization is called either of these acronyms);
- e-mail software (banning, restricting or having a 'health warning' on this phrase is totally unworkable);
- bulk e-mail software;
- bulk e-mail service;
- e-mail marketing;
- e-mail advertising;
- online advertising;
- online marketing;
- Web site promotion;
- e-mail lists;
- e-mail address lists;
- stealth e-mail;
- extractor (another totally unworkable one – what about all the other kinds of extractors?);
- harvester (another problem – what about, for example, the UK restaurant chain with this name?).

ABUSE BY E-MAIL

Spam may be annoying, and in some cases costly, but e-mail abuse has another side which can be more damaging – and expensive. Let's take the issue of the contents of the e-mails sent by your own staff: you make sure that all of your people have e-mail facilities but then can have no idea what is being sent out by them. Because they are using corporate e-mail addresses the recipient may believe that whatever is contained in the message represents company policy. Thus apart from the obvious messages that can include sensitive information or falsely accept liability on behalf of the organization, there are the new dangers of racist, sexist, offensive and/or pornographic material going out under your company's banner to the outside, or circulating internally. The Online Policy Group, a non-profit independent organization based in San Francisco, issued a definition of digital defamation that shows just how many individuals or groups you risk offending:

> *Digital Defamation involved online hate speech, defamation and/*
> *or profiling of various minority groups including, but not limited*
> *to, the lesbian, gay, bisexual, and transgender community, youth,*
> *the elderly, disabled, racial, ethnic, or religious minorities, and other*
> *traditionally under represented groups.*

Such communications can be more than just irritating, they can be expensive – as Norwich Union, the UK insurance company, found out in 1997. The company had to pay £450,000 in libel damages after its staff circulated untrue comments on an *internal* e-mail system alleging financial difficulties at Western Provident, a rival company. In the United States Chevron has had to pay US $2.2 million to settle a lawsuit which hinged on an e-mail message containing sexist comments; British Gas has had to pay £101,000 in a case of e-mail defamation.

What constantly surprises me is the ease with which e-mail users pour their woes, thoughts, vitriol, innermost feelings and anything else that is bothering them into e-mails. For some reason (which defies logic) many e-mail senders believe that their message will only be read by the person to whom it is addressed – leaving aside the inherent security problems in e-mail, have such users never noticed the 'forward' button on e-mail programs which can be used at will by the recipient? Even if such users appreciate the privacy/security problems, they reconcile themselves with the presence of a disclaimer on an e-mail. While such disclaimers are vital, it is a very moot point as to what practical effects they have; they might have some weight in a legal fight – but if you think a disclaimer will stop the recipient forwarding the message on to all and sundry, think again. E-mails on sex in particular are always good ones to pass around: the famous Norton Rose case demonstrates this observation. Claire Swire, and Bradley Chait, a lawyer at a London law firm, engaged in an exchange of e-mail concerning oral sex (which can found in full at www.whois claireswire.f2s.com). Mr Chait was obviously so impressed with a complimentary comment from Ms Swire that he felt duty bound to circulate it to a few of his closest friends. His message contained the usual disclaimers typical of a law firm – confidential, privileged, solely for the use of the recipient, etc. How many people ended up reading this e-mail will probably be never known – 20 million worldwide being one of the figures banded about by the media. Although highly publicized at the time, such exchange of niceties is not a rare occurrence. In October 2001 the *Liverpool Daily Post* reported that two Liverpool council workers had been suspended after sending 150 sexy e-mails to each other over a period of seven days. The messages were said to be 'sexually explicit'. At roughly the same time it was reported elsewhere that a member of the Press Association sent all of the organization's employees an e-mail intended for his girlfriend – presumably it wasn't just that week's shopping list.

Yet this problem is hardly new: in 1999 *The New York Times* dismissed 23 staff for sending offensive e-mails. At the time a spokesperson for the newspaper commented that 'the content (of the e-mails) was offensive and inappropriate. Creating a hostile work environment is illegal in America and employers are required to take action. [The event] was serious and violated our company values. Our e-mail policy is quite clear and was sent to all employees four months ago'. The simple truth, which is galling to organizations, is that employers can be held responsible for e-mails written by employees in the course of their employment, whether or not the employer consented to (or agreed with) the content of the message. Which is of course why every corporate e-mail should come with a disclaimer, every organization must have an e-mail usage policy and perhaps the monitoring of your staff's e-mails isn't such a bad idea after all. Added to all of this is the fact that e-mail should be viewed as just an important part of organizational records as any other document – as Microsoft discovered when evidence presented against it by the US Government in the long running anti-trust case consisted of internal e-mails composed by executives describing their plans to topple competitors.

Nobody really knows what protection e-mail disclaimers will give you in each and every situation; the fact that e-mails reach a global audience also means that their effectiveness (if any) will vary in different jurisdictions. In many cases their efficacy may be limited – as what really matters is the content of the e-mail. However, as they cost nothing, and may offer you some protection, it is foolish not to incorporate them (and establish a system whereby each and every e-mail sent by your organization has the disclaimer automatically added). Disclaimers come in all shapes, sizes and flavours: writing a suitable one for you is a bit of a pick and mix affair – so here are a few to play around with:

BREACH OF CONFIDENTIALITY AND ACCIDENTAL BREACH OF CONFIDENTIALITY

This e-mail and any files transmitted with it are confidential and intended solely for the use of the individual or entity to whom they are addressed. If you have received this e-mail in error please notify [the relevant person]. This e-mail contains confidential information and is intended only for the individual named. If you are not the named addressee you should not disseminate, distribute or copy this e-mail. Please notify the sender immediately by e-mail if you have received this e-mail by mistake and delete this e-mail from your system. If you are not the intended recipient you are notified that disclosing, copying, distributing or taking any action in reliance on the contents of this information is strictly prohibited.

AND WORTH ADDING...

If you are not the intended recipient of this communication, or any part of it, you may render yourself criminally liable by using the information contained in it in any way and/or communicating its contents to a third party.

ENTERING INTO CONTRACTS

No employee or agent of [your company] is authorized to conclude any binding agreement on behalf of [company] with another party by e-mail.

EMPLOYER'S LIABILITY

Any views or opinions presented in this e-mail are solely those of the author and do not necessarily represent those of the company. Employees of [company] are expressly required not to make defamatory statements and not to infringe or authorize any infringement of copyright or any other legal right by e-mail communications. Any such communication is contrary to company policy and outside the scope of the employment of the individual concerned. The company will not accept any liability in respect of such communication, and the employee responsible will be personally liable for any damages or other liability arising.

VIRUSES

WARNING: Computer viruses can be transmitted via e-mail. The recipient should check this e-mail and any attachments for the presence of viruses. The company accepts no liability for any damage caused by any virus transmitted by this e-mail. E-mail transmission cannot be guaranteed to be secure or error free as information could be intercepted, corrupted, lost, destroyed, arrive late or incomplete, or contain viruses. The sender therefore does not accept liability for any errors or omissions in the contents of this message, which arise as a result of e-mail transmission.

Warning: Although the company has taken reasonable precautions to ensure no viruses are present in this e-mail, the company cannot accept responsibility for any loss or damage arising from the use of this e-mail or attachments.

INTERCEPTION

It is not our normal practice to send reports, documents or similar confidential material by e-mail unless specifically requested to do so. If such material is sent by e-mail we can give no warranty as to its safe transmission and/or receipt, neither can we be held liable for any fraudulent/unlawful interception and subsequent use of such material by unauthorized third parties.

All of which means that by the time you have added all the relevant disclaimer information, it will be about three times as long as the average e-mail message!

Every organization must have a written policy relating to e-mail usage and abuse. As each business is different, a 'one size fits all' policy simply doesn't work. So listed below are the topics that such a policy must include – and don't forget this policy must also apply to sub-contractors, freelance workers, home workers and (subject to the exact circumstances) partners and suppliers:

- Efficient and permissible uses of e-mail: (what it can be used for).
- The fact that the organization reserves the right to monitor e-mail communications, and take action based on that monitoring.
- The rule that all communications and related information must be transmitted, stored and accessed in a confidential manner.
- Rules regarding accessing newsgroups.
- A definition of e-mail misuse which must list and define what the organization considers to be obscene, profane, racist, sexist and politically extreme. Additionally the organization must define what it would consider constitutes harassment by e-mail and what could create or add to a hostile working environment.
- A section forbidding the downloading of copyrighted images, documents or programs must be included.
- A clause concerning confidential information, and how it must not be transmitted to third parties without relevant consent, is recommended. (I'm actually not convinced that even if the relevant consent is given that information of this nature should be transmitted by e-mail.)
- A clause forbidding the use of company facilities to carry on any type of private actions or business for personal profit should appear. That being said, the definition of what private uses company e-mail can be used for is problematic. I have seen some recommendations in this area that deal with it very easily: no private e-mail. This seems to me to be both unrealistic and unworkable: for example, if a colleague in the same organization e-mails you and suggests that you meet for lunch, does this constitute personal e-mail? In a very narrow definition, yes – and that's why such tunnel vision will never work in practice.
- A rule not to download any files and/or programs without first checking such items using an approved anti-virus package.

When you have established what constitutes the organization's e-mail policy, you must then state clearly what will happen to any employee who violates it. One without the other is pointless. Again, each organization's disciplinary policy is subtly different, so it would be foolish to make too many generalizations. However, essentially, violation of your e-mail policy should be dealt with under your normal disciplinary procedure, which can result in the dismissal of the staff member(s) involved.

GIMME SHELTER

This chapter offers some hints, tips, ideas and suggestions to fight crime, fraud and risk in the digital age.

Our safety lies not in blindness, but in facing our dangers.

Johann Christoph Friedrich von Schiller (1759–1805)

There is absolutely no reason for you to read this chapter if you subscribe to any of the following excuses (sorry, reasons) for not being interested in, or implementing, digital security:

- We are not forced to do it, so we won't.
- We're no worse than anyone else.
- It is not part of our IT agenda.
- Our security is confidential information (which means we haven't got any, but don't want to admit it).
- We couldn't possibly discuss our security arrangements (usually said after those security arrangements have been substantially breached).
- No one is interested in our information.
- I don't have to worry because I never open e-mails or attachments from people I don't know.
- There are so many people on the Internet – no one will target me.

- It will never happen to me/us.
- Our security is the best in the world.
- Even if anyone breaks in (which they won't) we have nothing that could hurt us – even if it is published in full on the Web.
- It's not my responsibility – it's the board of directors'/management's/the IT department's baby.
- Somebody else in the organization (or if at home, in the family) will do it.
- When it happens, I'll be on holiday so it won't be my problem.
- We can't afford it.
- I haven't got any time to deal with this, I'm sorting out important things.
- I'm OK – when I bought my computer five years ago it came preloaded with a virus checker, and I haven't touched it since.
- No 12-year-old kid will dare to hack into my computer.
- I don't know very much about security, anyway.

I have never really subscribed to the mantra that security (of any type) is the responsibility of the board of directors and/or senior management or of the IT department, security and investigations department, the audit department – or anyone else specifically for that matter. Security should be everyone's concern and responsibility. If an organization seeks to hold one department totally responsible for digital security then their entire response to this key area will be doomed from the start. So whether you are a company director, line manager, security manager, operator or individual user the type of key issues that must concern you include, but certainly are not limited to:

- What digital security disasters are waiting to happen?
- What digital security disasters have already happened in your organization?
- What digital security disasters have happened (or are known to have happened, which is slightly different) at similar organizations or where there is a similar IT infrastructure?
- What does your organization do well in the security area? What does it do badly?
- Who are the key employees that have the best understanding of the digital security issues of your organization?
- What is the overall management stance to digital security? Among senior management, who are the supporters of security issues and who are the dissenters?

You must address these issues proactively, before you end up evaluating them in the eye of the storm of a disaster. The remainder of this chapter comprises various checklists to aid your task. However – and this is an important caveat – please do not think that these observations and suggestions are a finite list of what you must do, and if and when you have complied with each of them you will be totally safe. I hope you now realize (even if you didn't before) that risks in the digital age can change and be changed almost every nanosecond. You should therefore view the following suggestions as a bare minimum requirement, rather than a full 'belt and braces' solution.

How to create a secure organization – checklists of issues

Creating an organizational digital security culture

Creating a secure organizational environment starts at the top – it's as easy as that. Unfortunately it appears not to be as easy as that: in 2001 an Australian company, Com Tech, carried out a survey in the country that concluded that two thirds of business and decision makers in Australia say that IT security is a subject discussed at board level but then the responsibility for it is passed down to the organization's IT department. The Financial Services Authority (FSA) has already warned companies offering online services that directors and senior management must take their responsibilities more seriously or accept the responsibilities for their failures. The following questions need to be asked:

- Does your organization have a digital security policy? Has it been approved by management? Has it been implemented?
- Have you ever assessed the threats posed by digital crime? If so, how frequently do you review and update this risk assessment?
- Is there a stated procedure, which is followed, for the policy to be constantly reviewed and updated?
- Is there a digital security plan that implements the security policy?
- Are there stated policies for interfaces with external networks such as the Internet?
- Is there a digital security training plan?

- Are all staff trained in digital security, starting with their induction training?
- Is there a senior person responsible for digital security? (You can call this position what you want – as long as it exists.)
- Is there a digital security handbook? (Once again, what it is called is irrelevant.)
- Is there an organizational plan for responding to incidents? Has it ever been tested?
- Does your organization use network vulnerability scanning software to identify and qualify security threats?
- Does your organization have a sensible budget to enable the job to be done properly?

Controlling staff risks

- Are new staff vetted through references, credit checking and (if relevant) security clearance?
- Are new staff informed of digital security regulations?
- What is included in staff contracts regarding digital security, confidentiality and the procedure followed when infringements are identified?
- What procedures are in place regarding accessing internal systems and databases by staff away from their office or from home?
- Are procedures in place for staff who leave – covering, for example, return of equipment (portable computers, telephones, access cards, keys, identification badges, company credit cards), removal of system access authorities, checking files on PC. Do you conduct exit interviews?
- Are there written contracts with temporary/third party staff?
- What training (if any) do such staff have regarding digital security?
- What checking/vetting takes place regarding temporary staff? Have you established a contractual agreement for the supplier of such staff to vet them, if so you should audit the compliance of this. The bottom line is that you must have a system in place to vet such staff, as they are a particularly high risk element.
- Have you carried out due diligence checks of the company/ individual supplying temporary or third party staff?
- What type of identification badges are staff issued with? There is a school of thought (which I tend to agree with) that the worst

thing that you can do is issue a badge showing photograph, name and employee number. Staff members are prone to wander around before and after work with their badge still on and someone who really wanted to could either remove it or record the details from it. Police in some countries only show their ID number on a badge, so that they cannot be traced to their home address.

■ On a general level concerning staff risks, does the contractual agreement that staff sign include non-disclosure and non-compete clauses? Dependent on the nature of your business, you should also consider non-disclosure agreements with you partners and suppliers.

Controlling information risks

■ Does your organization have a system for classifying information so that different security measures can be applied to each class? Do you consider such categories as open, restricted, confidential and secret?
■ What access controls are applied to each different category?
■ Is confidential and secret information stored in a different program or database to open information?

Controlling software risks

■ What procedures exist for bringing data and/or software from outside of your organization?
■ Are there policies for security issues when systems are being developed?
■ Is there a procedure to monitor problems with hardware and software that your organization has installed, and is a system in place to ensure that security patches issued by developers or vendors are identified and implemented immediately?
■ What procedures are in place for the introduction of new software – particularly restricting individual users from loading new software?
■ Is there a procedure in place for evaluating the consequences on existing software and hardware by introducing new software?
■ Is there a routine for installing new software?
■ Is the access to system tools restricted and logged?

- Is critical software backed up and stored offsite?
- Is anti-virus software installed, automatically run daily and updated constantly?
- What due diligence is carried out on suppliers of software, particularly when they are previously unknown?
- Are extensive security tests carried out when software is developed in-house? Most security problems come from design and coding errors – not security specific features. Such tests will almost certainly be labour intensive and time consuming – but worth it in the end.
- What policies and procedures do you have in place regarding the use of pirated software? If it is discovered that you are running illegal copies of programs your organization may be fined and at the very least it will be extremely embarrassing.

Controlling hardware risks

- Are there procedures in place for bringing hardware into your organization from outside?
- Are there procedures in place for disposing of hardware, particularly in relation to clearing out effectively all information/data files?
- What rules exist in respect of private use of equipment?
- Are security controls included when specifying or purchasing new hardware?

Controlling risk through documentation

This is a key area that is sometimes ignored, but however unsexy it is, documented policies, procedures and checks are a critical area of digital security.

- Are systems and routines well documented?
- Are there procedure/control manuals covering hardware, software development and applications, communications and networks?
- Are all of your documents up to date and kept up to date?
- Do written rules exist covering staff responsibilities and authorities?
- Do you have a written plan documenting the steps to be taken when an incident occurs?

Controlling risk through physical security

You should not forget the obvious basic security tenets regarding the protection of physical and human assets.

- How are premises protected? Do you have relevant alarms and CCTV facilities?
- Are critical IT hardware facilities in a separate access controlled area?
- Do you have dedicated communication lines, which are protected? If you do not is the physical access to communications line secured?
- Do you carry out regular electronic sweeps of premises to ensure that no 'bugs', other listening devices and other offensive hardware are present?
- What type of entry and exit procedures do you have and what, if any, logs of such movements are there?
- If your physical assets were destroyed or severely damaged would you have a completely up-to-date backup offsite, so that all information could immediately be reconstituted? Digital data is actually far more robust than paper files: the latter can perish, burn, be lost or stolen.
- Are your systems and the information contained in them so critical that it warrants setting up a mirror system in a completely separate physical location?

Controlling risk through authentication, authorization, administration and audit procedures

In non-technical terms, authentication establishes who system users are; authorization establishes what each user can do; administration is the physical processes needed to ensure that users have access to the appropriate resources, and audit is the process of establishing what happened (or didn't).

- Do you have an authorization system that encompasses both users and resources?
- Does the system incorporate logging and alarm functions?
- What rules are in place regarding length and composition of passwords and PINs? (It should be mandatory that passwords cannot be less than six digits and must include both letters and numbers).

- Does the system allow reuse of old user IDs, passwords or PINs? (It shouldn't).
- Are there routines to automatically prompt users to change passwords at defined intervals?
- Is the default password on software packages automatically changed?
- Does the system restrict the number of log in attempts?
- Can users change their own access privileges?
- Do user IDs, passwords and PINs belong to individuals as opposed to groups, teams or departments?
- Are all these issues regularly audited and strict time periods enforced for suitable remedial action to be implemented?

EDUCATING YOUR USERS – AND THAT INCLUDES YOU

One of the most common complaints that I hear is that induction or ongoing training relating to hardware and software involves the box the equipment of software comes in being opened, installed and then the user being told to get on with it. Even worse is the user who knows something about technology – and as soon as his or her (though it's usually his) new toy is installed he or she cannot help but play with it incessantly. Of course this user has no need to read the manual, or be trained because he or she knows it all already. All users should be issued with guidelines as to their responsibilities: these should be signed and returned to the employer. At the very least, they give a basis on which to pursue disciplinary action when it all goes horribly wrong. Additionally users cannot claim ignorance. But remember – these guidelines also apply to you (and are equally applicable to home users, SMEs and one person businesses). The list below is by no means exhaustive, but provides a good starting point.

- The employer has an obligation to ensure that all users are fully trained in the operation of all hardware and software that they are required to use. This training will include information on security aspects.
- Users must not use any hardware without permission.
- Users must not attempt to access information, databases, systems and/or networks that they do have authorization to access.

- No hardware or software must be used for personal business without permission.
- If a user thinks that a virus exists on any piece of hardware, or any suspicious events have taken place on any hardware (or in relation to any equipment or software), he or she must report it to a designated person immediately.
- Users must not disclose any information held on digital systems to any third parties.
- Users must not disclose or share their password, user ID or any other similar items.
- Users must not use anyone else's password, user ID or similar item.
- Users must follow the organization's procedures regarding e-mail and Internet usage (which should be separate documents or appendices to this one).
- Users must not leave a computer unattended that is logged on to any system or network.

Having an incident response plan

- Be sure to record each and every action that you take, together with the date and time.
- You should discover and preserve evidence – it may seem irrelevant at the time, but you have no way of knowing what relevance/importance it may have.
- Remember that you should be always thinking about internal disciplinary procedures (if staff are involved) or criminal prosecution.
- When you discover a problem, notify relevant senior personnel immediately.
- You should limit the scope of the problem immediately.
- You must preserve all relevant documentation and audit logs.
- You must consider quickly what additional security measures should be taken immediately.
- Do you know which law enforcement authorities you should contact following an incident?

Preventing online fraud if you trade online

If you sell products or services online, you will be ripped off, period. This applies whether you are a large global banking organization or a one person business selling your wares to a new untapped international audience. If you sell online and accept credit cards (these two concepts go almost hand in hand) you will be hit by charge backs by credit card companies – so the risks are not theoretical, they go straight to your bottom line. Bear the following in mind:

- Beware of different billing and shipping/delivery addresses – many online suppliers refuse to deliver to anything other than the address on the credit card. If you must deliver to another address, at the very least get a signed authorization via fax before processing the order.
- Although this somewhat contradicts the whole point of the Internet, be both suspicious and cautious when sending goods overseas – if the order is fraudulent you will never get your money back.
- Many online merchants or service providers now do not accept orders from free, Web based or e-mail forwarding address. They insist on an ISP or domain based address – the logic being that such an address can be traced back to a real person. Some merchants physically check the domain names given to filter out any further free e-mail addresses that do not appear to be that at first site (the antifraud.com Web site has a long list of free e-mail domains and Web based non-ISP domains).
- Ask for phone and fax numbers, making them mandatory fields on any order forms. If in doubt, do the most basic thing by phoning the customer up. This can have various outcomes: you call a genuine customer thus you have achieved your objective; you call the genuine cardholder but he or she knows nothing about the order; or you call someone on the number given who has never heard of the 'cardholder'.
- Install syntax that enables you to record the IP address of the customer, so that you at least have somewhere to start if you need to trace him or her.

Securing your home computer

The information and data that is most precious, confidential and important to you will almost certainly be on your home PC or laptop: it is thus critically important that you secure these assets. Take this advice:

■ Never forget the obvious: computer thefts (particularly of laptops) are prevalent, so exercise care with these valuable pieces
of equipment. The thief may be only interesting in the hardware
itself, not the contents of it – but this is little consolation to you
when you lose all of your personal files.

■ If you work at home for an organization ensure that you are
aware of, and comply with, any policies and procedures that they
have in relation to IT equipment and software in remote sites.
You should also check their policies and procedures on the storing
of their confidential information on home computers.

■ Install anti-virus software and ensure that it is kept continually
up to date (see the Web directory of this book for excellent free
programs for personal use).

■ Back up your data regularly and then keep the backup in a
separate secure place.

■ Install a firewall and then ensure that it is kept continually up to
date (again, see the Web directory of this book for excellent free
programs for personal use).

■ Use a BIOS password and a screen saver password to prevent
unauthorized access to your confidential information.

■ Don't open unknown e-mail attachments – various viruses have
been distributed in this way, and no doubt will be in the future.

■ Do not use or distribute programs when their origins are unknown
to you.

■ Make sure that all your applications – particularly your application system – are kept up to date with the latest patches (easier
said than done, I know!).

■ If possible, when not in use, turn your computer off and/or
disconnect it from the network and/or Internet. If you are not
on the Internet, or your computer is turned off totally, no intruder
can gain access to it.

■ Make certain that you have a boot disk or recovery disk, so if
you suffer a catastrophic failure then with this and your backup
disc you can start again.

■ Change passwords on Internet sites frequently (very few Web
sites request you to do this as a matter of course once you have
signed up with them). Don't share your passwords with co-
workers, friends or even family – this could have horrendous
consequences if, as an example, money is removed from your
online bank account.

- Be careful about giving your credit card details over the Internet – unless you know who you are dealing with you could be sending your details straight to a fraudster or transmitting them across the ether with no security. Only give your credit card details to a site that uses encryption.

Securing your Web site

I am not a technical expert (as you might have gathered) and thus this section probably stretches my technical knowledge as far as it goes. The critical issue, though, is that most individuals and companies that operate Web sites leave the security of that site to the hosting provider, which is evidently a mistaken reliance, as the provider will not get attacked or defrauded, you will! Thus you must consider:

- Can your data be accessible to other users of the Web server?
- Are the external and internal firewalls of the Web hosting company configured correctly so that an attack can be recognized and responded to?
- Does the Web hosting company continuously monitor (and act upon) information about vulnerabilities?
- What tools does the Web hosting company use to monitor their network?
- What levels of physical security does the Web hosting company have? Online security is pointless if an attacker can get to your Web site easily from the premises of the company.
- Does your Web hosting company have clearly defined policies, procedures and standards for digital security? Do you get a copy of such documents?

E-mail security

As I write this, there have been some examples, particularly in the United States, of anthrax spores being delivered by normal terrestrial mail. E-mail, which has always been perceived as a notorious insecure way of communicating, has suddenly become a very sensible and secure (in a wider sense) method of getting a message across. I'm sure that all users would rather have a computer virus than a killer bacterial disease. Nevertheless, the new reliance on e-mail (which may have two diametrically opposite conclusions by either fading away or becoming the norm) makes lax e-mail security even more critical.

- Does your organization have a policy for e-mail use by employees and what constitutes abuse?
- Do all your organization's e-mails automatically include a disclaimer stating that the contents of the e-mail are the views and opinions of the sender and not necessarily those the company?
- Are employees instructed not to share e-mail passwords?
- Is what is acceptable e-mail use defined? Examples are business messages to co-workers, customers and suppliers together with short personal messages.
- Do you define exactly what unacceptable e-mail usage is? Examples are those involving personal business activities of staff, distributing chain letters or any messages containing lewd, harassing, offensive and/or pornographic material.
- Are your staff trained to realize that e-mails can be used as evidence in legal cases and thus any terms that imply or confirm slander, defamation and/or discrimination of any kind must be avoided?
- Are your staff trained to ensure that inappropriate messages, which could cause embarrassment for the organization and/or individual, are avoided? Remember the special advisor to a UK government minister who sent an e-mail on the afternoon of September 11 2001 suggesting that this would be a good day to release 'bad' news relating to the government's activities as it would be 'buried'.
- What are your procedures regarding sending confidential material and information by e-mail?
- What instructions do you have in place regarding deletion of e-mails?
- Are all users running an up-to-date virus checker that checks both incoming and outgoing e-mails and their attachments?

Minimizing losses when you buy online

As we have seen, you should not take at face value anything that appears on an individual' or company's Web site. The Internet does not confer any validity whatsoever on any Web sites located on it. Thus the advice to avoid fraudsters on the Internet operating scam Web sites is identical to the guidelines for avoiding suffering a fraud attack in general. The main points (already given in Chapter 5) bear repeating here along with some more advice:

- When you access a Web site of any unknown person and/or organization to establish any new business relationship you must validate that person's or organization's claims and history.
- Never forget: if any deal of offer appears to be too good to be true, turn it down – because it is.
- There are no such things as 'once in a lifetime opportunities' or 'guaranteed returns on investments' when the figures guaranteed are astronomical.
- Be suspicious.
- Question all transactions.
- Jealously guard all your personal and/or business information such as bank account details, credit card numbers.
- Don't sign any document before you have had it checked out – and don't agree to anything online or by e-mail until you have similarly had it checked out.
- Find out if the individual or company exists, and is registered with the necessary regulators or licensing authority.
- Find out how long the individual or company has been trading – who are the principals?
- Check out the filings of the subject company – it might be registered somewhere, but is it trading? If so does its financial status in any way reflect the deal being offered?
- Check out addresses and contact details of those approaching you (it still surprises me how many of these people use dead lines or business centres).
- Validate any documents presented for authenticity.
- Ask for references – but don't take them at face value.
- Ask for a prospectus and brochure.
- Carry out a media and Internet search on the individuals concerned.
- Don't pay for anything upfront unless you've dealt with the person/company before and know that the person/company is reputable.
- Don't be afraid to say 'No'.
- Don't be rushed – one key factor in many of these frauds is that the criminals try to rush you, usually saying that you must act quickly to take advantage of the unique opportunity.
- The Internet may be a great medium to promote fraud, but it is also a brilliantly effective way to search for information and detail on fraudsters. You may be surprised by what you find by searching – details of earlier investors who have lost money, for

example, or investigations that are going on into the company/ individual that is offering you the wonderful investment opportunity. I recommend searching on Dogpile, Google and Northern Light at the very least. Additionally it is fairly simple to confirm the owner of the domain name of the Web site you are dealing with; if it is a site on a free Web hosting provider, think very carefully about proceeding any further.

- If you have any doubt whatsoever, walk away – even if you are continually pressured to sign on the dotted line. (In fact, particularly if you are pressured to sign on the dotted line.)

Real time advice

Many – if not all – of the suggestions contained in this section are in broad terms, and I hope they will prompt you to examine the level of digital security present in your organization (whatever its size) and home. Yet the real way to combat digital crime, fraud and risk is in the fine detail: particularly where system vulnerabilities and intrusions are concerned. This is where it can get difficult for the mainstream user, as frequently the technical explanations and fixes resemble a now dead foreign language. One crucial resource, which does not rely on jargon or blinding you with science, is the SANS Institute (www.sans. org). Its Web site contains the SANS Institute/National Infrastructure Protection Center (NIPC) critical Internet security vulnerabilities list. As the site itself states, this schedule is a living document which is constantly updated. In November 2001 the site contained lists of Top 20 vulnerabilities split into three categories: general vulnerabilities, Windows vulnerabilities and Unix vulnerabilities. The site also gives step-by-step instructions and links to counter the problems. At the time of writing the top general vulnerabilities which comprise the first seven entries on the list were as follows:

- Default installs of operating systems and applications. In other words, when you install software the vendor makes it as easy as possible for the user, but by doing so more components than are needed are installed; these just sit on your system like open doors waiting for a visit from an intruder. Many of us almost certainly have no idea what programs are installed on our system, or if we do know this, we still are not fully aware of all of the components of each piece of software. Thus we do not maintain everything we have installed, and ignore any patches that are released. Every extra service or program provides another tool for an attacker.

- Accounts with no passwords or weak passwords. How many times can this obvious defect be repeated? The key vulnerability are accounts with easy to guess passwords, default passwords or no passwords at all. Any of these will be targeted by would be attackers. Among the remedies suggested is that you run a password cracking tool to determine just what weak or non-existent passwords are lurking on your system.

- Non-existent or incomplete backups. Think that you'll never need a backup version of all of your data? Think again: but even if you do back up regularly, do you ever check that the backup that you religiously perform every day (or week) actually works? Do you have procedures in place to restore the backup information? A further interesting (but often overlooked point) is that all of your confidential information is contained on the backup – so do you protect this information in the same way as the original? The key recommendation is to take backups daily.

- Large number of open ports. Open ports do, obviously, have legitimate uses – predominantly for legitimate users to access the system; but the more ports that you have open the more likely it is that an authorized person will access it too.

- Not filtering packets for correct incoming and outgoing addresses. It starts to get technical: but as we have seen, one of the methods used by attackers to disguise themselves is to spoof IP addresses. It is possible to filter both incoming and outgoing traffic on a network. While this will not solve all of the problems, it will give a high degree of protection.

- Non-existent or incomplete logging. In non-technical terms it's called keeping a record; in slightly technical terms it's (basically) called an audit trail. In essence a log records what has happened on your system – without it you are doomed, because you have no idea what happened in an attack, and thus you may be running a system that is now controlled by the attacker. Logs show what has happened, which systems are being attacked and which systems are being compromised. And one other crucial thing – go back to the third bullet point above, and back up your logs.

- Vulnerable common gateway interface (CGI) programs. Most Web servers are installed with sample CGI programs which provides a direct link from any user anywhere on the Internet to the operating system of the computer running the Web server. Such security loopholes are popular with intruders who have used them to deface Web sites, fraudulently obtain credit card information and establish back door entrances for future use.

And if the worst still happens. . .

Even if you action everything suggested in this chapter that is relevant to your operations and activities you will still not necessarily be secure. Somewhat perversely if you do everything you can there still remain problems – the major factor being the psychological one that you will begin to feel secure, but remember:

- Anti-virus software will make you safe: true, but only up to a point. It will protect against most viruses, but is worse than useless if it is not updated. Even then you may be retrospectively scanning for viruses that are already present. A real example of this happened to me: one of my PCs was running an up-to-date anti-virus program (one of the most well known ones, in fact). We decided to switch to new anti-virus software. As we booted up the PC it went no further – the new software immediately informed us that we had a virus, and it had been there for a few months.
- Firewall software will secure your system: true, but again only up to a point. Firewalls do offer a considerable degree of protection, but even they cannot protect you against every type and class of attack.
- The government/police/legal system will secure your computer and assets: no they won't and you can't rely on them in any way.

All of this may appear very daunting, if not downright impossible to deal with – but it is totally necessary. It is to be hoped that you will never suffer a serious digital attack, particularly one which will have serious repercussions on your reputation. Unfortunately even if you or your organization devote a substantial amount of time, effort and budget to these security issues, there are no guarantees that you will avoid being attacked.

If you are the subject of a major attack it is important that you realize that even if you/your organization has both an incident response plan and dedicated team to deal with the problem, you will almost certainly experience distinct phases of behaviour. Moreover, it is crucial to realize that a serious digital attack is no longer a technology problem, but a business crisis. Thus, while the technological response may be to ensure that any gaping holes in security are plugged to avoid recurrence, the general business objectives will be far wider and, at that particular stage, more important. The focus of these business activities will be on a combination of:

- Ensuring that any damage to the organization's reputation is minimized.
- Recovering stolen funds and information.
- If the matter has been reported to law enforcement agencies, ensuring that the perpetrators are brought to justice.
- Dealing with human resource and personnel issues if it is suspected or proven that staff members have been involved.

To understand the dynamic of a such an event and its results one should split it into four distinct phases. Let's look at each in turn.

The warning phase

The action taken on discovery of an attack or serious security breach is crucial – because if it goes wrong it can take hours, days, months or even years to undo. Some common mistakes are:

- Ignoring warning signs, suspicions or tip-offs.
- Doing nothing.
- Doing something but still placing blind faith in suspect staff members.
- Telling the individuals involved that they are suspects or being investigated – and then leaving them in place.
- Showing suspects material evidence.
- Destroying or tampering with evidence.
- Telling everybody that an attack has taken place.

It's no good either waiting for a fraud to happen or making it up as you go along. It is at this stage that your incident response plan comes into its own.

The acute phase

There are various decisions to be made in this phase of a crisis, some of which are fundamental. Do you report the event to law enforcement agencies? (This is the point where you find out if you have a policy on this topic that will be followed.) Is it worth going after the perpetrators? What legal action is required in respect of recovering funds/information or in respect of staff members suspected of being involved? Another key issue will entail assessing the risks to reputation of bad publicity. Media coverage is a guaranteed element of a digital crime if it is large or interesting (sex and crime are dynamic combinations for example). Moreover there is an ever-growing feeding frenzy for more and more news to satisfy both newsreaders and gatherers. It is relevant to realize that any event of this type carries with it the almost certain guarantee of a knock-on disaster, which could be more catastrophic than the fraud itself – media coverage, bad publicity and the inevitable long term fallout. Don't forget that bad publicity is 24 hour and global – as soon as any bad press goes on the Internet the whole world knows and containment is not an option. Unfortunately when dealing with reputational issues there is no middle ground – you either get it right or you don't. Thus don't wait to be asked – prepare your response in an open and honest manner stressing the decisive action that was taken when the event was discovered – or even better when YOU discovered it because of your robust and effective controls. Above all don't freeze – manage the dynamic and grasp it as an opportunity by recognizing a problem exists and taking quick decisions.

The clean-up phase

If staff members are involved in a criminal event then one of the prime objectives is to ensure that direct reoccurrences are eradicated. This can only be achieved if staff members involved are removed from the organization. In the UK dismissal can be achieved on 'the balance of probabilities' – the burden of proof is much less than that required in a criminal case. The disciplinary process should not only be brought to bear on those identified as being responsible for the fraud but also those staff members who may have assisted or exhibited contributory negligence.

The clean-up phase may entail becoming involved in a lengthy multi-jurisdictional police investigation and subsequent criminal prosecution. However, many organizational victims fear adverse publicity and conclude that if staff offenders have been dismissed they have been punished and future offences (*against that organization*) have been prevented. That stance is fine if the crime is confined to the organization's own staff, but if outsiders are involved there can be no alternative but to report the event to law enforcement authorities (let them take the decision on prosecution!). From my experience you can't expect cooperation from law enforcement authorities if you haven't made extensive efforts to police your own organization. It must be appreciated that criminal prosecutions are lengthy and time consuming with no guarantee of success. Two key factors that mitigate against a quick fix in terms of law enforcement investigation of digital crime cases are the technical complexity of such events combined with the possible complications of multi-jurisdictional matters – the danger is they 'disappear into a black hole'.

During this phase the amendments to hardware and software flaws identified by this attack will be achieved, after suitable testing.

The resolution phase

I have no idea what would constitute a successful resolution of a digital attack or related event. Some organizations would see it as their chief priority to avoid negative publicity and damage to reputation. On the other hand, the attack may be so catastrophic that the only objective is to recover funds because otherwise the company would go under. Other victim organizations may conclude that what is required is to bring those responsible to justice (which is far easier said than done). Another strong possibility is that if money or information is lost than the organization may face adverse litigation from customers, suppliers, shareholders or any other concerned parties who have suffered what they contend to be material loss. Just as likely, if the organization is officially regulated, is the probability of enforcement action by the relevant regulatory body. Obviously running underneath all these business implications is the need to resolve the technical issues that led to the problem in the first place. Some difficult decisions may have to be taken very quickly – if it cannot be guaranteed that you can eradicate the problems that caused the current predicament you may have no alternative but to shut down the product, service or access facility in which the problem surfaced. However, this could have catastrophic consequences. For example, if you run a sizeable online banking operation, and you have just lost millions in a digital attack in this area (involving the removal of funds from the accounts of innocent customers), could you seriously afford to shut down the entire operation? Just think of the bad press, not to mention the fact that none of your genuine customers would be able to access their funds.

In an ideal world the factors comprising a successful resolution of such a crisis would include:

- Recovery of stolen funds.
- Recovery of stolen information and data (and establishing what use such information was put to, where it was circulated and any other third parties who received copies of it).
- Identification of those responsible and successful criminal action against all participants – not just the low level operators.
- Minimal publicity, or if publicity is unavoidable, making sure that it is sympathetic to the victim organization.
- Successfully managing adverse reaction by staff, suppliers and, most importantly, customers (particularly – which is highly probable – when their money or information has been obtained by third parties).
- Quickly fixing the security lapses that occurred, and thus ensuring that the particular problem encountered can never recur.

Finally, don't forget that all of these comments in this section don't only apply to large organizations. They are equally applicable to organizations of any size – from government departments through charities to self-employed individuals.

SOME FINAL THOUGHTS. . .

> *Time has been transformed, and we have changed; it has advanced*
> *and set us in motion; it has unveiled its face, inspiring us with*
> *bewilderment and exhilaration.*
>
> *Kahlil Gibran*

> *You can never plan the future by the past.*
>
> *Edmund Burke*

We are now past the talismanic date of 2001 but no technology has
yet usurped its human creators. In many ways, the limits of technology
are now being realized. Certainly in the business world one obvious
constraining force constantly appears – that of financial viability.
Attempt to log on to excite.co.uk and you now find a blank screen
that regrets to inform you that www.excite.co.uk is no longer available;
Northern Light announced in January 2002 that it was refining its
business focus and would be discontinuing providing free Web
searches to the general public. In the wider world, the repercussions
of the events of September 11 2001 still echo. Corporate spending on
technology in 2001 was already well down on the previous year; this
trend was exacerbated after the terrorist attacks. Spending on security

183

has in the past become one of the first casualties when businesses tighten their money belts. Against this perceived wisdom is the possibility that after September 11 2001 we are in unchartered territory. Perhaps those events will facilitate both a recovery in technology spending and re-emphasis of the need for both digital security and digital tools to improve security in other business areas.

In the meantime things go on very much as normal: various end of year reviews for 2001 listed the worst digital hoaxes, problems, spams (or whatever you wish to call them). Such lists were uniformly a roll-call of the known, bad and ugly:

- Computer viruses and, just as prevalent, phony virus e-mails.
- E-mail messages soliciting donations for fraudulent charities. In a chilling demonstration of how sick some of these are, they were particularly common after September 11 2001, with various false claims for donations for victims and related charities.
- Fraudulent e-mails that claim to be from famous figures or organizations which out of the blue want to give you great riches. Too good to be true? You bet! So if you open your PC one morning and get an unsolicited e-mail from Bill Gates, Walt Disney Jr, AOL, the Gap (or anybody or thing similar) making such an offer, just press the delete button.
- Anything (virtually) from Nigeria. The whole range of stupidity from Nigeria has already defrauded victims out of more than US $5 billion: make sure that your hard-earned cash doesn't add to this total.

Added to all of this is the anticipation that viruses and worms will be additionally moving out of your PC and visiting mobile devices, pocket PCs and WAP/Smart phones. At the moment it is estimated that less than 5 per cent of wireless devices have anti-virus software, but many can be easily plugged into your PC. Experts are also concerned about new possibilities for transferring malicious code by text messaging on mobile phones. Added to this are hidden dangers in seemingly innocuous pastimes such as downloading ring tones for mobile phones (particularly where these are pirated versions).

The launch of the Microsoft XP operating system in 2001 also had a certain air of predictability. On December 20, Microsoft admitted that an inherent flaw allowed 'attackers to execute arbitrary code' on a PC running windows XP that is connected to the Internet. In plain English, hackers can enter your PC and roam at will: read your files, erase them, plant programs – you name it. Microsoft issued a warning that was headed 'Maximum Severity Rating: Critical', which urged users to download a software patch which would fix the problem and close the equivalent of an open door to your PC. Just one minor problem: the FBI's National Infrastructure Protection Center warned that the cure-all patch was actually insufficient.

And if all of this (and all that has gone before) doesn't give you sleepless nights than perhaps the sudden demise on January 22 2002 of Cloud Nine, an Internet service provider in Basingstoke, UK might just do so. In their own words, this is what happened to them:

> *Cloud Nine regret to announce that at 7:45 this morning the decision was taken to shut down our Internet connections with immediate effect.*

> *We tried overnight to bring our Web servers back online but were seeing denial of service attacks against all our key servers, including e-mail and DNS. These were of an extremely widespread nature.*

> *We felt we had a moral duty not to expose our customers to possible attacks as well.*

> *We must thank BT for all the help they provided us with, in trying to bring these attacks to an end. We worked with them for the last few weeks to investigate these problems but ultimately we did not believe that we could survive these attacks and that it would be in the best interests of both ourselves and our customers to close our Internet service and seek a transfer of our services to another ISP.*

> *We want to thank our customers for all the support over the last few days. Ultimately these attacks denied the service not to us but to many thousands of British businesses and ordinary people – this was an attack against everyone with no consideration for anyone!*

> *The company is solvent but if a sale of assets cannot take place quickly then an administrator will be appointed. We have had to pay our excellent staff to the end of the month and we feel really sorry for them as well and would like to thank them for all their efforts over the years and the commitment shown over the last few difficult days.*

> *All the directors are feeling absolutely gutted since we have all spent nearly 6 years building this company and its reputation to see it*

> *destroyed by a brazen act of cyber terrorism – well at this moment*
> *we can think of no words to express our true feelings.*

> *(Taken from a posting by Cloud Nine on ISP Review)*

Cloud Nine is merely an example of how digital attacks can destabilize – or ultimately destroy – a business. There have already been numerous other similar instances with, I suspect, many more to follow. The now defunct UK digital television provider ITN Digital had various problems including an estimated 100,000 pirate subscriber cards in circulation. To access the system a user needed a card to decode the signal. However the relevant encryption codes had been broken and publicised on the Internet (where else?). Additionally it has been estimated that another 100,000 legitimate customers had fraudulently upgraded their subscriptions using these codes.

Digital crime may not have the awful human consequences of terrorism, but in many ways this is a distinct advantage for those perpetrating it, in that they can successfully go about their business invisibly. The digital world is a globally unified one, which still has no regulatory or law enforcement controls. National intergovernmental agencies seem unable (or unwilling) to cooperate with one another. Industry has an uneasy alliance with government in this arena; Software and hardware manufacturers, on many occasions, appear to be blissfully (and irresponsibly) ignorant of the severe security flaws in the products that they are keen to sell us; there is very little regular cooperation on an international basis between law enforcement agencies; even if there was, no global legislation exists. Meanwhile many of us are heavily reliant on the global economy and the digital world – beginning each day by logging onto the Internet and checking our e-mail. In doing this we are entering a world which, in April 2002, the UK Department of Trade and Industry (DTI estimated could be costing UK firms £10 billion a year in losses due to digital attacks. After all of this, perhaps the Dark Avenger was right after all with his advice. Ladies and gentleman, welcome to the most important criminal arena of the 21st Century.

GLOSSARY

Access control   Essentially the feature in a system that allows or denies individual users, or groups of users, access to that system or parts of it. Access control should control each user in respect of what rights he or she has to read, amend and save records and/or data.

Altair 8080   A DIY computer kit in the United States, which came onto the market in March 1975. Selling for US $400 it was highly influential in suggesting the possibilities of a PC.

Analogue (analog – US)   The opposite of digital and now something of a condescending term. It refers to electronic transmission accomplished by adding signals of varying frequency or amplitude to carrier waves of a given frequency of alternating electromagnetic current. Broadcast and phone transmission have conventionally used analog technology. In a type of reverse reaction to the Digital Age, some performers and users have made the point of their continued use of analog technology.

Anonymity   A situation where you leave no trace or trail of your electronic activity on the Internet – particularly in respect of e-communication.

Anonymous remailer   Anonymous remailers wash e-mail, removing any identifying information such as the sender's name, address or any other personal details.

ATARI   Before Playstation there was Atari, a US company that dominated the computer game market in the early 1980s but then was overtaken by Sega and other similar companies.

Audit trail   Also known as investigative trail. In auditing terms a paper trail that confirms and validates a transaction and/or accounting entries. Thus if someone transfers money from one bank account to another the audit trail should include an authority from the customer, a confirmation that the transaction has been keyed and verification that the money has gone to the correct destination (from the right place). An audit trail should also record unauthorized activity – such as attempts within an organization to illegally access databases or systems.

Authentification   The process whereby an individual is identified, usually by a username and password. It is not the same as authorization, which is where individuals are given access rights to a system.

Backdoor   Also Trapdoor. As the name implies, a 'secret' or hidden entrance to a system or application built in by the designer and ostensibly left in place for testing or 'troubleshooting' reasons.

Bandwidth   In basic terms, how much data can be crammed onto a network. The wider the bandwidth, the greater amount of information that is available within the shorter time, so the more bandwidth you have the better if you want to listen to music, download quickly or watch streaming images on the Internet. Conversely the availability of greater bandwidth in certain countries (predominantly the United States) has facilitated more complex Web sites, which of course are impossible to access when bandwidth is at a minimum in less developed countries.

Biometrics   The study of measurable biological characteristics – which have been translated in computer security techniques as the automatic checking of such characteristics as fingerprints, speech and the retina. Biometrics has been the staple fare of science fiction films for the last 30 years (at least) and has been widely touted as the future of digital security, but has never quite made it on any high volume usage.

Broadband   In basic terms a transmission medium that is capable of carrying signals from multiple carriers on a single coaxial or fibre optic cable. Broadband can be used to transmit data, voice and video.

Browser   A software program developed for navigating the Internet, particularly the World Wide Web.

Bug   An error in the source code of program, which means that errors or unexpected results occur.

Byte   Basic unit of measurement for pieces of information.

Cache   The portion of the PC memory that is set aside for temporary storage such as Web sites that have been recently accessed.

Carnivore   The controversial FBI system that monitors e-mails and other traffic through ISPs. Also known as DCS1000.

CERN   Counseil Europeen pour la Recherche Nucleaire, based in Geneva, Switzerland. Now synonymous with the birth of the World Wide Web in 1989.

CD ROM   Essentially the same medium as a compact disc, but able to store up to 450 times as much data as a floppy disk.

CD-R   Compact disc recordable: a blank compact disc that can be written to, but not rewritten. This medium has become very popular for copying music CDs, but can also be used for storing data. In both cases the disc can be left 'open' so that additional files (or music tracks) can be added until the disk is finished or full. Discs normally hold up to 80 minutes of music or 700 MB of information.

CD-RW   Compact disc rewritable: in essence the same as a CD-R but with the capability to delete and rewrite information, thus to be used repeatedly.

Cookie   Information that a Web site places on your hard drive which can have various uses including recording information about where you go on the site; which language version of the site you want; rotating banner ads so that they do not repeat; allowing you to access certain information without the need to log in.

Cracker   A term devised by original hackers to distance themselves from later operators who broke into computer systems to obtain information, primarily for financial gain.

Critical infrastructure(s)   What drives the developed world: vital systems that are to some degree interdependent. Such systems are critical to the operation of national (and by inference in a global connected world) international economies and governments. Typically these comprise systems relating to defence, telecommunications, energy, financial services, manufacturing, water, transportation, health care, emergency services and governmental functions.

Cyberspace   Term coined by William Gibson in his 1984 novel *Necromancer* – but during the 1990s the influential Gibson seemed to rue his creation of this term when he commented 'They'll never let me forget it'. Essentially the space between pieces of connected hardware – phones, computers, networks, people.

Cyber stalking   Defined by the United States National Center for Victims of Crime as 'threatening behavior or unwanted advances directed at another using the Internet and other forms of online communication'.

Data integrity Refers to the validity and correctness of data held on computer. There are numerous ways in which data integrity can be compromised: keying errors; hardware malfunctions; natural or manmade disasters; errors when data is transmitted, updated or amended; bugs and viruses; cyber attacks.

Data packet The format in which data is transmitted over a network (including the Internet). The packet contains the data itself, addresses and anything other information to ensure that it ends up at the right place in one piece.

Decrypt The opposite of encrypt – to unscramble encrypted information.

Denial of service attacks These target systems, trying to make them inaccessible to legitimate users. Such attacks do not attempt to obtain credit card or other confidential data but they do attempt to make the system/computer crash or become so busy processing data that it is impossible to use. Also referred to as main bombs.

Digital In computer terms, digital refers to any system that is based on discontinuous data or events. Computers, for example, are digital because they can only distinguish between on and off or one and zero. All digital data must be encoded as a series on ones and zeroes. Ironically much of the Digital Age relies on conversion from analogue to digital and vice versa: modems convert digital information to an analogue signals for phone line transmission (and the other way around for incoming data); CDs store analogue forms (music) in a digital form, but when they are played the CD player reconverts the information back into analogue form so that we can listen to it.

Domain name A term relating to the Internet which identified one or more IP address. Domain names are used to identify specific Web pages. For example, in the www.proximalconsulting.com/index, the domain name is proximalconsulting.com. Every domain name has a suffix, which denotes which domain it belongs to. Originally these were limited to top level domains:

.gov – government agencies
.edu – educational institutions
.org – organizations (non-profit originally, but now commercial as well)
.mil – military
.com – commercial business
.net – network organizations

However the growth of the Internet has meant that numerous domain extensions or country domain extensions have been created (see Appendix 4).

DVD Digital versatile disc or digital video disc. Discs that hold between 4.7GB and 17GB, and thus have become very popular as a medium to buy prerecorded movies. They have excellent sound and vision quality using MPEG-2. DVD players are also backward compatible – they can play CD ROMs, CD-I disks, and video CD (newer DVD players can also play CD-Rs). Recordable DVD players are now available – at a price. From a counterfeiting point of view such equipment is a dream come true – as it gives perfect digital copies of any legitimate film already available on DVD.

Echelon The multi-nation cyber surveillance system that may or may not exist. If it does exist, we are still not certain what form it takes and what it is capable of. At worst it may be able to monitor every item of electronic communication.

Elint Electronic intelligence.

E-mail Electronic mail: a system for sending and receiving notes, memos, documents, images, sound files (you name it) between users across the Internet.

Encryption In simple terms, the translation/conversion of data into a secret code, thus achieving data security. Encryption is a subject that has become extremely complicated but perhaps should be viewed as the sending of coded messages. To decode (or decrypt) and thus access the data you must have the relevant key or password. Unencrypted data is known as plain text; cipher text is the term used for encrypted data. The two main types of encryption are asymmetric encryption, or public-key/symmetric encryption.

Firewall In non-technology terms, as the name implies, a firewall is a specially designed, constructed and positioned wall that stops (or at least controls) the spread of a fire. In computing terms a firewall is a device that controls the spread of a network threat. These days the highest threat comes courtesy of the Internet, where individuals wish to access networks and harm them. But a firewall can also regulate traffic within the network of the same company as well as protect the network from attacks originating on the Internet. For example, within a company a firewall can let department A access the files of department B, but prevent department B from accessing the files of department A. A firewall can consist of software, hardware or a combination of both.

Floppy disk   Also known as a diskette. The original 5.25 inch diskettes really were floppy hence the name. The smaller 3.5 inch disks have a storage capacity of 1.44 Mb, and are now too small to contain most single programs. They have therefore been replaced and superceded by CD-ROMs.

FTP   File transfer protocol. The protocol used for sending files across the Internet, mostly used for uploading pages to a Web site.

Future shock   A term coined by Alan Toffler in 1965, included in an influential book he published in 1970 about the reactions and problems of the rapid technological change that had occurred since the Second World War. The term has now passed into common usage and is used in many contexts (including forming the title of a Curtis Mayfield song).

Gigabyte(Gb)   Unit of measurement of data storage: approximately 1 billion bytes.

GSM   Global system for mobile communications, the standard defined by the European Telecommunications Standards Institute (ETSI) for mobile digital communications. The GSM standard has been adopted in most countries, using three different varieties. Dual band phones are now commonplace, but as the United States uses PCS-1900 only, you will need a tri-band mobile phone to receive and make calls in every country that uses GSM across the world.

Hacker   Individual who breaks into the computer or network of another. The term was coined at MIT (Massachusetts Institute of Technolgy) in respect of faster shortcuts for model railway trains and tracks. The model railway enthusiasts formed the nucleus of the original group of hackers that emerged there. The term has now gathered a certain amount of controversy in that 'ethical' hackers consider that the term does not apply to cyber criminals who access systems and databases for monetary gain – these should be described as 'crackers'.

Hacker ethic   Either a thieves' charter or a code of honour, depending on your point of view. Once upon a time hackers were viewed as paragons of democracy and anti-bureaucracy. There are various versions (and extensions) of the basic set of tenets, which are originally attributed to Steven Levy from his 1984 book *Hackers: Heroes of the computer revolution*. In essence the hacker ethic reads as follows:

Access to computers (and anything that might teach you something about how everything works) should be unlimited and total.
All information should be free.
Mistrust authority – promote decentralization.
Hackers should be judged by their hacking not bogus criteria such as degrees, age, race or position.
You can create art and beauty on a computer.
Computers can change your life for the better.

HAL   The HAL 9000 computer: the all seeing, all knowing on board computer in Stanley Kubrick's superlative *2001: A Space Odyssey*. In the film and beyond, HAL came to symbolize the fears, dangers and logical conclusion of a computer controlled future. Although various apocryphal tales exist as the meaning of the term HAL (such as each letter is the preceding one of IBM) the definition given by Arthur C Clarke and Kubrick is Heuristically programmed ALgoritmic computer.
Hard disk   A magnetic disk on which you can store computer data, and the basic component of any PC. The term *hard* is used to distinguish it from a soft, or *floppy*, disk. Hard disks hold more data and are faster than floppy disks. A hard disk, for example, can store anywhere from 10 megabytes to several gigabytes, whereas most floppies have a maximum storage capacity of 1.4 megabytes. The size of hard disks in PCs have been increasingly rapidly over the last 2–3 years.
Hoax   A wide range of hoaxes, constantly in existence and circulation, include programs that display spurious messages that some harm has been done, or will be done. A very popular hoax involves e-mails that warn about viruses that are incurable, untraceable or possessing any other attributes that will put the fear of god into the user. Just to confuse matters, it is not unknown for hoaxes to be reported as true events in the media, thus causing even more panic over a non-existent threat.
HTML   HyperText Markup Language – essentially the language that formats the Internet, instructing Web browsers how any document should look. It is written as text then converted to a Web page by the browser.
Hypertext   Used as the format on the World Wide Web, and one of the facets that makes the Web so user friendly and easy to navigate. It allows documents to link to other documents by making words, phrases or images 'clickable'. When you click on the link the second document opens, which should (in theory) be relevant to the word, phrase or image in the first document. Formatting of the relevant Web

site can open the linked page in a new window, or in the existing window to replace the current page. The reality can either work amazingly well or be completely disastrous – particularly if you end up opening numerous different windows.

Infosec Information security (predominantly but not exclusively in a military sense): protection of classified information that is stored on computers or transmitted electronically.

Internet A global network connecting millions of computers and their users accessing or exchanging news, data, opinions and commercial sites. As opposed to online services, the Internet is decentralized and each user can choose what information he or she chooses to access, from the dazzlingly confusing array available.

Internet service provider(ISP) A company that provides Internet accounts enabling users to access the Internet via telephone or cable lines. The user pays an annual or monthly set fee or a telephone charge by the minute; the ISP provides the software needed to dial up and the access telephone numbers required. ISPs usually also provide Web space, e-mail accounts and anything else that will get you to sign up and stay with them.

IP address Internet protocol address. In non-technical terms, every computer connected to the Internet has a unique numerical address. However, you may not have the same IP address each time that you access the Internet. Many ISPs use dynamic IP addresses as opposed to static ones and dynamic addresses are different each time you access the Internet. An IP address looks like this: 214.146.13.838. The basic format is a group of four numbers separated by points. The first part defines a specific pre-defined network while the second part defines the specific computer within that network. This address then ensures that replies to requests that you send are returned to the right place. If you want to know what your IP address is, go to http://www. lawrencegoetz.com/programs/ipinfo/.

IP spoofing Where unauthorized access is gained to a computer by the intruder sending messages to that computer indicating that message is coming from a trusted host. To achieve IP spoofing the intruder must find an IP address of a trusted host and then modify the packet headers so that it appears to the receiving computer that the packets are coming from that host.

ISDN Integrated services digital network – a system of digital end-to-end communication connections that has been available for the last 10 years.

Keystroke monitoring A device or software package that records every keystroke made by the user, who is unaware of such monitoring. The collected data is then transmitted to the person who is monitoring the activity.

Linux A fully fledged operating system that was started by Linus Torvalds, a Finnish student. Essentially developed as a collaborative democratic process on the Internet, Linux has now passed from being a cult to a serious operating system – having seen off various commercial competitors along the way. It is a sign of the times that a new laser printer I have just got proudly proclaims itself to be 'Linux compatible'. Remarkable too, as some commentators see it as the purest and most complete example of the hacker ethic.

Location One of the many glories of the Internet and e-mail is that you can access them from virtually anywhere in the world. Correct, up to a point: every location is equal, but some are more equal than others. In 2001 the most wired cities in the world were London, Amsterdam, Paris, New York, Frankfurt, Brussels, Geneva, Washington DC, Toronto and Montreal.

Logic bombs A logic bomb will lie dormant in a system until triggered by some event or specific system condition. When set off, the bomb will carry out a malicious act, or set of acts such as changing random data or making the disk unreadable. The trigger mechanism can be anything – amongst favorites are a specific date, a specific event or the number of times a certain thing is done (even the number of boot-ups). A logic bomb does not replicate itself.

Mainframe Remember large air-conditioned rooms the size of aircraft hangars housing the latest high tech computers, which were the size of traditional phone boxes? You must have been around in the 1970s and 1980s! Before personal computers had such incredible processing power as now, businesses and universities ran large mainframe computers that ran networks.

Malicious logic/malicious software A program whose purpose is to cause malicious/harmful/unauthorized actions. This is a collective term for such types as logic bomb, Trojan horse, virus and worm.

Megahertz (Mhz) Measure of the speed and power of a PCs processing chip.

Melissa virus From 1999, the Melissa virus infects Word documents and then very kindly e-mails itself to 50 people in your address book. The virus also infects Word documents and e-mails them as attachments (so there goes confidentiality). It spreads faster than any other virus.

MP3   A standard for the compression of digital audio. The sound obtained from a MP3 file is close to that of a CD, but is only one tenth of the file size. MP4 is a similar system but used for video compression.
MS-DOS   Microsoft Disk Operating System: the empire began with this first operating system from Microsoft.

Online   Interestingly this is now viewed as being connected to the Internet; prior to the Internet it was most commonly used to describe being connected to online individual services, such as Compuserve.
Operating system   The underlying software that manages all of the programs of a computer. Among those that have come (and in many cases gone) are DOS, OS/2, Unix, Windows and Linux. Every computer must have an operating system to run other programs together with basic tasks that are taken for granted such as recognizing input from the keyboard, sending output to the display screen and controlling peripheral devices such as modems, printers and disk drives. In larger systems the operating system is even more critical: effectively controlling users, access and security.

Packet sniffing   A software program is planted at remote junctions in a network which monitors information packets as they progress through the network. In this way user names and passwords are obtained by the hacker who then uses this information to break into the system.
Passwords   Perversely many of the crime problems in the Digital Age originate from some very basic problems – passwords being one of them. A password is a continuous set of numbers and/or letters that a user keys into a system to confirm that he or she is that particular user. Theoretically passwords should not be disclosed to any other person. However simple this concept is, it constantly causes major problems. People leave 'Post-it' notes on the PC that detail 'confidential' passwords; they appear to have almost a pathological need to tell others their passwords; choosing passwords seems to cause us problems – we pick words or numbers that we can easily remember, and thus create passwords that are easily guessed by others. Among favorites to be avoided are: the QWERTY top line of a keyboard; user's date of birth; maiden name, partner's/children's names; the user's own name (!) – surveys have shown that about half of the passwords used are the operator's name or nickname; a favourite football team/ film star/fantasy – surveys have shown that one third of users choose the name of their favourite football team or celebrity. Bear in mind

such passwords are also used for such things as uploading information and content to 'secure' Web sites.

Any name or real word should be avoided. Always pick a password that is a combination of both numbers and letters, is not similar to a previous password and then remember it. You should also have separate passwords for different sign-ons.

Phreaking   Hacking of the telephone system typically to make free long distance phone calls, have calls charged to someone else's bill or to tap phone lines.

PDA   Personal digital assistant: a computer about the size of a calculator with a touch sensitive screen (as opposed to a keyboard). Most PDAs have a contact management system (ie an address book), a diary and memo software. Many also offer Internet and e-mail access via a phone or mobile phone line.

Real time   Something that takes place on a computer at the same speed as it would in real life.

Script kiddie   A derogatory term given to those who try to break into systems by merely downloading a ready made script from the Internet and use it until he or she gets lucky. An example of this is Web site defacement.

Silicon Valley   A nickname for the area south of San Francisco that has an unusually high number of computer/IT companies; Silicon is the most used material to make semiconductors for chips. The term has also been hijacked in various other countries for their own 'silicon valley' geographical area or wannabe areas.

SIM   Subscriber identity module. The smart card used by all digital mobile phones. It holds the user's details and phone number so that the phone it is in can access the relevant network(s).

Source code   The original form of program instructions written in programming language. For the program to be executed it must be translated into machine language, which is in binary code and can be understood by a computer and directly executed. Source code is the only format that humans can read and understand. Purchased software is invariably in machine language only – you can therefore execute it, but not modify or amend it.

Spam   Unsolicited commercial e-mail: unwanted or 'junk' e-mail sent in large quantities to recipients who did not request it, would not chose to receive it, and when they do receive it, junk it – usually by just looking at the title of the message. Now a generic term, allegedly derived from the famous *Monty Python's Flying Circus* sketch, which in turn extolled the values of the canned luncheon meat. The term encompasses unsolicited bulk e-mail (UBE), unsolicited commercial e-mail (UCE) and make money fast (MMF) e-mails.

Trapdoor   *See* Backdoor.

Trojan horse   Just like in Homer's *Iliad* a Trojan horse is something that is apparently harmless (or even beneficial) but once it gains access turns out to be something else entirely. Trojan horses do not replicate like viruses and worms, but can still be extremely destructive. Trojan horses rely on users to install them, or they can be installed by intruders who have gained unauthorized access by other means. Then, an intruder attempting to subvert a system using a Trojan horse relies on other users running the Trojan horse to be successful. Among various Trojan horses that are common are anti-virus programs that actually install viruses and software upgrades that are nothing of the kind but which when loaded proceed to modify files and contact other remote systems.

URL   Uniform Resource Locator: the address of a document, image or other resource available on the Internet. An URL has three components that specify the protocol, server domain name and the file location. An example of this is www.proximalconsulting.com/index – which specifies the HTTP protocol (or access method), on the www.proximalconsulting.com server and the file '/index'.

Virus   A manmade malicious computer program designed to infuriate, annoy and ultimate damage and/or destroy computer files. Viruses usually spread by 'infected' files that are passed between computers. Five years ago the largest risk was probably caused by users inserting floppy disks that were infected into their PCs. Now the infinitely more critical risk is viruses originating via the Internet. Viruses can reproduce themselves, attach themselves to other programs, create copies of themselves. Viruses normally damage or corrupt data, use available memory, clutter up disk space and bring the system to an abrupt halt. The most dangerous types of viruses transmit across networks, exploiting security flaws. Running a anti-virus program that isn't up to date is almost worse than useless; even the best fully up-to-date anti-virus programs cannot protect against all viruses. Somewhat ironically, there is also a thriving market in hoax viruses, mostly through e-mails that claim to have latest information and demand that you pass them on.

WAP   Wireless Application Protocol. A global standard to enable mobile phones to have access to the Internet and related services.

Web site   A linked group of Web pages, normally dealing with a particular company, product, service, subject and/or person. Each Web site has its own distinctive.

WWW/World Wide Web/The Web   As recently as 1996 there was some doubt expressed as to just how popular the World Wide Web would be. The best description I know of the Web is that it is an application running on top of the Internet. It was conceived by Timothy Berners-Lee of CERN in 1989 when he invented the first workable hypertext system and is now the primary global online information repository.

Worm   The use of the word in this sense was originated in a 1982 research paper by John Shoch and Jon Hupp of the Xerox Palo Alto Research Center. However this paper derived the term from *The Shockwave Rider* by John Brunner, published in the early 1970s and now promoted as 'a cyberpunk story from the days before cyberpunk was a concept'. In the book a 'tapeworm' is used to erase previous identities computer program, virus or algorithm that is capable of disrupting a computer program. Normally a worm propagates/replicates itself across a computer network causing malicious damage such as using up resources (storage, processing time) and shutting the system down. The worm may copy itself from one disk drive to another or via e-mail. Worms appear to be the computer infection of choice, accounting for approximately half of the computer infections in 2000. Whereas in the past some technical knowledge would have been required to create worms, now worm generators can be downloaded from the Internet. A typical transmission mechanism for worms is in 'interesting e-mail attachments'; other worms need no human intervention and infect computers with specific security flaws and then seek out other computers that have the same flaw. Because of the power to replicate it is now being argued that worms have in effect caused denial of service attacks on the Internet because of the bandwidth consumed by them. In the roll-call of infamous worms are: the Anna Kournikova virus (2001); the Christmas Tree virus – possibly the first worm on a worldwide network that spread across BITNET in December 1987; the Cornell Internet Worm – which exploited computer security flaws in 1988 and infected about 5 per cent of those users connected to the protype Internet.

Zombie   A daemon is a perfectly legitimate process that runs in the background, performing a specific operation as a response to instructions or at a pre-specified time (e-mail handlers and print spoolers for example). However, if a hacker can implant a daemon in an innocent computer than that computer can perform various tasks unbeknown to the user. A computer 'taken over' in this way is known as a zombie. Zombies are predominantly used to launch denial of service attacks. The hacker sends commands to the zombie computer through one of its open ports. The zombie then transmits a massive amount of packets of useless data to a specific Web site, thus clogging it up and achieving a denial of service attack.

WEB DIRECTORY

If ever there was an industry in danger of eating itself, it must be the world of technology. There must be thousands, probably millions, of Web sites that cover every aspect (however obscure) of the digital world – and everything that led up to it. Thus this Web directory is totally subjective, comprising sites that I think are particularly useful, informative or just entertaining. Many of the sites listed have been chosen because they contain numerous links to other sites of relevance.

Search engines

If you want to search for any aspect of technology, security or any other related issues, try these:

www.google.com
An obvious choice, but nonetheless the best search engine in my opinion. Its simplicity is refreshing, but don't let that confuse you as to its immense capabilities. Another useful feature is the 'cached' feature – a snapshot of the site that Google took when it crawled the Web. One side effect of this is that you can often still access Web pages that have subsequently been removed.

www.northernlight.com
An often underrated search engine that, on many occasions, constantly surprises. Don't be put off by the fact that you have to pay for some articles and documents – it still efficiently finds free material. Equally, much of the chargeable material is worth the entrance price charged per article. It is particularly good for business information and obscure media articles. Now officially not available to the public, but can still be accessed at www.nlresearch.com.

Webferret
A software utility (bot) for Internet searching which, in its basic form, is available as a free download at www.zdnet.com/ferret/. Although it's been around for a relatively long time, Webferret often fills in any holes left by Google. It uses several search engines simultaneously but also roots out duplications of results.

News searches

If you want to keep up to date with what's happening in the digital world, try some of my particular favourites:

http://news.bbc.co.uk
One of the UK's most popular Web sites, and as to be expected, it has world beating news coverage. It has particularly good coverage of technology and digital security issues and news, together with having the advantage of keeping an amazingly extensive archive of previous news.

www.msnbc.com
A separate technology section with very good analysis of news and issues – very extensive with good links between stories.

www.newsfactor.com
There is a separate section on cybercrime on this exhaustive Web site. Highly recommended is the free daily cybercrime and security report which is delivered daily by e-mail and is one of the best of its kind. The report contains summaries of the stories that have hit the media in the previous 24 hours together with hyperlinks to the relevant source stories.

www.zdnet.co.uk and www.zdnet.com
Apart from the wide ranging coverage on technology in general these sites have good reporting on security issues, particularly the UK site which has a separate section on Net crime.

www.theregister.co.uk
Proudly proclaiming that the site is 'biting the hand that feeds IT', it has separate sections on Net security and anti-virus news together with a free general daily news digest, delivered by e-mail. It can almost invariably be relied upon to provide a left field view of what's going on.

Anti-virus software

www.grisoft.com
You must have an anti-virus program installed and it is essential that you keep it up to date. For personal users a free download is available of the AVG anti-virus program: you are then e-mailed with details of new updates (which are frequent) and the physical update progress is totally painless. I first read a rave review of this in *The Wall Street Journal* a couple of years ago, and haven't looked back since. As if to prove the point, when we installed the program on one of our PCs, it immediately identified a virus on reboot directly after installation that the previously installed (and well known) virus checker had singularly failed to notice. My recommendation of this program is completely independent and objective, and in the interests of impartiality, I should tell you that other anti-virus programs are of course available.

Firewall software

www.zonelabs.com
No, I haven't changed my stance – this is another non-sponsored evaluation. You must have a firewall, and this is the best. Free for personal users, and has a very good automatic notification of updates facility. The beauty of the program is that it runs automatically, so that you can forget about it. The company's Web site also contains useful information about general security related issues. Highly recommended.

Technology terms

Still confused by all those acronyms? There are numerous sites that decipher them for you; I think that these are the best:

www.its.bldrdoc.gov/projects/t1glossary2000/t1g2k.html
The American National Standard for Telecommunications Telecom Glossary – yes, I know it sounds like a site for anoraks, but actually is one of the best resources to look up the meaning of acronyms and technology terms. Obviously telecoms related but it has also been expanded to include Internet terms. This site has the great advantage of offering a variety of definitions for the same term from different sources. If a word or phrase isn't here it probably isn't worth knowing about. Highly recommended as an essential source.

www.whatis.com
Less technical than the above, but still excellent. Has some nice touches: the word of the day, the Top 20 words of the week and various 'fast references'.

www.Webopedia.com
Another essential online dictionary of Internet terms – also has term of the day, new terms and useful links. If the term you're looking for isn't in one of these three listings then it either isn't worth knowing or it doesn't exist!

Useful tools

www.checkdomain.com
There are many sites and companies that check whether a domain name is registered and if so, who is the owner. In my experience this site is one of the best because it covers almost every country in the world.

http://cyberatlas.Internet.com/big_picture/stats_toolbox/article
If a statistic about the Internet, its usage and much more besides is worth knowing it will be at this Web site which gives extensive information brought together from a variety of sources. Should you wish to amaze your friends and colleagues with little known facts then spend an hour here and fill your head with knowledge.

www.geektools.com
A useful collection of tools including a route tracer and 'who is' search facility.

www.domainstats.com
How many domains are there registered in Bouvet Island (.bv) or Djibouti – or anywhere else for that matter. The answers are on this list.

www.nielsen-netratings.com
A private joint venture between three companies that provides statistics on such topics as the Top 25 Internet advertisers, Top 10 banners and global Internet usage.

www.lawrencegoetz.com/programs/ipinfo/
I'm not sure how useful this site is (if at all); but if you want to know what your IP address is, this is the one for you.

www.dack.com/Web/bullshit.html
The Web Economy Bullshit Generator. How simple can it get to summon up meaningless phrases for your next corporate meeting? Just click on the button at this site and it will generate endless new terms such as 'maximize frictionless mindshare', 'cultivate 24/7 architectures', 'evolve synergistic vortals', 'drive turn-key interfaces' and 'reinvent world-class paradigms'. The 'critics comments' at the bottom of the page are almost as funny.

Internet abuse

http://abuse.net/
The Web site of the Network Abuse Clearinghouse, where you can report network abuse and abusive users. The site also has a good set of links including decoding single number network addresses, intrusion detection and prevention resource, and the spam tools mailing list.

www.doshelp.com
Essentially a personal Web site that tags itself as an 'intrusion and attack reporting center'. Among the sections on the site are: incident report, anti-virus tools, security tests, OS patchfiles, security sites, security tips and personal privacy.

www.emailabuse.org
A private Web site dedicated to 'informing users of abuse and providing them with the tools to avoid becoming a victim'. Includes a short, but interesting, section of links to anti-spam and anti-virus resources. Also good in this respect is the 'Fight Spam on the Internet' site at http://spam.abuse.net

www.fraud.org
The Web site of the (US) National Fraud Information Center & Internet Fraud Watch operated by the National Consumers League. The Internet Fraud Watch offers 'consumers advice about promotions in cyberspace and routes reports of suspected online and Internet fraud to the appropriate government agencies'.

History of the Internet and technology

Timelines describing the progress of technology in general and the Internet can be found at:
www.warbaby.com/biglist.html
www.historychannel.com/timeline/1940s.html
www.pbs.org/op6/nerds2.0.1/timeline
www.cyberstreet.com/hcs/museum/chron.htm
   Additionally the Living Internet at http://livingInternet.com provides clear information on how various aspects of the Internet work, how they were invented and security issues relating to them.

Government and official bodies

www.nipc.gov
The US National Infrastructure Protection Center's Web site is worth looking at for the current news together with various useful sections including US legal issues.

www.interpol.int
Check out the section on technology crime – the company checklist is a massive, highly informative document, which should be analysed and incorporated in any set of corporate security guidelines and procedures.

www1.ifccfbi.gov/index.asp
The Internet Fraud Complaints Center includes data on complaints that it has received, trends and current warnings.

www.cybercrime.gov
The Web site of the computer crime and intellectual property section of the Criminal Division of the US Department of Justice which contains incisive data on many aspects of computer and cyber crime including the latest press releases issued by the US Department of Justice which are in the main current information on their investigations and convictions achieved. This site is one of the best of its kind operated by the US Government.

General security and related issue Web sites

www.cert.org
The Web site of the CERT Coordination Center at the Software Engineering Institute, operated by Carnegie Mellon University. Obviously technical in nature, this site has detailed information on Internet security vulnerabilities, security alerts, long term analysis and training on key issues.

www.gocsi.com/
The Web site of the Computer Security Institute in California which contains, among other things, their annual Computer Crime and Security Survey together with various other relevant information and a good links page.

Viruses and anti-virus information

www.virusbtn.com
An international publication on computer virus prevention, recognition and removal with interesting information on its Web site including a list of links to other general anti-virus sites and anti-virus developers.

www.vmyths.com
Just as essential as information about viruses is details of what are hoaxes – and you'll find information here where the truth about computer virus myths and hoaxes is given in wonderful (and sometimes comical) detail.

www.sophos.com
Sophos is a large anti-virus software company; its Web site contains extensive and up-to-date details of the latest (and previous) viruses, Trojans and worms.

Internet fraud warning sites

Because of the very nature of the global reach of the Internet, there could never be one site that lists all the known scams, fraud types and criminals operating in cyberspace. Moreover, warnings that may be relevant to one person/organization may mean nothing to another. However, as a starting point I suggest you visit the following to filter out what is relevant to you:

www.ftc.gov – the US Federal Trade Commission, includes details on various scams and fraud types
www.fraud.org – the US National Consumers League
www.Internetfraud.usdoj.gov – the US Department of Justice site on Internet Fraud
www.cybercrime.gov
www.scambusters.com
www.Internet-101.com/hoax/ – which has a very extensive list of links to other relevant sites
www.fraudbureau.com
www.ccmostwanted.com
www.scamhound.com
www.netscalped.com

Information warfare

www.iwar.org.uk
The Information Warfare Site, which true to its name presents extensive documents and information on all things IW. Among the sections on the site are: computer security, critical infrastructure, crime and espionage, e-commerce, hacking and cracking, IO, intelligence, legal aspects, military affairs, psychological operations and terrorism. Highly recommended as the site consistently provides thought provoking commentary and analysis.

www.cipherwar.com
Good news links on current stories together with a huge archive directory of previous stories and separate sections on hackers and important documents. The site also contains a short (but valuable) list of 'approved hyperlinks'.

www.cryptome.org
What more do I need to say than quote the following: 'Cryptome welcomes documents for publication that are prohibited by governments worldwide, in particular material on cryptology, dual-use technologies, national security and intelligence – open, secret and classified – but not limited to those'.

www.psycom.net/iwar.1.html
A long page of interesting links on IW and related topics.

Hackers and hacking

www.2600.com
A classic – now available on news stands and the radio! Good current news articles (albeit on selective topics).

http://dmoz.org/Computers/Hacking
Not a Web site in itself, but an open directory listing of (at last count) 551 links to other Web sites that deal with all aspects of hacking (including an interesting 25 links to 'fake identification').

www.soci.niu.edu/~crypt/
The Crypt newsletter, which describes itself as 'a magazine highlighting stories from places very far removed from mannered computer culture. It presents intriguing case studies, analyses snapshots of Internet culture, computer crime, the world of information warfare and the old in spectacular collision with the new within American society. Warning: some satire included'.

www.totse.com
I've fairly deliberately ignored for the purpose of this directory sites that tell you how to hack, but this site is so extensive, illuminating and (on occasions) frightening that it is a 'must see'. The site itself says that it is about information rather than hacking – and it has a

point as there are sections on: computers, conspiracy, drugs, ego, erotica, fringe, hack, law, media, phreak, politics, privacy, religion, technology, viruses, zines. Allow a few days (seriously) to take in all that is here – but start with the hack section, and be surprised, shocked, amazed and very worried.

Also try www.defcon.org, www.hfactorx.org, www.phrack.com and http://rent-a-hacker.com/links2.htm

Privacy

www.privacilla.org
As the site says; 'your source for privacy policy from a free market, pro-technology perspective'. Very thorough analysis and reporting of a variety of topics under the headings of privacy fundamentals, privacy and government, privacy and business, online privacy, financial privacy and medical privacy.

Echelon

www.aclu.org/echelonwatch/index.html
There are hundreds of sites (of varying degrees of accuracy) about Echelon. This one is a very good place to start, with a comprehensive list of links to other Echelon sites in the resources section.

www.gwu.edu/~nsarchiv/NSAEBB/NSAEBB23/index.html
Large collection of NSA declassified documents mainly (but not exclusively) focusing on the creation, evolution and management of Echelon.

Humour

www.digicrime.com
The lighter side of the dark side, so to speak; but just to remind you that it is still a serious issue, the first two pages may just bring on a paranoia attack.

Obscure

www.bragi.com/classics/m/cm1814/mepd.html
Charles Mackay's 'Memoirs of Extraordinary Popular Delusions' can be found in its entirety on the Internet at various sites, this being one of them. Read it and weep – and show yourself that nothing changes, even though the risks of phony schemes and investments have been described for as long as they have existed.

INTERNATIONAL LAWS AND TREATIES

This book does not claim to be a legal textbook on the issues of crime, fraud and risk in the Digital Age. Apart from anything else, because of the very global nature of the problems, national legislation is somewhat limited in what it can achieve. For this reason, included is the full text of the Council of Europe Convention on Cybercrime, which is the first international convention that attempts to tackle the problem by establishing a common policy together with fostering international cooperation.

One would hope that legislation across the world is constantly changing to meet the dynamic challenges posed by the Digital Age: however, as some nations still do not yet have specific legislation related to these offences, I think it best not to hold one's breath.

This information in this section was current at December 1 2001 but is obviously subject to change.

Argentina

No special penal legislation.

Australia

Federal legislation:
COMMONWEALTH LAWS
CRIMES ACT 1914
PART VIA – OFFENCES RELATING TO COMPUTERS
Unlawful access to data in Commonwealth and other computers 76B.

(1) A person who intentionally and without authority obtains access to:
   (a) data stored in a Commonwealth computer; or
   (b) data stored on behalf of the Commonwealth in a computer that is not a Commonwealth computer; is guilty of an offence.
   Penalty: Imprisonment for 6 months.

(2) A person who:
   (a) with intent to defraud any person and without authority obtains access to data stored in a Commonwealth computer, or to data stored on behalf of the Commonwealth in a computer that is not a Commonwealth computer; or
   (b) intentionally and without authority obtains access to data stored in a Commonwealth computer, or to data stored on behalf of the Commonwealth in a computer that is not a Commonwealth computer, being data that the person knows or ought reasonably to know relates to:
      (i) the security, defence or international relations of Australia;
      (ii) the existence or identity of a confidential source of information relating to the enforcement of a criminal law of the Commonwealth or of a State or Territory;
      (iii) the enforcement of a law of the Commonwealth or of a State or Territory;
      (iv) the protection of public safety;
      (v) the personal affairs of any person;
      (vi) trade secrets;
      (vii) records of a financial institution; or
      (viii) commercial information the disclosure of which could cause advantage or disadvantage to any person; is guilty of an offence.
   Penalty: Imprisonment for 2 years.

(3) A person who:
   (a) has intentionally and without authority obtained access to data stored in a Commonwealth computer, or to data stored

on behalf of the Commonwealthh in a computer that is not a Commonwealth computer;

(b) after examining part of that data, knows or ought reasonably to know that the part of the data which the person examined relates wholly or partly to any of the matters referred to in paragraph (2)(b); and

(c) continues to examine that data; is guilty of an offence.

Penalty for a contravention of this subsection: Imprisonment for 2 years.

Unlawful access to data in Commonwealth and other computers by means of Commonwealth facility.
76D

(1) A person who, by means of a facility operated or provided by the Commonwealth or by a carrier, intentionally and without authority obtains access to data stored in a computer, is guilty of an offence.

Penalty: Imprisonment for 6 months.

(2) A person who:

(a) by means of a facility operated or provided by the Commonwealth or by a carrier, with intent to defraud any person and without authority obtains access to data stored in a computer; or

(b) by means of such a facility, intentionally and without authority obtains access to data stored in a computer, being data that the person knows or ought reasonably to know relates to:

(i) the security, defence or international relations of Australia;

(ii) the existence or identity of a confidential source of information relating to the enforcement of a criminal law of the Commonwealth or of a State or Territory;

(iii) the enforcement of a law of the Commonwealth or of a State or Territory;

(iv) the protection of public safety;

(v) the personal affairs of any person;

(vi) trade secrets;

(vii) records of a financial institution; or

(viii) commercial information the disclosure of which could cause advantage or disadvantage to any person; is guilty of an offence.

Penalty: Imprisonment for 2 years.

(3) A person who:
  (a) by means of a facility operated or provided by the Common-wealth or by a carrier, has intentionally and without authority obtained access to data stored in a computer;
  (b) after examining part of that data, knows or ought reasonably to know that the part of the data which the person examined relates wholly or partly to any of the matters referred to in paragraph (2)(b); and (c) continues to examine that data; is guilty of an offense.

Penalty for a contravention of this subsection: Imprisonment for 2 years.

Austria

Privacy Act 2000, effective as of January 1 2000:
Section 10:
§ 52. Administrative Penalty Clause

(1) Provided that the offence does not meet the statutory definition of a punishable action within the relevant jurisdiction of the court nor is threatened by a more severe punishment under a different administrative penalty clause, a minor administrative offence shall be pronounced with a fine of up to S 260.000. Parties who
  1. willfully obtain unlawful access to a data application or will-fully maintain discernable, unlawful, and deliberate access or
  2. intentionally transmit data in violation of the Data Secrecy Clause (§15), especially data that were entrusted to him/her according to §46 and §47, for intentional use for other purposes or
  3. use data contrary to a legal judgement or decision, withhold data, fail to correct false data, fail to delete data or
  4. intentionally delete data contrary to §26, Section 7.

Belgium

Articles on computer crime in the Belgium Criminal Code were adopted in November 2000.

IV. COMPUTER HACKING
Article 550(b) of the Criminal Code:

§1. Any person who, aware that he is not authorized, accesses or maintains his access to a computer system, may be sentenced to a term of imprisonment of 3 months to 1 year and to a fine of (Bfr 5,200–5m) or to one of these sentences.

    If the offence specified in §1 above is committed with intention to defraud, the term of imprisonment may be from 6 months to 2 years.

§2. Any person who, with the intention to defraud or with the intention to cause harm, exceeds his power of access to a computer system, may be sentenced to a term of imprisonment of 6 months to 2 years and to a fine of (BFr 5,200–20m) or to one of these sentences.

§3. Any person finding himself in one of the situations specified in §§ 1 and 2 and who either: accesses data which is stored, processed or transmitted by a computer system, or procures such data in any way whatsoever, or makes any use whatsoever of a computer system, or causes any damage, even unintentionally, to a computer system or to data which is stored, processed or transmitted by such a system, may be sentenced to a term of imprisonment of 1 to 3 years and to a fine of (BFr 5,200–10m) or to one of these sentences.

§4. The attempt to commit one of the offences specified in §§ 1 and 2 is sanctioned by the same sentences as the offence itself.

§5. Any person who, with intention to defraud or with the intention to cause harm, seeks, assembles, supplies, diffuses or commercializes data which is stored, processed or transmitted by a computer system and by means of which the offences specified in §§1–4 may be committed, may be sentenced to a term of imprisonment of 6 months to 3 years and to a fine of (BFr 5,200–20m) or to one of these sentences.

§6. Any person who orders or incites one of the offences specified in §§ 1–5 to be committed may be sentenced to a term of imprisonment of 6 months to 5 years and to a fine of (BFr 5,200–40m) or to one of these sentences.

§7. Any person who, aware that data has been obtained by the commission of one of the offences specified in §§1–3, holds, reveals or divulges to another person, or makes any use whatsoever of data thus obtained, may be sentenced to a term of imprisonment of 6 months to 3 years and to a fine of (BFr 5,200–20m) or to one of these sentences.

Brazil

No special penal legislation on unauthorized access. But law no. 9,983 of July 2000 has been adopted covering provisions:
'Entry of false data into the information system.
Art. 313–A. Entry, or facilitation on the part of an authorized employee of the entry, of false data, improper alteration or exclusion of correct data with respect to the computer system or the data bank of the public administration for purposes of achieving an improper advantage for himself or for some other person, or of causing damages.
Penalty – imprisonment for 2 to 12 years, and fine.'
'Unauthorized modification or alteration of the information system.
Art. 313–B. Modification or alteration of the information system or computer program by an employee, without authorization by or at the request of a competent authority.
Penalty – detention for 3 months to 2 years, and fine.'

Canada

Canadian Criminal Code Section 342.1 states:

(1) Everyone who, fraudulently and without color of right,
   (a) obtains, directly or indirectly, any computer service,
   (b) by means of an electro-magnetic, acoustic, mechanical or other device, intercepts or causes to be intercepted, directly or indirectly, any function of a computer system.
   (c) uses or causes to be used, directly or indirectly, a computer system with intent to commit an offence under paragraph (a) or (b) or an offence under section 430 in relation to data or a computer system, or
   (d) uses, possesses, traffics in or permits another person to have access to a computer password that would enable a person to commit an offence under paragraph (a), (b) or (c)
   is guilty of an indictable offence and liable to imprisonment for a term not exceeding ten years, or is guilty of an offence punishable on summary conviction.

Chile

Chile has a Law on Automated Data Processing Crimes no. 19.223, published June 7 1993.

Article 2:
Anyone illegally obtains access to or uses information contained in an information processing system, intercepts or interferes with it, shall be liable for imprisonment from a minor to a medium sentence.

People's Republic of China

Decree No. 147 of the State Council of the People's Republic of China, February 18 1994.
Regulations of The People's Republic of China on Protecting the Safety of Computer Information
System: Chapter 4 – Legal Responsibilities.
Article 23 – The public security organizations shall give warnings or may impose maximum fines of 5.000 Yuan on individuals and 15.000 Yuan on organizations in cases when they deliberately input a computer virus or other harmful data endangering a computer information system, or in a case when they sell special safety protection products for computer information systems without permission. Their illegal income will be confiscated and a fine shall be imposed in the amount of one to three times as much as the illegal income (if any).
See also Computer Information Network and Internet Security, Protection and Management Regulations, approved by the State Council, December 11 1997, and published December 30 1997.

Hong Kong

Telecommunication Ordinance: Section 27A: Unauthorized access to computer by telecommunication:

(1) Any person who, by telecommunication, knowingly causes a computer to perform any function to obtain unauthorized access to any program or data held in a computer commits an offence and is liable on conviction to a fine of US $20000.
(2) For the purposes of subsection (1)
    (a) the intent of the person need not be directed at
        (i) any particular program or data;
        (ii) a program or data of a particular kind; or
        (iii) a program or data held in a particular computer;
    (b) access of any kind by a person to any program or data held in a computer is unauthorized if he is not entitled to control

access of the kind in question to the program or data held in the computer and
  (i) he has not been authorized to obtain access of the kind in question to the program or data held in the computer by any person who is entitled;
  (ii) he does not believe that he has been so authorized; and
  (iii) he does not believe that he would have been so authorized if he had applied for the appropriate authority.
(3) Subsection (1) has effect without prejudice to any law relating to powers of inspection, search or seizure.
(4) Notwithstanding section 26 of the Magistrates Ordinance (Cap 227), proceedings for an offence under this section may be brought at any time within 3 years of the commission of the offence or within 6 months of the discovery of the offence by the prosecutor, whichever period expires first.

Section 161: Access to computer with criminal or dishonest intent.

(1) Any person who obtains access to a computer
  (a) with intent to commit an offence;
  (b) with a dishonest intent to deceive;
  (c) with a view to dishonest gain for himself or another; or
  (d) with a dishonest intent to cause loss to another, whether on the same occasion as he obtains such access or on any future occasion, commits an offence and is liable on conviction upon indictment to imprisonment for 5 years.
(2) For the purposes of subsection (1) 'gain' and 'loss' are to be construed as extending not only to gain or loss in money or other property, but as extending to any such gain or loss whether temporary or permanent; and
  (a) 'gain' includes a gain by keeping what one has, as well as gain by getting what one has not; and
  (b) 'loss' includes a loss by not getting what one might get, as well as a loss by parting with what one has.

Czech Republic

No special legislation on unauthorized access to computer systems, but the following provisions of the Criminal Code may be applicable: § 182 – Impairing and endangering the operation of public utility facilities.

§ 249 – Unauthorized use of other people's articles.
§ 257a – Damaging and misusing records in information stores.

Denmark

Penal Code Section 263:

(2) Any person who, in an unlawful manner, obtains access to another person's information or programs, which are meant to be used in a data processing system, shall be liable to a fine, to simple detention or to imprisonment for a term not exceeding 6 months.
(3) If an act of the kind described in subsection 1 or 2 is committed with the intent to procure or make oneself acquainted with information concerning trade secrets of a company or under other extraordinary aggravating circumstances, the punishment shall be increased to imprisonment for a term not exceeding 2 years.

Estonia

Estonian Criminal Code:
§ 269: Destruction of programs and data in a computer.
§ 270: Computer sabotage.
§ 271: Unauthorized use of computers, computer systems and networks.
§ 272: Damaging or interferes with computer network connections.
§ 273. Spreading of computer viruses.

Finland

Penal Code Chapter 38 Section 8:
Data trespass
Any person who, by using an identification code that does not belong to him or by breaking through a corresponding protective system unjustifiable, breaks into a computer system where data are processed, stored or transmitted electronically or other technical methods or into a separately protected part of such a system, shall be sentenced for data trespass to fines or imprisonment not exceeding one year.
Data trespass also includes any person who does not break into a computer system, but uses a special technical device to illegally obtain information that is stored in such a computer system.

This Section will only be applied if the act is not punishable as a more severe offense.

France

The new Penal Code, in effect since March 1 1993

Chapter III: ATTACKS ON SYSTEMS FOR AUTOMATED DATA PROCESSING

Article 323–1:
The act of fraudulently gaining access to, or maintaining, in all or part of an automated data processing system is punishable by imprisonment not exceeding one year and a fine of up to 100.000 FF.
Whenever this results in the suppression or modification of data contained in the system, or an alteration in the functioning of the system, the act is punished by imprisonment not exceeding two years and a fine up to 200.000 FF.

Article 323–2:
The act of hindering or of distorting the functioning of an automated data processing system is punishable by imprisonment not exceeding three years and a fine up to 300.000 FF.

Article 323–3:
The act of fraudulently introducing data into an automated data processing system or of fraudulently suppressing or modifying data contained therein is punishable by imprisonment not exceeding three years and a fine up to 300.000 FF.

Article 323–4:
Participation in a formed group or in an agreement with preparation in mind, characterized by one or more material acts, of one or more offenses provided for by Articles 323–1 to 323–3, is punishable by the sentences provided for the most serious offense committed.

Germany

Penal Code Section 202a. Data Espionage:

(1) Any person who obtains without authorization, for himself or for another, data which are not meant for him and which are specially protected against unauthorized access, shall be liable to imprisonment for a term not exceeding three years or to a fine.
(2) Data within the meaning of subsection 1 are only such as are stored or transmitted electronically or magnetically or in any form not directly visible.

Penal Code Section 303a: Alteration of Data

(1) Any person who unlawfully erases, suppresses, renders useless, or alters data (section 202a(2)) shall be liable to imprisonment for a term not exceeding two years or to a fine.
(2) The attempt shall be punishable.

Penal Code Section 303b: Computer Sabotage

(1) Imprisonment not exceeding five years or a fine shall be imposed on any person who interferes with data processing, which is of essential importance to another business, another's enterprise or an administrative authority by:
    1. committing an offense under section 300a(1) or
    2. destroying, damaging, rendering useless, removing, or altering a computer system or a data carrier.
(2) The attempt shall be punishable.

Greece

Criminal Code Article 370C§2:
Every one who obtains access to data recorded in a computer or in the external memory of a computer or transmitted by telecommunication systems shall be punished by imprisonment for up to three months or by a pecuniary penalty not less than ten thousand drachmas, under condition that these acts have been committed without right, especially in violation of prohibitions or of security measures taken by the legal holder. If the act concerns the international relations or the security of the State, he shall be punished according to Art. 148.
If the offender is in the service of the legal holder of the data, the act of the preceding paragraph shall be punished only if it has been explicitly prohibited by internal regulations or by a written decision of the holder or of a competent employee of his.

Hungary

Penal Code Section 300 C:
Computer Fraud

(1) Whoever, with the intent of obtaining for himself an unlawful gain, or by damaging, interferes with the results of electronic data processing, by altering programs, by erasing, by entering incorrect or incomplete data, or by other unlawful means commits an offence, imprisonment for a term not exceeding 3 years may be imposed.
(2) The punishment is
   a) imprisonment not exceeding 5 years whenever the fraudulent offence causes considerable damage.
   b) imprisonment from 2 years until 8 years whenever the fraudulent offence causes exceptional considerable damage.
(3) Whoever commits the offences under subsection (1)–(2) by using an electronic card for public or mobile telephone, or by altering the microprogram for the mobile telephone commits also fraud in connection with data.

Ireland

Criminal Damage Act, 1991:
Section 5:

(1) A person who without lawful excuse operates a computer –
   (a) within the State with intent to access any data kept either within or outside the State, or:
   (b) outside the State with intent to access any data kept within the State, shall, whether or not he accesses any data, be guilty of an offence and shall be liable on summary conviction to a fine not exceeding £500 or imprisonment for a term not exceeding 3 months or both.
(2) Subsection (1) applies whether or not the person intended to access any particular data or any category of data or data kept by any particular person.

Iceland

Penal Code § 228 Section 1:
The same penalty shall apply on any person who by unlawful manner obtains access to data or programs stored as data.

India

THE INFORMATION TECHNOLOGY ACT, 2000 (No. 21 of 2000)
CHAPTER XI
OFFENCES
66. Hacking into a computer system

(1) Whoever with the intent to cause or knowing that he is likely to cause wrongful loss or damage to the public or any person destroys or deletes or alters any information residing in a computer resource or diminishes its value or utility or affects it injuriously by any means, commits hacking.
(2) Whoever commits hacking shall be punished with imprisonment up to three years, or with fine which may extend up to two lakh rupees, or with both.

Israel

The Computer Law of 1995, Section 4:
Any person who unlawfully obtains access to data in a computer, shall be sentenced to imprisonment not exceeding three years.
With access to data means access to equipment connected to computers or access activated through such equipment, in addition to access defined as unlawful wiretapping according to the Law of 1979.

Italy

Penal Code Article 615: Unauthorized access into a computer or telecommunication systems:
Anyone who enters unauthorized into a computer or telecommunication system protected by security measures, or remains in it against the expressed or implied will of the one who has the right to exclude him, shall be sentenced to imprisonment not exceeding three years.
The imprisonment is from one until five years:

1) if the crime is committed by a public official or by an officer of a public service, through abuse of power or through violation of the duties concerning the function or the service, or by a person who practices – even without a licence – the profession of a private investigator, or with abuse of the capacity of a system operator.

2) if to commit the crime the culprit uses violence upon things or people, or if he is manifestedly armed.
3) if the deed causes the destruction or the damage of the system or the partial or total interruption of its working, or rather the destruction or damage of the data, the information or the programs contained in it.

Should the deeds of the 1st and 2nd paragraphs concern computer or telecommunication systems of military interest or (concerning) public order or public security or civil defence or whatsoever public interest, the penalty is – respectively – one to five years' or three to eight years' imprisonment. In the case provided for in the 1st paragraph, the crime is liable to punishment only after an action by the plaintiff; the other cases are prosecutioned 'ex-officio'.

–615 quarter: Illegal Possession and Diffusion of Access Codes to Computer or Telecommunication Systems:
Whoever, in order to obtain a profit for himself or for another or to cause damage to others, illegally gets hold of, reproduces, propagates, transmits or delivers codes, key-words or other means for the access to a computer or telecommunication system protected by safety measures, or however provides information or instructions fit to the above purpose, is punished with the imprisonment not exceeding one year and a fine not exceeding 10 million liras.
The penalty is imprisonment from one until two years and a fine from 10 until 20 million liras in the case of one of the circumstances numbered in 1 and 2 in the 4th paragraph of article 617 quarter.

–615 quinquies: Diffusion of Programs Aimed to Damage or to Interrupt a Computer System:
Whoever propagates, transmits or delivers a computer program – edited by himself or by another – with the aim and the effect to damage a computer or telecommunication system, the data or the programs contained or pertinent to it, or rather the partial or total interruption or an alteration in its working, is punished with imprisonment not exceeding two years and fined not exceeding 20 million liras.

Japan

Unauthorized Computer Access Law

Law No. 128 of 1999 (in effect from February 3 2000)
Husei access kinski hou
(Prohibition of acts of unauthorized computer access)

Article 3. No person shall conduct an act of unauthorized computer access.
2. The act of unauthorized computer access mentioned in the preceding paragraph means an act that falls under one of the following items:

(1) An act of making available a specific use which is restricted by an access control function by making in operation a specific computer having that access control function through inputting into that specific computer, via telecommunication line, another person's identification code for that access control function (to exclude such acts conducted by the access administrator who has added the access control function concerned, or conducted with the approval of the access administrator concerned or of the authorized user for that identification code);

(2) An act of making available a restricted specific use by making in operation a specific computer having that access control function through inputting into it, via telecommunication line, any information (excluding an identification code) or command that can evade the restrictions placed by that access control function on that specific use (to exclude such acts conducted by the access administrator who has added the access control function concerned, or conducted with the approval of the access administrator concerned; the same shall apply in the following item);

(3) An act of making available a restricted specific use by making in operation a specific computer, whose specific use is restricted by an access control function installed into another specific computer which is connected, via a telecommunication line, to that specific computer, through inputting into it, via a telecommunication, any information or command that can evade the restriction concerned.

(Prohibition of acts of facilitating unauthorized computer access)

Article 4. No person shall provide another person's identification code relating to an access control function to a person other than the access administrator for that access control function or the authorized user for that identification code, in indicating that it is the identification code for which specific computer's specific use, or at the request of a person who has such knowledge, excepting the case where such acts are conducted by that access administrator, or with the approval of that access administrator or of that authorized user.

(Penal provisions)

Article 8. A person who falls under one of the following items shall be punished with penal servitude for not more than one year or a fine of not more than 500,000 yen:
(1) A person who has infringed the provision of Article 3, paragraph 1.

Article 9. A person who has infringed the provision of Article 4 shall be punished with a fine of not more than 300,000 yen.

Latvia

The Criminal Law Section 241: Arbitrarily Accessing Computer Systems

(1) For a person who commits arbitrarily accessing an automated computer system, if opportunity for an outsider to acquire the information entered into the system is caused thereby, the applicable sentence is custodial arrest, or a fine not exceeding eighty times of monthly wage.
(2) For a person who commits the same acts, if breaching of computer software protective systems or accessing of communications lines is associated therewith, the applicable sentence is deprivation of liberty for a term not exceeding one year, or a fine not exceeding one hundred and fifty times the minimum monthly wage.

Luxembourg

The Act of July 15th 1993, relating to the reinforcement of the fight against financial crime and computer crime.

Section VI – concerning certain infractions in computer material.

Article 509–1 – Whoever fraudulently gains access or supports, wholly or in part, a system of data processing, shall be punished with imprisonment from two months until one year, or a fine from 10.000 to 250.000 F, or both.

The suppression or modification of the data contained in the system, or the alteration of the function of said system, is punishable by imprisonment from one to two years, and a fine from 50.000 to 500.000 F.

Malaysia

COMPUTER CRIMES ACT 1997
PART II
OFFENCES

(1) A person shall be guilty of an offence if
   (a) he causes a computer to perform any function with intent to secure access to any program or data held in any computer;
   (b) the access he intends to secure is unauthorized; and
   (c) he knows at the time when he causes the computer to perform the function that that is the case.
(2) The intent a person has to have to commit an offence under this section need not be directed at –
   (a) any particular program or data;
   (b) a program or data of any particular kind; or
   (c) a program or data held in any particular computer.

1. A person guilty of an offence under this section shall on conviction be liable to a fine not exceeding fifty thousand ringgit or to imprisonment not exceeding five years or to both.

Malta

CHAPTER 426
ELECTRONIC COMMERCE ACT
An act to provide in relation to electronic commerce and to provide for matters connected therewith or ancillary thereto.
PART VIII
COMPUTER MISUSE
Unlawful access to, or use of, information.
337 (C)

(1) A person who without authorization does any of the following acts shall be guilty of an offence against this article –

(a) uses a computer or any other device or equipment to access any data, software or supporting documentation held in that computer or on any other computer, or uses, copies or modifies any such data, software or supporting documentation;

(b) outputs any data, software or supporting documentation from the computer in which it is held, whether by having it displayed or in any other manner whatsoever;

(c) copies any data, software or supporting documentation to any storage medium other than that in which it is held or to a different location in the storage medium in which it is held;

(d) prevents or hinders access to any data, software or supporting documentation;

(e) impairs the operation of any system, software or the integrity or reliability of any data;

(f) takes possession of or makes use of any data, software or supporting documentation;

(g) installs, moves, alters, erases, destroys, varies or adds to any data, software or supporting documentation;

(h) discloses a password or any other means of access, access code or other access information to any unauthorized person;

(i) uses another person's access code, password, user name, electronic mail address or other means of access or identification information in a computer;

(j) discloses any data, software or supporting documentation unless this is required in the course of his duties or by any other law.

(2) For the purpose of this Sub-title:

(a) a person shall be deemed to act without authorization if he is not duly authorized by an entitled person;

(b) a person shall be deemed to be an entitled person if the person himself is entitled to control the activities defined in paragraphs (a) to (j) of sub article (1) or in paragraphs (a) and (b) of article 4 of this Sub-title.

(3) For the purpose of sub article (1):

(a) a person shall be deemed to have committed an offence irrespective of whether in the case of any modification; such modification is intended to be permanent or temporary;

(b) the form in which any software or data is output and in particular whether or not it represents a form in which, in the case of software, it is capable of being executed or, in the case of data, it is capable of being processed by a computer, is immaterial.

(4) For the purposes of paragraph (f) of sub article (1), a person who for the fact that he has in his custody or under his control any data, computer software or supporting documentation which he is not authorized to have, shall be deemed to have taken possession of it.

Offences and Penalties
337 (F)

(1) Without prejudice to any other penalty established under this Sub-title, any person who contravenes any of the provisions of this Sub-title shall be guilty of an offence and shall be liable on conviction to a fine (multa) not exceeding ten thousand liri or to imprisonment for a term not exceeding four years, or to both such fine and imprisonment.

(2) Where any such offence constitutes an act which is in any way detrimental to any function or activity of Government, or hampers, impairs or interrupts in any manner whatsoever the provision of any public service or utility, whether or not such service or utility is provided or operated by any Government entity, the penalty shall be increased to a fine (multa) of not less than one hundred liri and not exceeding fifty thousand liri or to imprisonment for a term from three months to ten years, or both such fine and imprisonment.

Mauritius

The Information Technology (Miscellaneous Provision) Act 1998
Act No. 18 of 1998

Penal Code Section 369A. Computer misuse
Any person who –

(a) wilfully and in defiance of the rights of another person, impedes or tampers with the operation of a computer;
(b) wilfully and in defiance of the rights of another person, directly or indirectly introduces data into a computer or suppresses or modifies any data which it contained or the method of treatment or transmission of such data;

(c) knowingly makes use of a document referred to in paragraph (c);
(d) without the consent of the person to whom a computer is entrusted, gains access to, or so maintains himself in, the computer;
(e) shall commit an offence and shall, on conviction, be liable to penal servitude for a term not exceeding 10 years and to a fine not exceeding 100,000 rupees.

369A. Aggravating circumstance.
A person who commits an offence under section 369A(e) shall, on conviction, be liable to penal servitude for a term not exceeding 20 years and to a fine not exceeding 200,000 rupees where, as a result of the commission of the offence, data contained in the computer is suppressed or modified or the operation of the computer is altered.

The Netherlands

Criminal Code Article 138a:
Any person who intentionally and unlawfully accesses an automated system for the storage or processing of data, or part of such a system, shall be liable, as guilty of breach of computer peace, to term of imprisonment not exceeding six months or a fine of 10.000 guilders if he:

(a) Breaks through a security system, or
(b) obtains access by a technical intervention, with the help of false signals or a false key or by acting in a false capacity.

New Zealand

No special penal legislation, but the Crimes Amendment (No 6) Bill contains the following:
Section 305ZE deals with accessing a computer system for dishonest purpose. Two offences are created.
The first provides that it is an offence
– to directly or indirectly access any computer system or part thereof
– and dishonestly or by deception and without claim of right – actually obtain any property, privilege, service, pecuniary advantage, benefit or valuable consideration or cause loss to any other person.

The second provides an offence
– of access without obtaining any of the above or causing such loss, but deals with the person who intentionally obtains access with the purpose of obtaining property or causing loss.
Section 305ZF deals with damaging or interfering with a computer system.
A Select Committee has to report back to the Parliament by June 30 2000.

Norway

Penal Code § 145:
Any person who unlawfully opens a letter or other closed document or in a similar manner gains access to its contents, or who breaks into another person's locked depository shall be liable to fines or to imprisonment for a term not exceeding 6 months.
The same penalty shall apply to any person who by breaking a protective device or in a similar manner, unlawfully obtains access to data or programs, which are stored or transferred by electronic or other technical means.
If damage is caused by the acquisition or use of such unauthorized knowledge, or if the felony is committed for the purpose of obtaining for any person an unlawful gain, imprisonment for a term not exceeding 2 years may be imposed.
Accomplices shall be liable to the same penalty.
Public prosecution will only be instituted when the public interest so requires.

Penal Code § 151 b:
Any person who by destroying, damaging, or putting out of action any data collection or any installation for supplying power, broadcasting, telecommunication, or transport causes comprehensive disturbance in the public administration or in community life in general shall be liable to imprisonment for a term not exceeding 10 years.
Negligent acts of the kind mentioned in the first paragraph shall be punishable by fines or imprisonment for a term not exceeding one year.
Accomplices shall be liable to the same penalty.

Penal Code § 261:
Any person who unlawfully uses or disposes of any chattel that belongs to another person and thereby obtains for himself or another a considerable gain, or inflicts on the person entitled thereto a considerable loss, shall be liable to imprisonment for a term not exceeding three years. The penalty for aiding and abetting is the same. Under especially extenuating circumstances fines may be imposed.
A public prosecution will only be instituted when requested by the aggrieved person unless it is required in the public interest.

Penal Code § 291:
Any person who unlawfully destroys, damages, renders useless or wastes an object that wholly or partly belongs to another shall be guilty of vandalism.
The penalty for vandalism shall be fines or imprisonment for a term not exceeding one year. An accomplice shall be liable to same penalty.
A public prosecution will only be instituted when requested by the aggrieved person unless it is required in the public interest.

Peru

Relevant amendments have been made to the country's Penal Code.

Poland

The Penal Code:
Article 267

§ 1. Whoever, without being authorized to do so, acquires information not destined for him, by opening a sealed letter, or connecting to a wire that transmits information or by breaching electronic, magnetic or other special protection for that information, shall be subject to a fine, the penalty of restriction of liberty or the penalty of deprivation of liberty for up to 2 years.

§ 2. The same punishment shall be imposed on anyone, who, in order to acquire information to which he is not authorized access, installs or uses tapping, visual detection or other special equipment.

§ 3. The same punishment shall be imposed on anyone who imparts to another person the information obtained in the manner specified in § 1 or 2.

§ 4. The prosecution of the offence specified in § 1–3 shall occur on a motion of the injured person.

Article 268

§ 1. Whoever, not being himself authorized to do so, destroys, damages, deletes or alters a record of essential information or otherwise prevents or makes it significantly difficult for an authorized person to obtain knowledge of that information, shall be subject to a fine, or the penalty of deprivation of liberty for up to 2 years.
§ 2. If the act specified in § 1 concerns the record on an electronic information carrier, the perpetrator shall be subject to the penalty of deprivation of liberty for up to 3 years.
§ 3. Whoever, by committing an act specified in § 1 or 2, causes a significant loss of property shall be subject to the penalty of deprivation of liberty for a term of between 3 months and 5 years.
§ 4. The prosecution of the offence specified in § 1-3 shall occur on a motion of the injured person.

Article 269

§1. Whoever destroys, deletes or changes a record on an electronic information carrier, having a particular significance for national defence, transport safety, operation of the government or other state authority or local government, or interferes with or prevents automatic collection and transmission of such information, shall be subject to the penalty of deprivation of liberty for a term of between 6 months and 8 years.
§ 2. The same punishment shall be imposed on anyone who commits the act specified in §1 by damaging a device used for the automatic processing, collection or transmission of information.

Portugal

Criminal Information Law of August 17 1991:
Chapter 1 Article 7:

1. Any person who, without authorization, obtains for himself or another person an unlawful gain or use by any manner accessing an information system or network, shall be sentenced to imprisonment not exceeding one year, or to a fine and imprisonment not exceeding 120 days.

2. Imprisonment not exceeding three years or a fine if the person concerned obtains access to information by breaking the security rules.
3. Imprisonment for a term of one year not exceeding five years when:
   (a) the person concerned by obtaining access to information acquires knowledge of trade secrets or confidential data protected by law,
   (b) the gain or use results in comprehensive values.

Philippines

REPUBLIC ACT NO. 8792
AN ACT PROVIDING FOR THE RECOGNITION AND USE OF ELECTRONIC COMMERCIAL AND NON-COMMERCIAL TRANS-ACTIONS, PENALTIES FOR UNLAWFUL USE THEREOF, AND OTHER PURPOSES

PART V: FINAL PROVISIONS
Sec. 33. Penalties – The following Acts shall be penalized by fine and/or imprisonment, as follows:
a) Hacking or cracking which refers to unauthorized access into or interference in a computer system/server or information and communication system; or any access in order to corrupt, alter, steal or destroy using a computer or other similar information and communication devices, without the knowledge and consent of the owner of the computer or information and communications system, including the introduction of computer viruses and the like, resulting in the corruption, destruction, alteration, theft or loss of electronic data messages or electronic document shall be punished by a minimum fine of one hundred thousand pesos (P100,000.00) and a maximum commensurate to the damage incurred and a mandatory imprisonment of six (6) months to three (3) years.

Singapore

Chapter 50A: Computer misuse Act.
Section 3. Unauthorized access to computer material.

(1) Any person who knowingly causes a computer to perform any function for the purpose of securing access without authority to any program or data held in any computer shall be guilty of an

offence and shall be liable on conviction to a fine not exceeding $5,000 or to imprisonment for a term not exceeding 2 years or to both and, in case of a second or subsequent conviction, to a fine not exceeding $ 10, 000 or to imprisonment for a term not exceeding 3 years or to both.

(2) If any damage is caused as a result of an offence under this section, a person convicted of the offence shall be liable to a fine not exceeding $ 50,000 or to imprisonment for a term not exceeding 7 years or to both.

Section 4: Access with intent to commit or facilitate commission of offence.

(1) Any person who causes a computer to perform any function for the purpose of securing access to any program or data held in any computer with intent to commit an offence to which this section applies, shall be guilty of an offence.

(2) This section shall apply to an offence involving property, fraud, dishonesty or which causes bodily harm and which is punishable on conviction with imprisonment for a term of not less than 2 years.

(3) Any person guilty of an offence under this section shall be liable on conviction to a fine not exceeding $ 50,000 or to imprisonment for a term not exceeding 10 years or to both.

South Africa

No special legislation, but
The South African Law Commission has published a Discussion Paper on Computer-related crime, with a closing date for comments: July 2 2001. The Paper is a preliminary proposal for reform in respect of unauthorized access to computers, unauthorized modification of computer data and software applications, and related aspects. And includes:

CHAPTER 2
OFFENCES
Unauthorized access to or obtaining of applications or data in computer system.
Art. 2 Any person who intentionally and without authority to do so accesses or obtains any application or data held in a computer system, is guilty of an offence.

Spain

No special penal legislation, but the following provisions in the Penal Code may be applicable:
Title X
CRIMES AGAINST PRIVACY, THE RIGHT TO FREEDOM FROM INJURY TO REPUTATION AND DOMESTIC PRIVACY

CHAPTER 1
Discovery and revelation of secrets:
Article 197

SECTION 1 ON FRAUD
Article 264 no.2

Sweden

The Data Act of 1973 (amendments in 1986 and 1990) § 21:
A person who without authorization secures access to a recording for electronic data processing, or alters or deletes or adds to such a recording, shall be sentenced for data trespass to pay a fine or to imprisonment for at most two years, unless the deed is criminalized in the Criminal Code or in the 1990 Protection of Trade Secrets Act. As a recording is also regarded information being transferred via an electronic or other similar aid to be used for electronic data processing. Attempt and preparation shall be punished as stated in Chapter 23 of the Criminal Code, unless the completed crime would have been regarded as petty.

Switzerland

Penal Code Article 143bis: Unauthorized access to data processing system.
Anyone, who without authorization, and without the intent of procuring an unlawful gain, accesses a data processing system which (is) specially protected against unauthorized access, by electronic devices, shall be sentenced to imprisonment or fines.

Tunisia

No special penal legislation.

Turkey

Penal Code Section 525/a:

Any person who unlawfully obtains programs, data or any other components from an automated data processing system, shall be sentenced to imprisonment from one to three years and a heavy fine ranging from one to fifteen million Turkish Liras.

Any person who uses, transmits or reproduces a program, data or any other component within an automated data processing system with intent to cause loss to another shall be sentenced to the same penalty stated above.

United Kingdom

Computer Misuse Act 1990
Chapter 18
Unauthorized access to computer material:

1. (1) A person is guilty of an offence if –
   (a) he causes a computer to perform any function with the intent to secure access to any program or data held in any computer,
   (b) the access he intends to secure is unauthorized, and
   (c) he knows at the time when he causes the computer to perform the function that that is the case.
   (2) The intent a person has to have to commit an offence under this section need not be directed at:
   (a) any particular program or data,
   (b) a program or data of any particular kind, or
   (c) a program or data held in any particular computer.
   (3) A person guilty of an offence under this section shall be liable on summary conviction to imprisonment for a term not exceeding six months or to a fine not exceeding level 5 on the standard scale or to both.

2. (1) A person is guilty of an offence under this section if he commits an offence under section 1 above ('the unauthorized access offence') with intent
   (a) to commit an offence to which this section applies; or
   (b) to facilitate the commission of such an offence (whether by himself or by any other person); and the offence he intends

to commit or facilitate is referred to below in this section as the further of

(2) This section applies to offences
  (a) for which the sentence is fixed by law; or
  (b) for which a person of twenty-one years of age or over (not previously convicted) may be sentenced to imprisonment for a term of five years (or, in England and Wales, might be so sentenced but for the restrictions imposed by section 33 of the Magistrates Courts Act 1980).

(3) It is immaterial for the purposes of this section whether the further offence is to be committed on the same occasion as the unauthorized access offence or on any future occasion.

(4) A person may be guilty of an offence under this section even though the facts are such that the commission of the further offence is impossible.

(5) A person guilty of an offence under this section shall be liable.
  (a) on summary conviction, to imprisonment for a term not exceeding the statutory maximum or to both; and
  (b) on conviction on indictment, to imprisonment for a term not exceeding five years or to a fine or to both.

3. (1) A person is guilty of an offence if –
  (a) he does any act, which causes an unauthorized modification of the contents of any computer; and
  (b) at the time when he does the act he has the requisite intent and the requisite knowledge.

(2) For the purposes of subsection (1)(b) above the requisite intent is an intent to cause a modification of the contents of any and by so doing –
  (a) to impair the operation of any computer;
  (b) to prevent or hinder access to any program or data held in any computer; or
  (c) to impair the operation of any such program or the reliability of any such data.

(3) The intent need not be directed at –
  (a) any particular computer;
  (b) any particular program or data or program or data of any particular kind; or
  (c) any particular modification or a modification of any particular kind.

(4) For the purposes of subsection (1)(b) above the requisite knowledge is knowledge that any modification he intends to cause is unauthorized.

(5) It is immaterial for the purposes of this section whether an unauthorized modification or any intended effect of it of a kind mentioned in subsection (2) above is, or is intended to be, permanent or merely temporary.

(6) For the purposes of the Criminal Damage Act 1971 a modification of the contents of a computer shall not be regarded as damaging any computer or computer storage medium unless its effect on that computer or computer storage medium impairs its physical condition.

(7) A person guilty of an offence under this section shall be liable –

    (a) on summary conviction, to imprisonment for a term not exceeding six months or to a fine not exceeding the statutory maximum or to both; and

    (b) on conviction on indictment, to imprisonment for a term not exceeding five years or to a fine or to both.

United States

Federal legislation:
UNITED STATES CODE
TITLE 18. CRIMES AND CRIMINAL PROCEDURE

PART I – CRIMES

CHAPTER 47– FRAUD AND FALSE STATEMENTS
(As amended October 3 1996)

Section 1030. Fraud and related activity in connection with computers.
(a) Whoever –

(1) having knowingly accessed a computer without authorization or exceeding authorized access, and by means of such conduct having obtained information that has been determined by the United States Government pursuant to an Executive order or statute to require protection against unauthorized disclosure for reasons of national defense or foreign relations, or any restricted data, as defined in paragraph y of section 11 of the Atomic Energy Act of 1954, with reason to believe that such information so obtained could be used to the injury of the United States, or to the advantage of any foreign nation willfully communicates, delivers, transmits, or causes to be communicated, delivered, or transmitted, or attempts to communicate, deliver, transmit or cause to be communicated, delivered, or transmitted the same to any person not

entitled to receive it, or willfully retains the same and fails to deliver it to the officer or employee of the United States entitled to receive it;

(2) intentionally accesses a computer without authorization or exceeds authorized access, and thereby obtains –

  (A) information contained in a financial record of a financial institution, or of a card issuer as defined in section 1602 (n) of title 15, or contained in a file of a consumer reporting agency on a consumer, as such terms are defined in the Fair Credit Reporting Act (15 U.S.C. 1681 et seq.);

  (B) information from any department or agency of the United States; or

  (C) information from any protected computer if the conduct involved an interstate or foreign communication;

(3) intentionally, without authorization to access any nonpublic computer of a department or agency of the United States, accesses such a computer of that department or agency that is exclusively for the use of the Government of the United States or, in the case of a computer not exclusively for such use, is used by or for the Government of the United States and such conduct affects that use by or for the Government of the United States;

(4) knowingly and with the intent to defraud, accesses a protected computer without authorization, or exceeds authorized access, and by means of such conduct furthers the intended fraud and obtains anything of value, unless the object of the fraud and the thing obtained consists only of the use of the computer and the value of such use is not more than $ 5,000 in any one-year period;

(5)

  (A) knowingly causes the transmission of a program, information, code, or command, and as a result of such conduct, intentionally causes damage without authorization, to a protected computer;

  (B) intentionally accesses a protected computer without authorization, and as a result of such conduct recklessly causes damage; or

  (C) intentionally accesses a protected computer without authorization, and as a result of such conduct, causes damage;

(6) knowingly and with intent to defraud traffics (as defined in section 1029) in any password or similar information through which a computer may be accessed without authorization, if

  (A) such trafficking affects interstate or foreign commerce; or

   (B) such computer is used by or for the Government of the United States;

(7) with intent to extort from any person, firm, association, educational institution, financial institution, government entity, or other legal entity, any money or thing of value, transmits in interstate or foreign commerce any communication containing any threat to cause damage to a protected computer; shall be punished as provided in subsection (c) of this section.

   (b) Whoever attempts to commit an offense under subsection (a) of this section shall be punished as provided in subsection (c) of this section.

   (c) The punishment for an offense under subsection (a) or (b) of this section is –

      (1) (A) a fine under this title or imprisonment for not more than ten years, or both, in the case of an offense under subsection (a) (1) of this section which does not occur after a conviction for another offense under this subsection, or an attempt to commit an offense punishable under this subparagraph; and

      (B) a fine under this title or imprisonment for not more than twenty years, or both, in the case of an offense under subsection (a) (1) of this section which occurs after a conviction for another offense under this subsection, or an attempt to commit an offense punishable under this subparagraph; and

      (2) (A) a fine under this title or imprisonment for not more than one year, or both, in the case of an offense under subsection (a) (2), (a) (3), (a) (5) (C) or (a) (6) of this section which does not occur after a conviction for another offense under this subsection, or an attempt to commit an offense punishable under this subparagraph; and

      (B) a fine under this title or imprisonment for not more than 5 years, or both, in the case of an offense under subsection (a) (2) if-

        (i) the offense was committed for purposes of commercial advantage or private financial;

        (ii) the offense was committed in furtherance of any criminal or tortuous act in violation of the Constitution or laws of the United States; or

        (iii) the value of the information obtained exceeds $5,000;

C)   a fine under this title or imprisonment for not more than ten years, or both, in the case of an offense under subsection (a) (2), (a) (3) or (a) (6) of this section which occurs after a conviction for another offense under this subsection, or an attempt to commit an offense punishable under this subparagraph; and

(3) (A)   a fine under this title or imprisonment for not more than five years, or both, in the case of an offense under subsection (a) (4), (a) (5) (A), (a) (5) (B), or (a) (7) of this section which does not occur after a conviction for another offense under this section, or an attempt to commit an offense punishable under this subparagraph; and

(B)   a fine under this title or imprisonment for not more than ten years, or both, in the case of an offense under subsection (a) (4), (a) (5) (A), (a) (5) (B), (a) (5) (C), or (a) (7) of this section which occurs after a conviction for another offense under this section, or an attempt to commit an offense punishable under this subparagraph; and

(d)   The United States Secret Service shall, in addition to any other agency having such authority, have the authority to investigate offenses under subsections (a) (2) (A), (a) (2) (B), (a) (3), (a) (4),(a) (5) and (a) (6) of this section. Such authority of the United States Secret Service shall be exercised in accordance with agreement which shall be entered into by the Secretary of the Treasury and the Attorney General.

(f)   This section does not prohibit any lawfully authorized investigative, protective, or intelligence activity of a law enforcement agency of the United States, a State, or a political subdivision of a State or of an intelligence agency of the United States.

(g)   Any person who suffers damage or loss by reason of a violation of the section may maintain a civil action against the violator to obtain compensatory damages and injunctive relief or other equitable relief. Damages for violations involving damage as defined in subsection (e) (8) (A) are limited to economic damages. No action may be brought under this subsection unless such action is begun within 2 years of the date of the act complained of or the date of the discovery of the damage.

(h) The Attorney General and the Secretary of Treasury shall report to the Congress annually, during the first 3 years following the date of the enactment of this subsection, concerning investigations and prosecutions under section 1030 (a) (5) of Title 18, United States Code.

Alabama Computer Crime Act – Ala. Code §§ 13A–8–100 to 13A–8–103

Alaska Stat. §§ 11.46.200(a)(3), 11.46.484(a)(5), 11.46.740, 11.46.985, 11.46.990, 11.81.900(a)(46) & (52)

Arizona. Rev. Stat. Ann. §§ 13-2301(E), 13–2316

Arkansas. Code §§ 5–41–101 to –107 Cal. Penal Code §§ 484j, 499c, 502, 502.01, 502.7(h), 503, 1203.047, 2702

Colorado. Rev. Stat. §§ 18–5.5–101 to 18.5.5–102

Connecticut. Gen. Stat. §§ 53a–250 to 53a–261 Computer–Related Offenses

Delaware Code Ann. tit. 11, §§ 931–939 Computer–Related Offenses

Florida Computer Crimes Act – Fla. Stat. ch. 815; Fla. Stat. ch. 934, Fla. Stat. ch. 775;

Georgia Code Ann. §§ 16–7–22; Computer Systems Protection Act – Ga. Code Ann. §§ 16–9–90 to 16–9–94

Hawaii. Rev. Stat. §§ 708–891 to –893 Computer Crime,

Idaho Code §§ 18–2201 to –2202, 26–1220, 48–801

Illinois. Rev. Stat., ch. 38, §§ 16D–1 to –7 Computer Crime Prevention Law

Indiana. Code § 35–43–1–4; Ind. Code § 35–43–2–3; Ind. Code § 35–43–4–1 ; Ind. Code § 35–43–4–2 ; Ind. Code § 35–43–4–3 ; Ind. Code § 35–43–5–1; Ind. Code § 35–43–7–3

Iowa Code §§ 716A.1 to 716A.16

Kansas. Stat. Ann. § 21–3755

Kentucky. Rev. Stat. Ann. §§ 434.840 to 434.860

Louisiana. Rev. Stat. Ann. §§ 14:73.1 to 14:73.5

Maine. Rev. Stat. Ann. tit. 17–A, ch. 18, §§ 431–433

Maryland. Code Ann., Crim. Law §§ 27–45A, 27–145, 27–146, 27–340

Massachussets. Gen. L. ch. 266, §§ 30, 60A

Michhigan. Comp. Laws §§ 752.791 to 752.797

Minnesota. Stat. ch. 609 Crimes Against Commerce

Missippi. Code Ann. ch. 45 Computer Crimes

Missouri. Rev. Stat. §§ 569.093–.099

Montana Code Ann. §§ 45–1–205(4), 45–2–101, 45–6–310, 45–6–311

Nebraska. Rev. Stat. §§ 28–1341 to –1348 Computer Crimes Act
Nevada. Rev. Stat. §§ 205.473 –.477, 205.481, 205.485, 205.491 Crimes
Against Property; Unlawful Acts Regarding Computers
New Hampshire Rev. Stat. Ann. §§ 638:16–:19
New Jersey Stat. Ann. §§ 2A:38A–1 to –6, 2C:20–1, 2C:20–23 to –34
New Mexico Stat. Ann. §§ 30–45–1 to 30–45–7 Computer Crimes Act –
New York Penal Law § 156.05; § 156.10; § 156.20; § 156.25; § 156.26; §
156.27; § 156.30; § 165.15
North Carolina Gen Stat. §§ 14–453 to –457 Computer–Related Crime
North Dakota Cent. Code §§ 12.1–06.1–01, 12.1–06.1–08
Ohio Rev. Code Ann. §§ 2901.01(J), (M); 2901.1(I); 2901.12; 2912.01(F),
(L)-(R), (T); 2913.04 (B), (D); 2913.42; 2913.81; 2933.41(A)(7)
Oklahoma. Stat. Ann. tit. 21, §§ 1951–1958
Oregon Rev. Stat. § 164.377. Computer crime
Pennsylvania. Cons. Stat. § 3933
Rhode Island Gen. Laws § 11–52–1 to 11–52–8
South Carolina Code Ann. §§ 16–16–10 to 16–16–40 Computer Crime
Act
South Dakota Codifed Laws Ann. §§ 43–43B–1 to 43–43B–8
Tennessee Computer Crimes Act: Tenn. Code Ann. §§ 39–14–601 to
39–14–603
Texas. Penal Code Ann. §§ 33.01– .05
Utah Code Ann. §§ 76–6–701 to 76–6–705
Virginia Computer Crimes Act: Va. Code §§ 18.2–152.1 thru 18.2–152.14
Washington. Rev. Code § 9A.52.110; Wash. Rev. Code § 9A.52.120; §
9A.52.130
West Virginia Va. Code §§ 61–3C–1 to 61–3C–21
Wisconsin. Stat. §§ 943.70
Wyoming. Stat. § 6–3–401

The Council of Europe Convention on Cybercrime

Budapest, 23.XI.2001
Preamble
The member States of the Council of Europe and the other States
signatory hereto,

Considering that the aim of the Council of Europe is to achieve a
greater unity between its members;

Recognizing the value of fostering co-operation with the other States
parties to this Convention;

Convinced of the need to pursue, as a matter of priority, a common criminal policy aimed at the protection of society against cybercrime, *inter alia,* by adopting appropriate legislation and fostering international co-operation;

Conscious of the profound changes brought about by the digitalization, convergence and continuing globalization of computer networks;

Concerned by the risk that computer networks and electronic information may also be used for committing criminal offences and that evidence relating to such offences may be stored and transferred by these networks;

Recognizing the need for co-operation between States and private industry in combating cybercrime and the need to protect legitimate interests in the use and development of information technologies;

Believing that an effective fight against cybercrime requires increased, rapid and well-functioning international co-operation in criminal matters;

Convinced that the present Convention is necessary to deter action directed against the confidentiality, integrity and availability of computer systems, networks and computer data as well as the misuse of such systems, networks and data by providing for the criminaliaztion of such conduct, as described in this Convention, and the adoption of powers sufficient for effectively combating such criminal offences, by facilitating their detection, investigation and prosecution at both the domestic and international levels and by providing arrangements for fast and reliable international co-operation;

Mindful of the need to ensure a proper balance between the interests of law enforcement and respect for fundamental human rights as enshrined in the 1950 Council of Europe Convention for the Protection of Human Rights and Fundamental Freedoms, the 1966 United Nations International Covenant on Civil and Political Rights and other applicable international human rights treaties, which reaffirm the right of everyone to hold opinions without interference, as well as the right to freedom of expression, including the freedom to seek, receive, and impart information and ideas of all kinds, regardless of frontiers, and the rights concerning the respect for privacy;

Mindful also of the right to the protection of personal data, as conferred, for example, by the 1981 Council of Europe Convention for the Protection of Individuals with regard to Automatic Processing of Personal Data;

Considering the 1989 United Nations Convention on the Rights of the Child and the 1999 International Labor Organization Worst Forms of Child Labor Convention;

Taking into account the existing Council of Europe conventions on co-operation in the penal field, as well as similar treaties which exist between Council of Europe member States and other States, and stressing that the present Convention is intended to supplement those conventions in order to make criminal investigations and proceedings concerning criminal offences related to computer systems and data more effective and to enable the collection of evidence in electronic form of a criminal offence;

Welcoming recent developments, which further advance international understanding and co-operation in combating cybercrime, including action taken by the United Nations, the OECD, the European Union and the G8;

Recalling Committee of Ministers Recommendations No. R (85) 10 concerning the practical application of the European Convention on Mutual Assistance in Criminal Matters in respect of letters rogatory for the interception of telecommunications, No. R (88) 2 on piracy in the field of copyright and neighboring rights, **No. R (87) 15** regulating the use of personal data in the police sector, No. R (95) 4 on the protection of personal data in the area of telecommunication services, with particular reference to telephone services, as well as No. R (89) 9 on computer-related crime providing guidelines for national legislatures concerning the definition of certain computer crimes and No. R (95) 13 concerning problems of criminal procedural law connected with information technology;

Having regard to Resolution No. 1 adopted by the European Ministers of Justice at their 21st Conference (Prague, 10 and 11 June 1997), which recommended that the Committee of Ministers support the work on cybercrime carried out by the European Committee on Crime Problems (CDPC) in order to bring domestic criminal law provisions closer to each other and enable the use of effective means of investigation into such offences, as well as to Resolution No. 3 adopted at the 23rd Conference of the European Ministers of Justice (London, 8 and 9 June 2000), which encouraged the negotiating parties to pursue their efforts with a view to finding appropriate solutions to enable the largest possible number of States to become parties to the Convention and acknowledged the need for a swift and efficient system of international co-operation, which duly takes into account the specific requirements of the fight against cybercrime;

Having also regard to the Action Plan adopted by the Heads of State and Government of the Council of Europe on the occasion of their Second Summit (Strasbourg, 10 and 11 October 1997), to seek common responses to the development of the new information technologies based on the standards and values of the Council of Europe;

Have agreed as follows:

Chapter I – Use of terms

Article 1 – Definitions
For the purposes of this Convention:

a) 'computer system' means any device or a group of interconnected or related devices, one or more of which, pursuant to a program, performs automatic processing of data;
b) 'computer data' means any representation of facts, information or concepts in a form suitable for processing in a computer system, including a program suitable to cause a computer system to perform a function;
c) 'service provider' means:
i) any public or private entity that provides to users of its service the ability to communicate by means of a computer system, and
ii) any other entity that processes or stores computer data on behalf of such communication service or users of such service;
d) 'traffic data' means any computer data relating to a communication by means of a computer system, generated by a computer system that formed a part in the chain of communication, indicating the communication's origin, destination, route, time, date, size, duration, or type of underlying service.

Chapter II – Measures to be taken at the national level
Section 1 – Substantive criminal law

Title 1 – Offences against the confidentiality, integrity and availability of computer data and systems

Article 2 – Illegal access
Each Party shall adopt such legislative and other measures as may be necessary to establish as criminal offences under its domestic law, when committed intentionally, the access to the whole or any part of a computer system without right. A Party may require that the offence be committed by infringing security measures, with the intent of obtaining computer data or other dishonest intent, or in relation to a computer system that is connected to another computer system.

Article 3 – Illegal interception

Each Party shall adopt such legislative and other measures as may be necessary to establish as criminal offences under its domestic law, when committed intentionally, the interception without right, made by technical means, of non-public transmissions of computer data to, from or within a computer system, including electromagnetic emissions from a computer system carrying such computer data. A Party may require that the offence be committed with dishonest intent, or in relation to a computer system that is connected to another computer system.

Article 4 – Data interference

1. Each Party shall adopt such legislative and other measures as may be necessary to establish as criminal offences under its domestic law, when committed intentionally, the damaging, deletion, deterioration, alteration or suppression of computer data without right.
2. A Party may reserve the right to require that the conduct described in paragraph 1 result in serious harm.

Article 5 – System interference

Each Party shall adopt such legislative and other measures as may be necessary to establish as criminal offences under its domestic law, when committed intentionally, the serious hindering without right of the functioning of a computer system by inputting, transmitting, damaging, deleting, deteriorating, altering or suppressing computer data.

Article 6 – Misuse of devices

1. Each Party shall adopt such legislative and other measures as may be necessary to establish as criminal offences under its domestic law, when committed intentionally and without right:
   a) the production, sale, procurement for use, import, distribution or otherwise making available of:
      i) a device, including a computer program, designed or adapted primarily for the purpose of committing any of the offences established in accordance with the above Articles 2 through 5;
      ii) a computer password, access code, or similar data by which the whole or any part of a computer system is capable of being accessed, with intent that it be used for the purpose

of committing any of the offences established in Articles 2 through 5; and

b) the possession of an item referred to in paragraphs a.i or ii above, with intent that it be used for the purpose of committing any of the offences established in Articles 2 through 5. A Party may require by law that a number of such items be possessed before criminal liability attaches.

2. This article shall not be interpreted as imposing criminal liability where the production, sale, procurement for use, import, distribution or otherwise making available or possession referred to in paragraph 1 of this article is not for the purpose of committing an offence established in accordance with Articles 2 through 5 of this Convention, such as for the authorized testing or protection of a computer system.

3. Each Party may reserve the right not to apply paragraph 1 of this article, provided that the reservation does not concern the sale, distribution or otherwise making available of the items referred to in paragraph 1 a.ii of this article.

Title 2 – Computer-related offences

Article 7 – Computer-related forgery
Each Party shall adopt such legislative and other measures as may be necessary to establish as criminal offences under its domestic law, when committed intentionally and without right, the input, alteration, deletion, or suppression of computer data, resulting in inauthentic data with the intent that it be considered or acted upon for legal purposes as if it were authentic, regardless whether or not the data is directly readable and intelligible. A Party may require an intent to defraud, or similar dishonest intent, before criminal liability attaches.

Article 8 – Computer-related fraud
Each Party shall adopt such legislative and other measures as may be necessary to establish as criminal offences under its domestic law, when committed intentionally and without right, the causing of a loss of property to another person by:

a) any input, alteration, deletion or suppression of computer data;
b) any interference with the functioning of a computer system, with fraudulent or dishonest intent of procuring, without right, an economic benefit for oneself or for another person.

Title 3 – Content-related offences

Article 9 – Offences related to child pornography

1. Each Party shall adopt such legislative and other measures as may be necessary to establish as criminal offences under its domestic law, when committed intentionally and without right, the following conduct:
   a) producing child pornography for the purpose of its distribution through a computer system;
   b) offering or making available child pornography through a computer system;
   c) distributing or transmitting child pornography through a computer system;
   d) procuring child pornography through a computer system for oneself or for another person;
   e) possessing child pornography in a computer system or on a computer-data storage medium.
2. For the purpose of paragraph 1 above, the term 'child pornography' shall include pornographic material that visually depicts:
   a) a minor engaged in sexually explicit conduct;
   b) a person appearing to be a minor engaged in sexually explicit conduct;
   c) realistic images representing a minor engaged in sexually explicit conduct.
3. For the purpose of paragraph 2 above, the term 'minor' shall include all persons under 18 years of age. A Party may, however, require a lower age-limit, which shall be not less than 16 years.
4. Each Party may reserve the right not to apply, in whole or in part, paragraphs 1, sub-paragraphs d) and e), and 2, sub-paragraphs b) and c).

Title 4 – Offences related to infringements of copyright and related rights

Article 10 – Offences related to infringements of copyright and related rights

1. Each Party shall adopt such legislative and other measures as may be necessary to establish as criminal offences under its domestic law the infringement of copyright, as defined under the law of that

Party, pursuant to the obligations it has undertaken under the Paris Act of 24 July 1971 revising the Bern Convention for the Protection of Literary and Artistic Works, the Agreement on Trade-Related Aspects of Intellectual Property Rights and the WIPO Copyright Treaty, with the exception of any moral rights conferred by such conventions, where such acts are committed willfully, on a commercial scale and by means of a computer system.

2. Each Party shall adopt such legislative and other measures as may be necessary to establish as criminal offences under its domestic law the infringement of related rights, as defined under the law of that Party, pursuant to the obligations it has undertaken under the International Convention for the Protection of Performers, Producers of Phonograms and Broadcasting Organizations (Rome Convention), the Agreement on Trade-Related Aspects of Intellectual Property Rights and the WIPO Performances and Phonograms Treaty, with the exception of any moral rights conferred by such conventions, where such acts are committed willfully, on a commercial scale and by means of a computer system.

3. A Party may reserve the right not to impose criminal liability under paragraphs 1 and 2 of this article in limited circumstances, provided that other effective remedies are available and that such reservation does not derogate from the Party's international obligations set forth in the international instruments referred to in paragraphs 1 and 2 of this article.

Title 5 – Ancillary liability and sanctions

Article 11 – Attempt and aiding or abetting

1. Each Party shall adopt such legislative and other measures as may be necessary to establish as criminal offences under its domestic law, when committed intentionally, aiding or abetting the commission of any of the offences established in accordance with Articles 2 through 10 of the present Convention with intent that such offence be committed.

2. Each Party shall adopt such legislative and other measures as may be necessary to establish as criminal offences under its domestic law, when committed intentionally, an attempt to commit any of the offences established in accordance with Articles 3 through 5, 7, 8, and 9.1.a) and c) of this Convention.

3. Each Party may reserve the right not to apply, in whole or in part, paragraph 2 of this article.

Article 12 – Corporate liability

1. Each Party shall adopt such legislative and other measures as may be necessary to ensure that legal persons can be held liable for a criminal offence established in accordance with this Convention, committed for their benefit by any natural person, acting either individually or as part of an organ of the legal person, who has a leading position within it, based on:
   a) a power of representation of the legal person;
   b) an authority to take decisions on behalf of the legal person;
   c) an authority to exercise control within the legal person.
2. In addition to the cases already provided for in paragraph 1 of this article, each Party shall take the measures necessary to ensure that a legal person can be held liable where the lack of supervision or control by a natural person referred to in paragraph 1 has made possible the commission of a criminal offence established in accordance with this Convention for the benefit of that legal person by a natural person acting under its authority.
3. Subject to the legal principles of the Party, the liability of a legal person may be criminal, civil or administrative.
4. Such liability shall be without prejudice to the criminal liability of the natural persons who have committed the offence.

Article 13 – Sanctions and measures

1. Each Party shall adopt such legislative and other measures as may be necessary to ensure that the criminal offences established in accordance with Articles 2 through 11 are punishable by effective, proportionate and dissuasive sanctions, which include deprivation of liberty.
2. Each Party shall ensure that legal persons held liable in accordance with Article 12 shall be subject to effective, proportionate and dissuasive criminal or non-criminal sanctions or measures, including monetary sanctions.

Section 2 – Procedural law

Title 1 – Common provisions

Article 14 – Scope of procedural provisions

1. Each Party shall adopt such legislative and other measures as may be necessary to establish the powers and procedures provided for

in this section for the purpose of specific criminal investigations or proceedings.

2. Except as specifically provided otherwise in Article 21, each Party shall apply the powers and procedures referred to in paragraph 1 of this article to:
   a) the criminal offences established in accordance with Articles 2 through 11 of this Convention;
   b) other criminal offences committed by means of a computer system; and
   c) the collection of evidence in electronic form of a criminal offence.

3. a) Each Party may reserve the right to apply the measures referred to in Article 20 only to offences or categories of offences specified in the reservation, provided that the range of such offences or categories of offences is not more restricted than the range of offences to which it applies the measures referred to in Article 21. Each Party shall consider restricting such a reservation to enable the broadest application of the measure referred to in Article 20.
   b) Where a Party, due to limitations in its legislation in force at the time of the adoption of the present Convention, is not able to apply the measures referred to in Articles 20 and 21 to communications being transmitted within a computer system of a service provider, which system:
      i) is being operated for the benefit of a closed group of users, and
      ii) does not employ public communications networks and is not connected with another computer system, whether public or private, that Party may reserve the right not to apply these measures to such communications. Each Party shall consider restricting such a reservation to enable the broadest application of the measures referred to in Articles 20 and 21.

Article 15 – Conditions and safeguards

1. Each Party shall ensure that the establishment, implementation and application of the powers and procedures provided for in this Section are subject to conditions and safeguards provided for under its domestic law, which shall provide for the adequate protection of human rights and liberties, including rights arising pursuant to obligations it has undertaken under the 1950 Council of Europe Convention for the Protection of Human Rights and Fundamental

Freedoms, the 1966 United Nations International Covenant on Civil and Political Rights, and other applicable international human rights instruments, and which shall incorporate the principle of proportionality.

2. Such conditions and safeguards shall, as appropriate in view of the nature of the procedure or power concerned, *inter alia*, include judicial or other independent supervision, grounds justifying application, and limitation of the scope and the duration of such power or procedure.

3. To the extent that it is consistent with the public interest, in particular the sound administration of justice, each Party shall consider the impact of the powers and procedures in this section upon the rights, responsibilities and legitimate interests of third parties.

Title 2 – Expedited preservation of stored computer data

Article 16 – Expedited preservation of stored computer data

1. Each Party shall adopt such legislative and other measures as may be necessary to enable its competent authorities to order or similarly obtain the expeditious preservation of specified computer data, including traffic data, that has been stored by means of a computer system, in particular where there are grounds to believe that the computer data is particularly vulnerable to loss or modification.

2. Where a Party gives effect to paragraph 1 above by means of an order to a person to preserve specified stored computer data in the person's possession or control, the Party shall adopt such legislative and other measures as may be necessary to oblige that person to preserve and maintain the integrity of that computer data for a period of time as long as necessary, up to a maximum of ninety days, to enable the competent authorities to seek its disclosure. A Party may provide for such an order to be subsequently renewed.

3. Each Party shall adopt such legislative and other measures as may be necessary to oblige the custodian or other person who is to preserve the computer data to keep confidential the undertaking of such procedures for the period of time provided for by its domestic law.

4. The powers and procedures referred to in this article shall be subject to Articles 14 and 15.

Article 17 – Expedited preservation and partial disclosure of traffic data

1. Each Party shall adopt, in respect of traffic data that is to be preserved under Article 16, such legislative and other measures as may be necessary to:
   a) ensure that such expeditious preservation of traffic data is available regardless of whether one or more service providers were involved in the transmission of that communication; and
   b) ensure the expeditious disclosure to the Party's competent authority, or a person designated by that authority, of a sufficient amount of traffic data to enable the Party to identify the service providers and the path through which the communication was transmitted.
2. The powers and procedures referred to in this article shall be subject to Articles 14 and 15.

Title 3 – Production order

Article 18 – Production order

1. Each Party shall adopt such legislative and other measures as may be necessary to empower its competent authorities to order:
   a) a person in its territory to submit specified computer data in that person's possession or control, which is stored in a computer system or a computer-data storage medium; and
   b) a service provider offering its services in the territory of the Party to submit subscriber information relating to such services in that service provider's possession or control.
2. The powers and procedures referred to in this article shall be subject to Articles 14 and 15.
3. For the purpose of this article, the term 'subscriber information' means any information contained in the form of computer data or any other form that is held by a service provider, relating to subscribers of its services other than traffic or content data and by which can be established:
   a) the type of communication service used, the technical provisions taken thereto and the period of service;
   b) the subscriber's identity, postal or geographic address, telephone and other access number, billing and payment information, available on the basis of the service agreement or arrangement;

c) any other information on the site of the installation of communication equipment, available on the basis of the service agreement or arrangement.

Title 4 – Search and seizure of stored computer data

Article 19 – Search and seizure of stored computer data

1. Each Party shall adopt such legislative and other measures as may be necessary to empower its competent authorities to search or similarly access:
   a) a computer system or part of it and computer data stored therein; and
   b) a computer-data storage medium in which computer data may be stored in its territory.
2. Each Party shall adopt such legislative and other measures as may be necessary to ensure that where its authorities search or similarly access a specific computer system or part of it, pursuant to paragraph 1.a, and have grounds to believe that the data sought is stored in another computer system or part of it in its territory, and such data is lawfully accessible from or available to the initial system, the authorities shall be able to expeditiously extend the search or similar accessing to the other system.
3. Each Party shall adopt such legislative and other measures as may be necessary to empower its competent authorities to seize or similarly secure computer data accessed according to paragraphs 1 or 2. These measures shall include the power to:
   a) seize or similarly secure a computer system or part of it or a computer-data storage medium;
   b) make and retain a copy of those computer data;
   c) maintain the integrity of the relevant stored computer data;
   d) render inaccessible or remove those computer data in the accessed computer system.
4. Each Party shall adopt such legislative and other measures as may be necessary to empower its competent authorities to order any person who has knowledge about the functioning of the computer system or measures applied to protect the computer data therein to provide, as is reasonable, the necessary information, to enable the undertaking of the measures referred to in paragraphs 1 and 2.
5. The powers and procedures referred to in this article shall be subject to Articles 14 and 15.

Title 5 – Real-time collection of computer data

Article 20 – Real-time collection of traffic data

1. Each Party shall adopt such legislative and other measures as may be necessary to empower its competent authorities to:
   a) collect or record through the application of technical means on the territory of that Party, and
   b) compel a service provider, within its existing technical capability:
      i) to collect or record through the application of technical means on the territory of that Party; or
      ii) to co-operate and assist the competent authorities in the collection or recording of, traffic data, in real-time, associated with specified communications in its territory transmitted by means of a computer system.
2. Where a Party, due to the established principles of its domestic legal system, cannot adopt the measures referred to in paragraph 1.a, it may instead adopt legislative and other measures as may be necessary to ensure the real-time collection or recording of traffic data associated with specified communications transmitted in its territory, through the application of technical means on that territory.
3. Each Party shall adopt such legislative and other measures as may be necessary to oblige a service provider to keep confidential the fact of the execution of any power provided for in this article and any information relating to it.
4. The powers and procedures referred to in this article shall be subject to Articles 14 and 15.

Article 21 – Interception of content data

1. Each Party shall adopt such legislative and other measures as may be necessary, in relation to a range of serious offences to be determined by domestic law, to empower its competent authorities to:
   a) collect or record through the application of technical means on the territory of that Party, and
   b) compel a service provider, within its existing technical capability:
      i) to collect or record through the application of technical means on the territory of that Party, or
      ii) to co-operate and assist the competent authorities in the collection or recording of, content data, in real-time, of

specified communications in its territory transmitted by means of a computer system.

2. Where a Party, due to the established principles of its domestic legal system, cannot adopt the measures referred to in paragraph 1.a), it may instead adopt legislative and other measures as may be necessary to ensure the real-time collection or recording of content data on specified communications in its territory through the application of technical means on that territory.

3. Each Party shall adopt such legislative and other measures as may be necessary to oblige a service provider to keep confidential the fact of the execution of any power provided for in this article and any information relating to it.

4. The powers and procedures referred to in this article shall be subject to Articles 14 and 15.

Section 3 – Jurisdiction

Article 22 – Jurisdiction

1. Each Party shall adopt such legislative and other measures as may be necessary to establish jurisdiction over any offence established in accordance with Articles 2 through 11 of this Convention, when the offence is committed:
   a) in its territory; or
   b) on board a ship flying the flag of that Party; or
   c) on board an aircraft registered under the laws of that Party; or
   d) by one of its nationals, if the offence is punishable under criminal law where it was committed or if the offence is committed outside the territorial jurisdiction of any State.

2. Each Party may reserve the right not to apply or to apply only in specific cases or conditions the jurisdiction rules laid down in paragraphs 1.b through 1.d of this article or any part thereof.

3. Each Party shall adopt such measures as may be necessary to establish jurisdiction over the offences referred to in Article 24, paragraph 1, of this Convention, in cases where an alleged offender is present in its territory and it does not extradite him or her to another Party, solely on the basis of his or her nationality, after a request for extradition.

4. This Convention does not exclude any criminal jurisdiction exercised by a Party in accordance with its domestic law.

5. When more than one Party claims jurisdiction over an alleged offence established in accordance with this Convention, the Parties involved shall, where appropriate, consult with a view to determining the most appropriate jurisdiction for prosecution.

Chapter III – International co-operation

Section 1 – General principles
Title 1 – General principles relating to international co-operation

Article 23 – General principles relating to international co-operation
The Parties shall co-operate with each other, in accordance with the provisions of this chapter, and through the application of relevant international instruments on international co-operation in criminal matters, arrangements agreed on the basis of uniform or reciprocal legislation, and domestic laws, to the widest extent possible for the purposes of investigations or proceedings concerning criminal offences related to computer systems and data, or for the collection of evidence in electronic form of a criminal offence.

Title 2 – Principles relating to extradition

Article 24 – Extradition

1. a) This article applies to extradition between Parties for the criminal offences established in accordance with Articles 2 through 11 of this Convention, provided that they are punishable under the laws of both Parties concerned by deprivation of liberty for a maximum period of at least one year, or by a more severe penalty.
   b) Where a different minimum penalty is to be applied under an arrangement agreed on the basis of uniform or reciprocal legislation or an extradition treaty, including the European Convention on Extradition (ETS No. 24), applicable between two or more parties, the minimum penalty provided for under such arrangement or treaty shall apply.
2. The criminal offences described in paragraph 1 of this article shall be deemed to be included as extraditable offences in any extradition treaty existing between or among the Parties. The Parties undertake to include such offences as extraditable offences in any extradition treaty to be concluded between or among them.

3. If a Party that makes extradition conditional on the existence of a treaty receives a request for extradition from another Party with which it does not have an extradition treaty, it may consider this Convention as the legal basis for extradition with respect to any criminal offence referred to in paragraph 1 of this article.

4. Parties that do not make extradition conditional on the existence of a treaty shall recognize the criminal offences referred to in paragraph 1 of this article as extraditable offences between themselves.

5. Extradition shall be subject to the conditions provided for by the law of the requested Party or by applicable extradition treaties, including the grounds on which the requested Party may refuse extradition.

6. If extradition for a criminal offence referred to in paragraph 1 of this article is refused solely on the basis of the nationality of the person sought, or because the requested Party deems that it has jurisdiction over the offence, the requested Party shall submit the case at the request of the requesting Party to its competent authorities for the purpose of prosecution and shall report the final outcome to the requesting Party in due course. Those authorities shall take their decision and conduct their investigations and proceedings in the same manner as for any other offence of a comparable nature under the law of that Party.

7. a) Each Party shall, at the time of signature or when depositing its instrument of ratification, acceptance, approval or accession, communicate to the Secretary General of the Council of Europe the name and address of each authority responsible for making or receiving requests for extradition or provisional arrest in the absence of a treaty.

   b) The Secretary General of the Council of Europe shall set up and keep updated a register of authorities so designated by the Parties. Each Party shall ensure that the details held on the register are correct at all times.

Title 3 – General principles relating to mutual assistance

Article 25 – General principles relating to mutual assistance

1. The Parties shall afford one another mutual assistance to the widest extent possible for the purpose of investigations or proceedings concerning criminal offences related to computer systems and data, or for the collection of evidence in electronic form of a criminal offence.

2. Each Party shall also adopt such legislative and other measures as may be necessary to carry out the obligations set forth in Articles 27 through 35.

3. Each Party may, in urgent circumstances, make requests for mutual assistance or communications related thereto by expedited means of communication, including fax or e-mail, to the extent that such means provide appropriate levels of security and authentication (including the use of encryption, where necessary), with formal confirmation to follow, where required by the requested Party. The requested Party shall accept and respond to the request by any such expedited means of communication.

4. Except as otherwise specifically provided in articles in this chapter, mutual assistance shall be subject to the conditions provided for by the law of the requested Party or by applicable mutual assistance treaties, including the grounds on which the requested Party may refuse co-operation. The requested Party shall not exercise the right to refuse mutual assistance in relation to the offences referred to in Articles 2 through 11 solely on the ground that the request concerns an offence which it considers a fiscal offence.

5. Where, in accordance with the provisions of this chapter, the requested Party is permitted to make mutual assistance conditional upon the existence of dual criminality, that condition shall be deemed fulfilled, irrespective of whether its laws place the offence within the same category of offence or denominate the offence by the same terminology as the requesting Party, if the conduct underlying the offence for which assistance is sought is a criminal offence under its laws.

Article 26 – Spontaneous information

1. A Party may, within the limits of its domestic law and without prior request, forward to another Party information obtained within the framework of its own investigations when it considers that the disclosure of such information might assist the receiving Party in initiating or carrying out investigations or proceedings concerning criminal offences established in accordance with this Convention or might lead to a request for co-operation by that Party under this chapter.

2. Prior to providing such information, the providing Party may request that it be kept confidential or only used subject to conditions. If the receiving Party cannot comply with such request, it shall

notify the providing Party, which shall then determine whether the information should nevertheless be provided. If the receiving Party accepts the information subject to the conditions, it shall be bound by them.

Title 4 – Procedures pertaining to mutual assistance requests in the absence of applicable international agreements

Article 27 – Procedures pertaining to mutual assistance requests in the absence of applicable international agreements

1. Where there is no mutual assistance treaty or arrangement on the basis of uniform or reciprocal legislation in force between the requesting and requested Parties, the provisions of paragraphs 2 through 9 of this article shall apply. The provisions of this article shall not apply where such treaty, arrangement or legislation exists, unless the Parties concerned agree to apply any or all of the remainder of this article in lieu thereof.
2. a) Each Party shall designate a central authority or authorities responsible for sending and answering requests for mutual assistance, the execution of such requests or their transmission to the authorities competent for their execution.
   b) The central authorities shall communicate directly with each other;
   c) Each Party shall, at the time of signature or when depositing its instrument of ratification, acceptance, approval or accession, communicate to the Secretary General of the Council of Europe the names and addresses of the authorities designated in pursuance of this paragraph;
   d) The Secretary General of the Council of Europe shall set up and keep updated a register of central authorities designated by the Parties. Each Party shall ensure that the details held on the register are correct at all times.
3. Mutual assistance requests under this article shall be executed in accordance with the procedures specified by the requesting Party, except where incompatible with the law of the requested Party.
4. The requested Party may, in addition to the grounds for refusal established in Article 25, paragraph 4, refuse assistance if:
   a) the request concerns an offence which the requested Party considers a political offence or an offence connected with a political offence, or

b) it considers that execution of the request is likely to prejudice its sovereignty, security, *ordre public* or other essential interests.

5. The requested Party may postpone action on a request if such action would prejudice criminal investigations or proceedings conducted by its authorities.

6. Before refusing or postponing assistance, the requested Party shall, where appropriate after having consulted with the requesting Party, consider whether the request may be granted partially or subject to such conditions as it deems necessary.

7. The requested Party shall promptly inform the requesting Party of the outcome of the execution of a request for assistance. Reasons shall be given for any refusal or postponement of the request. The requested Party shall also inform the requesting Party of any reasons that render impossible the execution of the request or are likely to delay it significantly.

8. The requesting Party may request that the requested Party keep confidential the fact of any request made under this chapter as well as its subject, except to the extent necessary for its execution. If the requested Party cannot comply with the request for confidentiality, it shall promptly inform the requesting Party, which shall then determine whether the request should nevertheless be executed.

9. a) In the event of urgency, requests for mutual assistance or communications related thereto may be sent directly by judicial authorities of the requesting Party to such authorities of the requested Party. In any such cases, a copy shall be sent at the same time to the central authority of the requested Party through the central authority of the requesting Party.

b) Any request or communication under this paragraph may be made through the International Criminal Police Organization (Interpol).

c) Where a request is made pursuant to sub-paragraph a) of this article and the authority is not competent to deal with the request, it shall refer the request to the competent national authority and inform directly the requesting Party that it has done so.

d) Requests or communications made under this paragraph that do not involve coercive action may be directly transmitted by the competent authorities of the requesting Party to the competent authorities of the requested Party.

e) Each Party may, at the time of signature or when depositing its instrument of ratification, acceptance, approval or accession, inform the Secretary General of the Council of Europe that, for reasons of efficiency, requests made under this paragraph are to be addressed to its central authority.

Article 28 – Confidentiality and limitation on use

1. When there is no mutual assistance treaty or arrangement on the basis of uniform or reciprocal legislation in force between the requesting and the requested Parties, the provisions of this article shall apply. The provisions of this article shall not apply where such treaty, arrangement or legislation exists, unless the Parties concerned agree to apply any or all of the remainder of this article in lieu thereof.

2. The requested Party may make the supply of information or material in response to a request dependent on the condition that it is:
   a) kept confidential where the request for mutual legal assistance could not be complied with in the absence of such condition, or
   b) not used for investigations or proceedings other than those stated in the request.

3. If the requesting Party cannot comply with a condition referred to in paragraph 2, it shall promptly inform the other Party, which shall then determine whether the information should nevertheless be provided. When the requesting Party accepts the condition, it shall be bound by it.

4. Any Party that supplies information or material subject to a condition referred to in paragraph 2 may require the other Party to explain, in relation to that condition, the use made of such information or material.

Section 2 – Specific provisions
Title 1 – Mutual assistance regarding provisional measures

Article 29 – Expedited preservation of stored computer data

1. A Party may request another Party to order or otherwise obtain the expeditious preservation of data stored by means of a computer system, located within the territory of that other Party and in respect of which the requesting Party intends to submit a request for mutual assistance for the search or similar access, seizure or similar securing, or disclosure of the data.

2. A request for preservation made under paragraph 1 shall specify:
   a) the authority seeking the preservation;
   b) the offence that is the subject of a criminal investigation or proceedings and a brief summary of the related facts;
   c) the stored computer data to be preserved and its relationship to the offence;
   d) any available information identifying the custodian of the stored computer data or the location of the computer system;
   e) the necessity of the preservation; and
   f) that the Party intends to submit a request for mutual assistance for the search or similar access, seizure or similar securing, or disclosure of the stored computer data.

3. Upon receiving the request from another Party, the requested Party shall take all appropriate measures to preserve expeditiously the specified data in accordance with its domestic law. For the purposes of responding to a request, dual criminality shall not be required as a condition to providing such preservation.

4. A Party that requires dual criminality as a condition for responding to a request for mutual assistance for the search or similar access, seizure or similar securing, or disclosure of stored data may, in respect of offences other than those established in accordance with Articles 2 through 11 of this Convention, reserve the right to refuse the request for preservation under this article in cases where it has reasons to believe that at the time of disclosure the condition of dual criminality cannot be fulfilled.

5. In addition, a request for preservation may only be refused if:
   a) the request concerns an offence which the requested Party considers a political offence or an offence connected with a political offence, or
   b) the requested Party considers that execution of the request is likely to prejudice its sovereignty, security, *ordre public* or other essential interests.

6. Where the requested Party believes that preservation will not ensure the future availability of the data or will threaten the confidentiality of or otherwise prejudice the requesting Party's investigation, it shall promptly so inform the requesting Party, which shall then determine whether the request should nevertheless be executed.

7. Any preservation effected in response to the request referred to in paragraph 1 shall be for a period not less than sixty days, in order to enable the requesting Party to submit a request for the search or

similar access, seizure or similar securing, or disclosure of the data. Following the receipt of such a request, the data shall continue to be preserved pending a decision on that request.

Article 30 – Expedited disclosure of preserved traffic data

1. Where, in the course of the execution of a request made pursuant to Article 29 to preserve traffic data concerning a specific communication, the requested Party discovers that a service provider in another State was involved in the transmission of the communication, the requested Party shall expeditiously disclose to the requesting Party a sufficient amount of traffic data to identify that service provider and the path through which the communication was transmitted.
2. Disclosure of traffic data under paragraph 1 may only be withheld if:
   a) the request concerns an offence which the requested Party considers a political offence or an offence connected with a political offence; or
   b) the requested Party considers that execution of the request is likely to prejudice its sovereignty, security, *ordre public* or other essential interests.

Title 2 – Mutual assistance regarding investigative powers

Article 31 – Mutual assistance regarding accessing of stored computer data

1. A Party may request another Party to search or similarly access, seize or similarly secure, and disclose data stored by means of a computer system located within the territory of the requested Party, including data that has been preserved pursuant to Article 29.
2. The requested Party shall respond to the request through the application of international instruments, arrangements and laws referred to in Article 23, and in accordance with other relevant provisions of this chapter.
3. The request shall be responded to on an expedited basis where:
   a) there are grounds to believe that relevant data is particularly vulnerable to loss or modification; or
   b) the instruments, arrangements and laws referred to in paragraph 2 otherwise provide for expedited co-operation.

Article 32 – Trans-border access to stored computer data with consent or where publicly available
A Party may, without the authorization of another Party:

a) access publicly available (open source) stored computer data, regardless of where the data is located geographically; or
b) access or receive, through a computer system in its territory, stored computer data located in another Party, if the Party obtains the lawful and voluntary consent of the person who has the lawful authority to disclose the data to the Party through that computer system.

Article 33 – Mutual assistance in the real-time collection of traffic data

1. The Parties shall provide mutual assistance to each other in the real-time collection of traffic data associated with specified communications in their territory transmitted by means of a computer system. Subject to the provisions of paragraph 2, this assistance shall be governed by the conditions and procedures provided for under domestic law.
2. Each Party shall provide such assistance at least with respect to criminal offences for which real-time collection of traffic data would be available in a similar domestic case.

Article 34 – Mutual assistance regarding the interception of content data
The Parties shall provide mutual assistance to each other in the real-time collection or recording of content data of specified communications transmitted by means of a computer system to the extent permitted under their applicable treaties and domestic laws.

Title 3 – 24/7 Network

Article 35 – 24/7 Network

1. Each Party shall designate a point of contact available on a twenty-four hour, seven-day-a-week basis, in order to ensure the provision of immediate assistance for the purpose of investigations or proceedings concerning criminal offences related to computer systems and data, or for the collection of evidence in electronic form of a criminal offence. Such assistance shall include facilitating, or,

if permitted by its domestic law and practice, directly carrying out the following measures:

a) the provision of technical advice;

b) the preservation of data pursuant to Articles 29 and 30;

c) the collection of evidence, the provision of legal information, and locating of suspects.

2. a) A Party's point of contact shall have the capacity to carry out communications with the point of contact of another Party on an expedited basis.

b) If the point of contact designated by a Party is not part of that Party's authority or authorities responsible for international mutual assistance or extradition, the point of contact shall ensure that it is able to co-ordinate with such authority or authorities on an expedited basis.

3. Each Party shall ensure that trained and equipped personnel are available, in order to facilitate the operation of the network.

Chapter IV – Final provisions

Article 36 – Signature and entry into force

1. This Convention shall be open for signature by the member States of the Council of Europe and by non-member States which have participated in its elaboration.

2. This Convention is subject to ratification, acceptance or approval. Instruments of ratification, acceptance or approval shall be deposited with the Secretary General of the Council of Europe.

3. This Convention shall enter into force on the first day of the month following the expiration of a period of three months after the date on which five States, including at least three member States of the Council of Europe, have expressed their consent to be bound by the Convention in accordance with the provisions of paragraphs 1 and 2.

4. In respect of any signatory State which subsequently expresses its consent to be bound by it, the Convention shall enter into force on the first day of the month following the expiration of a period of three months after the date of the expression of its consent to be bound by the Convention in accordance with the provisions of paragraphs 1 and 2.

Article 37 – Accession to the Convention

1. After the entry into force of this Convention, the Committee of Ministers of the Council of Europe, after consulting with and obtaining the unanimous consent of the Contracting States to the Convention, may invite any State which is not a member of the Council and which has not participated in its elaboration to accede to this Convention. The decision shall be taken by the majority provided for in Article 20.d. of the Statute of the Council of Europe and by the unanimous vote of the representatives of the Contracting States entitled to sit on the Committee of Ministers.
2. In respect of any State acceding to the Convention under paragraph 1 above, the Convention shall enter into force on the first day of the month following the expiration of a period of three months after the date of deposit of the instrument of accession with the Secretary General of the Council of Europe.

Article 38 –Territorial application

1. Any State may, at the time of signature or when depositing its instrument of ratification, acceptance, approval or accession, specify the territory or territories to which this Convention shall apply.
2. Any State may, at any later date, by a declaration addressed to the Secretary General of the Council of Europe, extend the application of this Convention to any other territory specified in the declaration. In respect of such territory the Convention shall enter into force on the first day of the month following the expiration of a period of three months after the date of receipt of the declaration by the Secretary General.
3. Any declaration made under the two preceding paragraphs may, in respect of any territory specified in such declaration, be withdrawn by a notification addressed to the Secretary General of the Council of Europe. The withdrawal shall become effective on the first day of the month following the expiration of a period of three months after the date of receipt of such notification by the Secretary General.

Article 39 – Effects of the Convention

1. The purpose of the present Convention is to supplement applicable multilateral or bilateral treaties or arrangements as between the Parties, including the provisions of:

- the European Convention on Extradition, opened for signature in Paris, on 13 December 1957 (ETS No. 24);
- the European Convention on Mutual Assistance in Criminal Matters, opened for signature in Strasbourg, on 20 April 1959 (ETS No. 30);
- the Additional Protocol to the European Convention on Mutual Assistance in Criminal Matters, opened for signature in Strasbourg, on 17 March 1978 (ETS No. 99).

2. If two or more Parties have already concluded an agreement or treaty on the matters dealt with in this Convention or have otherwise established their relations on such matters, or should they in future do so, they shall also be entitled to apply that agreement or treaty or to regulate those relations accordingly. However, where Parties establish their relations in respect of the matters dealt with in the present Convention other than as regulated therein, they shall do so in a manner that is not inconsistent with the Convention's objectives and principles.

3. Nothing in this Convention shall affect other rights, restrictions, obligations and responsibilities of a Party.

Article 40 – Declarations

By a written notification addressed to the Secretary General of the Council of Europe, any State may, at the time of signature or when depositing its instrument of ratification, acceptance, approval or accession, declare that it avails itself of the possibility of requiring additional elements as provided for under Articles 2, 3, 6 paragraph 1.b), 7, 9 paragraph 3, and 27, paragraph 9.e).

Article 41 – Federal clause

1. A federal State may reserve the right to assume obligations under Chapter II of this Convention consistent with its fundamental principles governing the relationship between its central government and constituent States or other similar territorial entities provided that it is still able to co-operate under Chapter III.

2. When making a reservation under paragraph 1, a federal State may not apply the terms of such reservation to exclude or substantially diminish its obligations to provide for measures set forth in Chapter II. Overall, it shall provide for a broad and effective law enforcement capability with respect to those measures.

3. With regard to the provisions of this Convention, the application of which comes under the jurisdiction of constituent States or other similar territorial entities, that are not obliged by the constitutional system of the federation to take legislative measures, the federal government shall inform the competent authorities of such States of the said provisions with its favorable opinion, encouraging them to take appropriate action to give them effect.

Article 42 – Reservations

By a written notification addressed to the Secretary General of the Council of Europe, any State may, at the time of signature or when depositing its instrument of ratification, acceptance, approval or accession, declare that it avails itself of the reservation(s) provided for in Article 4, paragraph 2, Article 6, paragraph 3, Article 9, paragraph 4, Article 10, paragraph 3, Article 11, paragraph 3, Article 14, paragraph 3, Article 22, paragraph 2, Article 29, paragraph 4, and Article 41, paragraph 1. No other reservation may be made.

Article 43 – Status and withdrawal of reservations

1. A Party that has made a reservation in accordance with Article 42 may wholly or partially withdraw it by means of a notification addressed to the Secretary General of the Council of Europe. Such withdrawal shall take effect on the date of receipt of such notification by the Secretary General. If the notification states that the withdrawal of a reservation is to take effect on a date specified therein, and such date is later than the date on which the notification is received by the Secretary General, the withdrawal shall take effect on such a later date.
2. A Party that has made a reservation as referred to in Article 42 shall withdraw such reservation, in whole or in part, as soon as circumstances so permit.
3. The Secretary General of the Council of Europe may periodically enquire with Parties that have made one or more reservations as referred to in Article 42 as to the prospects for withdrawing such reservation(s).

Article 44 – Amendments

1. Amendments to this Convention may be proposed by any Party, and shall be communicated by the Secretary General of the Council

of Europe to the member States of the Council of Europe, to the non-member States which have participated in the elaboration of this Convention as well as to any State which has acceded to, or has been invited to accede to, this Convention in accordance with the provisions of Article 37.

2. Any amendment proposed by a Party shall be communicated to the European Committee on Crime Problems (CDPC), which shall submit to the Committee of Ministers its opinion on that proposed amendment.

3. The Committee of Ministers shall consider the proposed amendment and the opinion submitted by the CDPC and, following consultation with the non-member States Parties to this Convention, may adopt the amendment.

4. The text of any amendment adopted by the Committee of Ministers in accordance with paragraph 3 of this article shall be forwarded to the Parties for acceptance.

5. Any amendment adopted in accordance with paragraph 3 of this article shall come into force on the thirtieth day after all Parties have informed the Secretary General of their acceptance thereof.

Article 45 – Settlement of disputes

1. The European Committee on Crime Problems (CDPC) shall be kept informed regarding the interpretation and application of this Convention.

2. In case of a dispute between Parties as to the interpretation or application of this Convention, they shall seek a settlement of the dispute through negotiation or any other peaceful means of their choice, including submission of the dispute to the CDPC, to an arbitral tribunal whose decisions shall be binding upon the Parties, or to the International Court of Justice, as agreed upon by the Parties concerned.

Article 46 – Consultations of the Parties

1. The Parties shall, as appropriate, consult periodically with a view to facilitating:
   a) the effective use and implementation of this Convention, including the identification of any problems thereof, as well as the effects of any declaration or reservation made under this Convention;

b) the exchange of information on significant legal, policy or technological developments pertaining to cybercrime and the collection of evidence in electronic form;

c) consideration of possible supplementation or amendment of the Convention.

2. The European Committee on Crime Problems (CDPC) shall be kept periodically informed regarding the result of consultations referred to in paragraph 1.

3. The CDPC shall, as appropriate, facilitate the consultations referred to in paragraph 1 and take the measures necessary to assist the Parties in their efforts to supplement or amend the Convention. At the latest three years after the present Convention enters into force, the European Committee on Crime Problems (CDPC) shall, in co-operation with the Parties, conduct a review of all of the Convention's provisions and, if necessary, recommend any appropriate amendments.

4. Except where assumed by the Council of Europe, expenses incurred in carrying out the provisions of paragraph 1 shall be borne by the Parties in the manner to be determined by them.

5. The Parties shall be assisted by the Secretariat of the Council of Europe in carrying out their functions pursuant to this article.

Article 47 – Denunciation

1. Any Party may, at any time, denounce this Convention by means of a notification addressed to the Secretary General of the Council of Europe.

2. Such denunciation shall become effective on the first day of the month following the expiration of a period of three months after the date of receipt of the notification by the Secretary General.

Article 48 – Notification

The Secretary General of the Council of Europe shall notify the member States of the Council of Europe, the non-member States which have participated in the elaboration of this Convention as well as any State which has acceded to, or has been invited to accede to, this Convention of:

a) any signature;

b) the deposit of any instrument of ratification, acceptance, approval or accession;

c) any date of entry into force of this Convention in accordance with Articles 36 and 37;

d) any declaration made under Article 40 or reservation made in accordance with Article 42;

e) any other act, notification or communication relating to this Convention.

In witness whereof the undersigned, being duly authorized thereto, have signed this Convention.

Done at Budapest, this 23rd day of November 2001, in English and in French, both texts being equally authentic, in a single copy which shall be deposited in the archives of the Council of Europe. The Secretary General of the Council of Europe shall transmit certified copies to each member State of the Council of Europe, to the non-member States which have participated in the elaboration of this Convention, and to any State invited to accede to it.

DOMAIN EXTENSIONS

.ac	– Ascension Island	.ad	– Andorra
.ae	– United Arab Emirates	.af	– Afghanistan
.ag	– Antigua and Barbuda	.ai	– Anguilla
.al	– Albania	.am	– Armenia
.an	– Netherlands Antilles	.ao	– Angola
.aq	– Antarctica	.ar	– Argentina
.as	– American Samoa	.at	– Austria
.au	– Australia	.aw	– Aruba
.az	– Azerbaijan	.ba	– Bosnia and Herzegovina
.bb	– Barbados	.bd	– Bangladesh
.be	– Belgium	.bf	– Burkina Faso
.bg	– Bulgaria	.bh	– Bahrain
.bi	– Burundi	.bj	– Benin
.bm	– Bermuda	.bn	– Brunei Darussalam
.bo	– Bolivia	.br	– Brazil
.bs	– Bahamas	.bt	– Bhutan
.bv	– Bouvet Island	.bw	– Botswana
.by	– Belarus	.bz	– Belize
.ca	– Canada	.cc	– Cocos (Keeling) Islands
.cd	– Congo, Democratic Republic of the	.cf	– Central African Republic
.cg	– Congo, Republic of	.ch	– Switzerland
.ci	– Cote d'Ivoire	.ck	– Cook Islands

.cl	– Chile		.cm	– Cameroon
.cn	– China		.co	– Colombia
.cr	– Costa Rica		.cu	– Cuba
.cv	– Cap Verde		.cx	– Christmas Island
.cy	– Cyprus		.cz	– Czech Republic
.de	– Germany		.dj	– Djibouti
.dk	– Denmark		.dm	– Dominica
.do	– Dominican Republic		.dz	– Algeria
.ec	– Ecuador		.ee	– Estonia
.eg	– Egypt		.eh	– Western Sahara
.er	– Eritrea		.es	– Spain
.et	– Ethiopia		.fi	– Finland
.fj	– Fiji		.fk	– Falkland Islands (Malvina)
.fm	– Micronesia, Federal State of		.fo	– Faroe Islands
.fr	– France		.ga	– Gabon
.gd	– Grenada		.ge	– Georgia
.gf	– French Guiana		.gg	– Guernsey
.gh	– Ghana		.gi	– Gibraltar
.gl	– Greenland		.gm	– Gambia
.gn	– Guinea		.gp	– Guadeloupe
.gq	– Equatorial Guinea		.gr	– Greece
.gs	– South Georgia and the South Sandwich Islands		.gt	– Guatemala
.gu	– Guam		.gw	– Guinea-Bissau
.gy	– Guyana		.hk	– Hong Kong
.hm	– Heard and McDonald Islands		.hn	– Honduras
.hr	– Croatia/Hrvatska		.ht	– Haiti
.hu	– Hungary		.id	– Indonesia
.ie	– Ireland		.il	– Israel
.im	– Isle of Man		.in	– India
.io	– British Indian Ocean Territory		.iq	– Iraq
.ir	– Iran (Islamic Republic of)		.is	– Iceland
.it	– Italy		.je	– Jersey
.jm	– Jamaica		.jo	– Jordan
.jp	– Japan		.ke	– Kenya
.kg	– Kyrgyzstan		.kh	– Cambodia
.ki	– Kiribati		.km	– Comoros

.kn	– Saint Kitts and Nevis	.kp	– Korea, Democratic People's Republic
.kr	– Korea, Republic of	.kw	– Kuwait
.ky	– Cayman Islands	.kz	– Kazakhstan
.la	– Lao People's Democratic Republic	.lb	– Lebanon
.lc	– Saint Lucia	.li	– Liechtenstein
.lk	– Sri Lanka	.lr	– Liberia
.ls	– Lesotho	.lt	– Lithuania
.lu	– Luxembourg	.lv	– Latvia
.ly	– Libyan Arab Jamahiriya	.ma	– Morocco
.mc	– Monaco	.md	– Moldova, Republic of
.mg	– Madagascar	.mh	– Marshall Islands
.mk	– Macedonia, Former Yugoslav Republic	.ml	– Mali
.mm	– Myanmar	.mn	– Mongolia
.mo	– Macau	.mp	– Northern Mariana Islands
.mq	– Martinique	.mr	– Mauritania
.ms	– Montserrat	.mt	– Malta
.mu	– Mauritius	.mv	– Maldives
.mw	– Malawi	.mx	– Mexico
.my	– Malaysia	.mz	– Mozambique
.na	– Namibia	.nc	– New Caledonia
.ne	– Niger	.nf	– Norfolk Island
.ng	– Nigeria	.ni	– Nicaragua
.nl	– Netherlands	.no	– Norway
.np	– Nepal	.nr	– Nauru
.nu	– Niue	.nz	– New Zealand
.om	– Oman	.pa	– Panama
.pe	– Peru	.pf	– French Polynesia
.pg	– Papua New Guinea	.ph	– Philippines
.pk	– Pakistan	.pl	– Poland
.pm	– St. Pierre and Miquelon	.pn	– Pitcairn Island
.pr	– Puerto Rico	.ps	– Palestinian Territories
.pt	– Portugal	.pw	– Palau
.py	– Paraguay	.qa	– Qatar
.re	– Reunion Island	.ro	– Romania
.ru	– Russian Federation	.rw	– Rwanda
.sa	– Saudi Arabia	.sb	– Solomon Islands
.sc	– Seychelles	.sd	– Sudan
.se	– Sweden	.sg	– Singapore

.sh	– St. Helena	.si	– Slovenia
.sj	– Svalbard and Jan Mayen Islands	.sk	– Slovak Republic
.sl	– Sierra Leone	.sm	– San Marino
.sn	– Senegal	.so	– Somalia
.sr	– Suriname	.st	– Sao Tome and Principe
.sv	– El Salvador	.sy	– Syrian Arab Republic
.sz	– Swaziland	.tc	– Turks and Caicos Islands
.td	– Chad	.tf	– French Southern Territories
.tg	– Togo	.th	– Thailand
.tj	– Tajikistan	.tk	– Tokelau
.tm	– Turkmenistan	.tn	– Tunisia
.to	– Tonga	.tp	– East Timor
.tr	– Turkey	.tt	– Trinidad and Tobago
.tv	– Tuvalu	.tw	– Taiwan
.tz	– Tanzania	.ua	– Ukraine
.ug	– Uganda	.uk	– United Kingdom
.um	– US Minor Outlying Islands	.us	– United States
.uy	– Uruguay	.uz	– Uzbekistan
.va	– Holy See (City Vatican State)	.vc	– Saint Vincent and the Grenadines
.ve	– Venezuela	.vg	– Virgin Islands (British)
.vi	– Virgin Islands (US)	.vn	– Vietnam
.vu	– Vanuatu	.wf	– Wallis and Futuna Islands
.ws	– Western Samoa	.ye	– Yemen
.yt	– Mayotte	.yu	– Yugoslavia
.za	– South Africa	.zm	– Zambia
.zw	– Zimbabwe		

Note: One of the prime reasons for including a complete list of domain extensions is so that the registry location of a website can be easily established. Very often, particularly with "dubious" websites there is an immediate inconsistency between the site's claimed location and domain registry. Sites such as www.checkdomain.com provide full details of the registrant of individual websites.

REFERENCES AND FURTHER READING

In researching and writing this book I have used and made reference to the publications listed below, which are also recommended for further reading. I have also listed here the Web sites and print sources I used while researching this book.

BOOKS

Brunner, J (1984) *Shockwave Rider*, Del Ray Books, New York

Fialka, J J (1997) *War by Other Means: Economic espionage in America*, W W Norton & Company, New York

Hafner, K and Markoff, J (1993) *Cyber Punk: Outlaws and hackers on the computer frontier*, Corgi, London

Hale, C (ed) *Wired Style: Principles of English usage in the digital age*, Hard Wired, California

Kahaner L, (1998) *Competitive Intelligence*, Simon & Schuster, New York

Levy, S (1984) Hackers: *Heroes of the Computer Revolution*, Penguin, New York

Lilley, P (2000) *Dirty Dealing: The untold truth about global money laundering*, Kogan Page, London

Power, R (2000) *Tangled Web: Tales of digital crime from the shadows of cyberspace*, Que, Indianapolis

Statalla, M and Quittner J (1995) *Masters of Deception: The gang that ruled cyberspace*, Harper Collins, New York

Sterling, B (1992*) The Hacker Crackdown: Law and disorder on the electronic frontier*, Bantam, New York

United Kingdom Audit Commission (1994) *Opportunity Makes a Thief: An analysis of computer abuse*, Audit Commission Publications, Abingdon

United Kingdom Audit Commission (1998) *Ghost in the machine: An analysis of IT fraud and abuse*, Audit Commission Publications, Abingdon

WEB SITES

Interpol (accessed 16 May 2001) IT Security and crime prevention methods, *Interpol* (online)
http://www.interpol.int/public/technologycrime/crimeprev/itsecurity.asp

Interpol (accessed 16 May 2001) Company Checklist, *Interpol* (online)
http://www.interpol.int/public/technologycrime/crimeprev/companychecklist.asp

Sophos (accessed 01 November 2001) Virus Info, *Sophos* (online)
htttp://www.sophos.com/virusinfo/infofeed/

Maxus (accessed 30 May 2001) Maxus Credit Cards Datapipe (online)
http://www.pc-radio.com/maxus.htm

Nerds (accessed 09 May 2001) Glossary of Geek, *PBS Nerds 2.0.1* (online) http://www.pbs.org/oph/nerds2.0.1/geek_glossary/

Cyberstreet (accessed 05 May 2001) A Chronology of Computer History, *Cyberstreet* (online)
http://www.cyberstreet.com/hcs/museum/chron.htm

PBS (accessed 20 May 2001) Timeline, *PBS Life on the Internet* (online)
http://www.pbs.org/internet/timeline/timeline-txt.html

History Channel (accessed 20 November) Technology Timeline, *History Channel* (online) http://www.historychannel.com/timeline/1940s.html

PRINT SOURCES

Sunday Business newspaper (UK)
Computeractive magazine (UK)
Web User Magazine (UK)
The Times newspaper (UK)
The Daily Telegraph newspaper (UK)
The Financial Times
The Business FT weekend magazine
MoneyWeek magazine (UK)
The Sunday Times newspaper (UK)
The Independent on Sunday newspaper (UK)
The Wall Street Journal (US)
USA Today (US)
The New York Times (US)
The Los Angeles Times (US)

GENERAL WEB SITE SOURCES

In researching this book I have made use of the following online sources:
www.zonelabs.com: Zonelabs
www.webopedia.com: Webopedia Online Dictionary & Search Engine
www.totse.com: Totse
www.abcnews.com: ABC News
www.ananova.com: Ananova
www.usatoday.com: USA Today
www.cybercrime.gov: Cybercrime
www.fraud.org: Internet fraud watch
www.wired.com: Wired
www.guardian.co.uk: Guardian Unlimited
www.computerworld.com: Computerworld
www.bbc.co.uk: BBCi
www.msnbc.com: Msnbc
www.computeruser.com: Computer User
www.zdnet.com: ZDNet
www.cnn.com: CNN
www.theregister.co.uk: The Register
www.newsbytes.com: Newsbytes

www.netratings.com: Netratings
http://66.129.1.101/top20.htm: Sans Institute
www.iwar.org.uk: IWS – The Information Warfare Site
www.cybersource.com: Cybersource
www.sec.gov: US Securities and Exchange Commission
www.sophos.com: Sophos Anti-Virus
www.cert.org: CERT Co-ordination centre

A note of thanks

Much of the basic research for this book was done by James Lilley, to whom I express my great thanks for doing such a good job – any technical errors, though, are mine not his.

INDEX